A Jungian and Evolutionary Approach to Psychology and Culture

This ground-breaking book re-positions C.G. Jung's legacy, and the field of analytical psychology, within the panorama of contemporary knowledge in neurobiology, psychology, culture and anthropology.

Within this new volume, Stefano Carta aims to provide a new, up-to-date way of understanding Jung's work, and to show the effect to which his central positions can be better understood in relation to topics such as the nature of the psyche, of the self, of the collective unconscious, and of archetypal theory. This book describes, with extensive substantiations and an original discussion, the transformation of psychological processes into cultural ones, leading to the formation of various forms of symbolic institutions.

Spanning two volumes, which are also accessible as standalone books, and with international appeal and original and interdisciplinary in scope, they will be of great interest to Jungian scholars and analysts as well as students and those on Jungian-oriented training courses.

Stefano Carta is a psychologist and a Jungian analyst graduate at the C.G. Jung Institute in Zurich. He is Professor of Dynamic and Clinical Psychology and Ethnopsychology at the University of Cagliari, Italy, and has been Honorary Professor at the Department of Psychoanalytic Studies at the University of Essex, UK. He is a member of the International Association of Analytical Psychology and former President of the Associazione Italiana di Psicologia Analitica (AIPA). Among his many publications, he has edited the entry "Psychology" in three volumes for the *Encyclopaedia of Life Support Systems* by UNESCO.

A Jungian and Evolutionary Approach to Psychology and Culture

The Infinite Ladder

Volume 2

Stefano Carta

Routledge
Taylor & Francis Group

LONDON AND NEW YORK

Designed cover image: M.C. Escher, Tetrahedral Planetoid.
Copyright of the M.C. Escher Company.

First published 2025
by Routledge
4 Park Square, Milton Park, Abingdon, Oxon OX14 4RN

and by Routledge
605 Third Avenue, New York, NY 10158

*Routledge is an imprint of the Taylor & Francis Group, an informa
business*

British Library Cataloguing-in-Publication Data
A catalogue record for this book is available from the British
Library

ISBN: 978-1-032-95768-5 (hbk)
ISBN: 978-1-032-95767-8 (pbk)
ISBN: 978-1-003-58646-3 (ebk)

DOI: 10.4324/9781003586463

Typeset in Times New Roman
by Apex CoVantage, LLC

Contents

The discussions we are having here could be represented pictorially by a helix; we keep on coming back to the same point, only on different levels of the helix.
W. R. Bion (2014). *Brazilian Lectures. Rio de Janeiro, 1974.*
In: *The Complete Works of W.R. Bion*, Vol VII. London: Karnak, p. 82

collective schemas are the ones that are of most interest to ethnologists, for they constitute one of the principal means of constructing shared cultural meanings. They may be defined as psychic, sensorimotor and emotional dispositions that are internalized thanks to experience acquired in a given social environment. These make it possible to exercise at least three types of skills: first, to structure the flow of perception in a selective fashion, granting a preeminence in signification to particular traits and processes that can be observed in the environment; second, to organize both practical activity and the expression of thoughts and emotions in accordance with relatively standardized scenarios; and third, to provide a framework for typical interpretations of patterns of behavior and events—interpretations that are acceptable and can be communicated within a community in which the habits of life that they convey are regarded as normal.
P. Descola (2013). *Beyond Nature and Culture.*
Chicago, London: The University of Chicago Press, p. 101

Chapter 1

Structures, history and problems within an anthropological perspective

In the first volume, I tried to discuss Jung's motivational theory and relate it to biology through what he called the psychization process. I discussed how the progressive transformation from the pre-psychic innate dispositional human endowment made of affects and feelings (which motivate the ignition and organization of the whole psyche) and the sensory-motor apparatus (which provides the material to give particular structure and representational forms to these affects) may representationally redescribe themselves into individual idiosyncratic psychologies that express themselves in personal contents – meaningful behaviors, thoughts and modes of apprehension. Thus, until now, I have been interpreting Jung's psychization process (vol. I, § 3) to situate it within a co-evolutionary environment.

This discussion was essentially aimed at placing the *numinosum* and its relationship with the religious strata of the collective unconscious back into the center, as it represents the deepest and most immediate expression of the affects at work. Furthermore, I have been trying to reaffirm Jung's paradigmatic principle of the dispositional nature of the brainmind to preserve analytical psychology from becoming some sort of sophisticated neo-behaviorism, or a mere adaptive perspective, such as that theorized by Ego-psychology. In pursuing this aim, I argued that such a dispositional nature expresses itself through innate structures, which, in an upward spiral movement of progressive abstraction/spiritualization and universalization, describe something like a helicoidal pattern while diversifying in number and quality.

Starting from biological constraints, I referred to the role of conceptual primitives, innate inferential systems and ontological categories, not as pure intellectual products of an epistemic knowledge but as an expression of the development of primary affects into secondary and tertiary emotions. This is the area studied (just to quote some authors) by Colin Trevarthen, Daniel Stern, Louis Sander or Michael Tomasello – a developmental area in which a theory of mind is developed and, finally, a new perspective of cooperation and fairness based on transcending values emerges. The cognitive representations of such an emotional transformation are what Bion called "emotional thoughts" and describe what I called "gnostic knowledge". Such a knowledge, now extended far beyond the individual's Ego-centered limits into the open space of we-ness and sociality, will keep giving form to the

DOI: 10.4324/9781003586463-1

original innate affects that, on their way, become always more differentiated, complex and spiritually refined feelings and emotions.

While in the first volume I discussed the progressive transformation of biology into psychology, in this second volume, I will try to show a further transformation from psychology to culture. In my perspective, this is how the soul takes back its pivotal position and role of a transformer *between* biology and anthropology, precisely as Marsilio Ficino argued when he wrote about the "anima copula mundi" ("the soul, bind of all things" [literally: "of the world"]). I think that this view of the psyche as a transformer of what we call the "biological" into the "symbolic" (or the "spiritual") domain is very similar to Jung's view of symbol-formation as he discussed in his *Symbols of Transformation* (1911/1956).

As we will see from Marshall Sahlins' discussion on kinship, from this perspective, the symbolic realm and culture cannot be reductively interpreted through biological principles (as much of sociobiology has done) but must be related to psychology as the middle, transformational area between what we, in our Western, naturalistic ontology (Descola, 2021), call the "body" and the social community, bound by symbolic and ethical ties.[1]

In the next pages, I will argue that the biological and psychological constraints that make it possible to feel and think, while at the same time limiting what is "easy to be thought and felt" within an environment, may also apply to those more complex emotional representations that constitute a culture. In simpler words, I will try to verify if and how, for contemporary research, the hypothesis of cultural universal "contents" (therefore, patterns and meanings) is tenable or not.

Before starting this discussion, I think it is "philosophically" correct to refer to the issue of the relationship between innate and learned factors within the new realm that I am about to explore now: the realm of society and culture. I am not interested in discussing the whole history of such an issue, as this would mean to write another book devoted just to this. What I think will suffice is to recall an opinion for which mental structures, à la Lévi-Strauss, and history not only can interact but cannot *not* do so. This is the position of Marshall Sahlins, who has been without doubt one of the contemporary giants of his discipline – anthropology.

Sahlins introduced the concept of the "structure of the conjuncture" to describe his view of history. Located between cultural expectations of what an event should look like, what and how it should mean and how individuals exploit it for their own historically meaningful purposes, the "conjuncture" is the space where history is produced.

In his *Islands of History* (1985), Sahlins shows how to study the conjuncture's "structure" by focusing on a particularly notorious arrival: that of Captain Cook on the island of Kauai in 1778, followed by his murder by the Hawaiians the following year. According to Sahlins (1995), Cook's fate was the outcome of a singular confluence of perceptions. To the Hawaiians, Cook might have appeared as if he were reenacting the ritual of the "dying god" Lono, who returns every year only to be killed again in a confrontation with the king. Hence, from this perspective, a "cultural structure" was at work. To his British comrades, on the other hand, it seemed like the Hawaiians murdered Cook because he accidentally offended them

by violating a taboo. Hence, from this other perspective, the protagonist is a historical event that took place. Each perspective implies its own kind of cultural logic,
the former a *ritual logic*, the latter a *causal logic*.

Sahlins' reference to a ritual logic is ingenious and heuristic. In fact, as I will
try to discuss later, the structure of rituals manifests something like a repeating,
somehow synchronic and nonhistorical pattern at work. I will argue that the fact
that, *seen from a biological point of view*, this feature of rituals – their structural
logic – is analogous to a constrained "pattern of behavior", now transposed at a
social, cultural level.

For Sahlins, both perspectives must be given weight in a thorough historical
analysis, and this is what I am trying to do by taking into consideration the role
of what acts as an invariant – a structure – in interaction with variable, diverse
"historical" events that happen to every individual. In my perspective, the historical nature to which I am referring has to do with the individuals' relational present
and past environment (i.e., with the transgenerational transmission of psychological contents) *and structures* through intersubjective and social relationships. This
perspective directly involves the relationship between archetypal, cultural and personal complexes. Figure 1.1 shows how Shalin's structure of the conjuncture may
be translated in these terms.

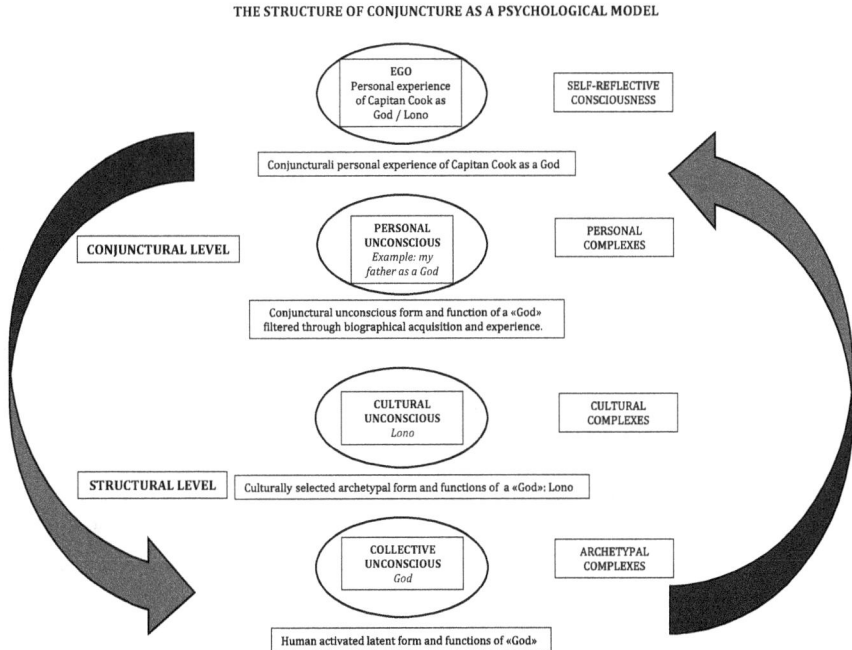

THE STRUCTURE OF CONJUNCTURE AS A PSYCHOLOGICAL MODEL

EGO
Personal experience
of Capitan Cook as
God / Lono

SELF-REFLECTIVE
CONSCIOUSNESS

Conjuncturall personal experience of Capitan Cook as a God

CONJUNCTURAL LEVEL

PERSONAL
UNCONSCIOUS
*Example: my
father as a God*

PERSONAL
COMPLEXES

Conjunctural unconscious form and function of a «God»
filtered through biographical acquisition and experience.

CULTURAL
UNCONSCIOUS
Lono

CULTURAL
COMPLEXES

STRUCTURAL LEVEL

Culturally selected archetypal form and functions of a «God»: Lono

COLLECTIVE
UNCONSCIOUS
God

ARCHETYPAL
COMPLEXES

Human activated latent form and functions of «God»

Figure 1.1 The circular relationship between archetypal, cultural and individual
complexes invariants.

The clarification of this first issue on the possible integration between invariants (in Sahlins' case, cultural structures) and (historical) events is necessary to earn the epistemological legitimacy of transposing the principle of biological invariants (constraints) to a psychological and cultural level.

A second crucial topic that must be taken into consideration when dealing with culture regards reductionism and the claim for which mental and even cultural facts can be wholly explained through the direct reference to biological principles. This is the approach of sociobiology and, to a certain extent, of evolutionary psychology. In fact, this transposition from the biological domain all the way up to the anthropological one *must* avoid reductionism. One example of non-reductionism is Sahlins' discussion on the "structure of conjunctures"; another one is the way he saw the relationship between consanguinity and kinship (vol. I, § 6.1).

Since we are discussing the legitimacy of some aspects of Jung's theory, the issue of reductionism becomes quite relevant for the relation between the biological nature of the collective unconscious, psychology and culture. In fact, one should not reduce culture to psychology and psychology to biology (and, further, biology to physics); the point is how they holistically interact.

Approaching anthropology, I need to express an important disagreement with Jung. This passage from the Tavistock Lectures might help me to clarify my position:

> There is nothing mystical about the collective unconscious. It is just a new branch of science, and it is really common sense to admit the existence of unconscious collective processes. For, though a child is not born conscious, his mind is not a tabula rasa. The child is born with a definite brain, and the brain of an English child will work not like that of an Australian black fellow. But in the way of a modern English person. The brain is born with the finished structure, It will work in a modern way, but this brain has its history. It has been built up in the course of millions of years and represents a history of which it is the result. Naturally, it carries with it the traces of the history, exactly like the body, and if you grow down into the basic structure of the mind, you naturally find traces of the archaic mind.
>
> (Jung, 1935, § 84)

Here, Jung's words basically express a racist theory, even if he was benevolent with the "other others" (as Renos Papadopoulos would say) and, for example, spoke of the Navajo Indian Mountain Lake as "my friend Mountain Lake".

Although I suspect that the most fundamental ontological layer is mathematics, the theory that I am trying to defend from a bottom-up perspective is a theory that at its base rests on biology (which does not mean at all that biology can "explain" it) and, therefore on the "collective unconscious". So I agree with Jung on the legitimacy to hypothesize a sufficiently unique brainmind common to our species – *Homo sapiens*. My disagreement is on the idea that the *brain* of an "Australian black fellow" is different from that of the British child (benevolently hoping that Jung is referring to an Australian child, as he might be referring to an Australian adult!). This is a racist and reductive statement, which has no evidence and carries enormous obvious ethical implications.

Now, the point is *not* that the brains are different, in fact because all brains are always different; there is not one brain exactly like another for genetic, maturational and developmental reasons. Furthermore, recent studies show that the brain *is* affected and modified by complex trauma (Schore, 2013). The issue at stake here is the categorization and generalization into a set of fixed biological differences of psychological and, at this point, *cultural* differences.

As I argued in the first volume, my hypothesis is that the precocial brain functions in a constrained way, which interacts with the altricial brain to produce different psychological and cultural solutions to universal problems that are felt and are thinkable within those constraints. This is implicit in von Uexküll's theory of the *Umwelt*. Therefore, I want to distinguish the variations that occur during ontogenesis from the invariant set-up of phylogenesis: the individual (and his personal and cultural complexes) from the species (the collective unconscious). This is an important point – for myself also a personal professional issue[2] – as I am aware that the inclusion of species-specific invariants risks being used in a racist way to differentiate on a biological basis individual and personal cultural differences.

What we need to do is to correct a Jung's residual Lamarckism, not to exclude it completely (as we saw discussing the origin of the innate inferential systems or the perspective of developmental evolutionary biology, which has somehow rehabilitated Lamarck) but to define its limits in relation to what we know today of how epigenetic transmission works. In fact, not only the brain but also the DNA remains deeply immersed in its co-evolutionary environment of which it is part, starting from the cytoplasm in which the cellular nucleus is immersed.

On an individual psychological basis, while I am convinced of the existence of a True (dispositional) Self and of a teleological development, I also think that we must be careful as to how we conceptualize the relationship between (innate) temperament and acquired character. Therefore, when in the following pages I deal with cultural matters, I will consider culture as a creative, innovative emergence from a human endowment common to the whole species. Such precocial endowment carries limits and constraints, but it does not define subsets made of black, white or yellow or Australian, Swiss or Italian brains.

Notes

1 In other ontologies, like the animist ontology, this discussion should have been organized in a very different way.
2 I was among those who signed the open letter on Jung's position on the "Africans" (Samuels, 2018).

References

Descola, P. (2021). *Oltre Natura e Cultura*. Milano: Cortina.
Jung, C.G. (1911/1956). Symbols of Transformation. In: The *Collected Works of C.G. Jung*, vol. 5. London: Routledge.
Jung, C.G. (1935/1972). The Tavistock Lectures. In: *The Collected Works of C.G. Jung*, vol. 15. London: Routledge.

Sahlins, M. (1985). *Islands of History*. Chicago: Chicago University Press.

Sahlins, M. (1995). *How 'Natives' Think. About Captain Cook, for Example*. Chicago: Chicago University Press.

Samuels, A. (2018). Open letter from a group of Jungians on the question of Jung's writings on and theories about "Africans". *British Journal of Psychotherapy*, 34, 4.

Schore, A. (2013). Relational Trauma, Brain Development and Dissociation. In: Ford, D., Curtois, C.A. (eds) *Treating Complex Traumatic Stress Disorders in Children and Adolescents*. New York: Guilford Press.

Singer, T., Kaplinsky, C. (2009). The Cultural Complex. In: Stein, M. (ed) *Jungian Psychoanalysis*. Chicago: Open Court.

Chapter 2

From affective images to cultures

In this chapter, I will argue that complex symbolic images, concepts and values – like Jung's archetypal images – emerge from the interaction between empirical experience (within the co-evolutionary field, starting from the mother-infant relationship) and Mandler's conceptual primitives, which dispositionally emerge in the mind and organize cognitive experience.

The complexity of these contents is a product of a process of *reflection* (as in Jung's instinct of reflection, which seems to me to be the basis for Karmiloff-Smith's representational redescription) through which biological affective-sensory-motor constraints are abstracted as *conceptual primitives*, which are then generalized and metaphorized first in ontological categories, then in a plurality of diversified specific cultural contents.

As we will see, this process is possible because of the existence of the mind's specific *susceptibilities*. Such susceptibilities may be also at the origin of the fact that all the natural languages might not only share the same deep syntactical structure (Chomsky) but also the same nuclear semantics (vol. II, § 9.3). In fact, from a limited number of linguistic meanings (words), the infinite complexity and diversity of possible concepts and narratives may arise. This seems similar to the semantic narrative content of myths and fairy tales, which, through diversified contents, may reveal the same constrained formative process. These contents are individual representations transformed into cultural *beliefs*, *narratives* and *folk theories*, which have a *contagious character*. This character determines the easiness by which these contents spread in the minds of other members of a social group.

For Jung, what is needed to mentalize whatever autonomously emerges from the body as sensations and affects is a representation, an "image". If such an image expresses a relevant emotion, it is a symbolic *image*, an image that should express and integrate both worlds – that of factual perceptions and that of sensations. Too much affectivity will "disturb" the factual image (all the way to psychosis), too little will transform one's experience in a traumatic fact and the person in a normotic, *banal* subject (as Annah Arendt calls it).

As I said when discussing the relationship between precocial and altricial competences and functions, for a psychic content to enter into Ego-consciousness, its original autonomy (its intrinsically alien, depersonalizing nature) must transcend

DOI: 10.4324/9781003586463-2

itself into a meaningful, personal, altricial experience. The point is that, when a pre-cocial content enters the altricial realm (which is de-specialized), it does so imbued of a *numinous* emotional cloud as a form of anxiety. In fact, I consider affects as precocial and primary and secondary emotions as altricial. It is the symbolic image that, due to its intrinsic characteristics, will provide the *adequate form* – a representation – for such an unconscious, "atmospheric" content, transforming the affect into a primary or secondary emotion, a relational function addressed to an intersubjective, social and cultural relationship.

In his *Symbols of Transformation* (1911/1956), Jung discusses the nature of symbolic images. They are the transcendent function's product of the transforma-tion of mere perception into meaningful sensations – hence, representations of the libido. In a few words, the symbolic realm is what makes it possible not to go crazy precisely because the symbol can transform psychic energy into a meaningful psy-chological experience, and for the purpose of my discussions, the symbolic realm may also be thought of as the realm of *culture*.

Jung had a precise theory as to how the symbol and culture transform and shape (i.e., make psychologically workable, thinkable and shareable) such alien numi-nous irruptions, which correspond to those ancestral functional modules formed during evolutionary time – the archetypes. In connection to the symbolic fabric of culture, Jung's theory has been seriously taken as a possible model for the process of the generations of abductions[1] and cultural discovery by epistemologists and information technology researchers (Magnani, 2018).

Jung's anthropological example of the transformation of psychic energy is that of the Wachandi of Australia (Jung, 1928). The Wachandi dig a hole in the ground, oval in shape, and set about with bushes so that it looks like a woman's genitals. Then they dance around this hole, holding their spears in front of them in imitation of an erect penis. As they dance round, they thrust their spears into the hole, shout-ing, *"Pulli nira, pulli nira, wataka!" (non fossa, non fossa, sed cunnus!)* ("Not the hole, not the hole, but a vagina". My transl.). During the ceremony, none of the participants is allowed to look at a woman. (Jung, 1928)

Here, Jung clearly sees culture – we should better say the socially shared psy-chic symbol – as a transformer of energy. According to Jung, for a symbolic inter-pretive perspective (in anthropology, see Turner, 1967), the ritual artifact built on the ground is the following:

> an analogue of the female genitals, the object of natural instinct. By the reiter-ated shouting and the ecstasy of the dance they suggest to themselves that the hole is really a vulva, and in order not to have this illusion disturbed by the real object of instinct, none may look at a woman. There can be no doubt that this is a canalization of energy and its transference to an analogue of the original object by means of the dance (which is really a mating-play, as with birds and other animals) and by imitating the sexual act.

This dance has a special significance as an earth-impregnation ceremony and therefore takes place in the spring. It is a magical act for the purpose of transferring libido to the earth, whereby the earth acquires a special psychic value and becomes an object of expectation. The mind then busies itself with the earth, and in turn is affected by it, so that there is a possibility and even a probability that man will give it his attention, which is the psychological prerequisite for cultivation.

(Jung, 1928, p. 43)

From an epistemological perspective:

It is clear that the artifact renders possible special cognitive processes also thanks to that ritual character which encourages interesting and fruitful inferential cognitive routines. Indeed, the psychic values, which – in psychoanalytic terms – relate to those inferential possibilities, can be "picked up" and so learnt by other members of the community still ignorant of those cognitive chances. The birth of agriculture is at stake, indeed Jung contends that "the mind then busies itself with the earth, and in turn is affected by it" and this fact favors the attention of human beings to create the psychological prerequisite for cultivation. Agriculture did in fact arise, though not exclusively, from the formation of sexual analogies.

(Magnani, 2018, p. 149)

Such a "cognitive" function of the symbol makes it possible to transform primary affects into a well-organized intersubjective experience and eventually into social representations, specific techniques for the transformation, hence, culturalization, of nature – a social idiom and a language. This was also Jung's vision, or Ernesto de Martino's (2023), for whom ethno-psychiatry deals with understanding the specificity of the forms in which a culture tries to govern suffering and crisis through specific social institutions.

For de Martino, the symbol is a container equivalent to the destructive "natural" crisis produced by the irruption in a person's life of what he calls "Nature". This "Nature" is precisely the primary, raw, unthought affect, whose effect is a "de-historification" of the human "presence" (Heidegger's *Dasein*) – something that Jung might have called a regression to a collective unconscious way of functioning. Therefore, culture, myth, ritual and all cultural *techniques are, for de Martino (and for Jung, or Bion), "vital" techniques of defense from "Nature".*

What makes it possible for these contents to spread in the minds of the other individuals that belong to the social group in such a way is that, emerging from *innate psychological precocial constraints*, they are *susceptible* to be thought and remembered by each individual's mind *in a common co-evolutionary* (now *social*) *environment*. These contents, therefore, express *susceptibilities* emerging from the combination of conceptual primitives, dispositional inferences, ontological categories and primary meanings universally present (and expressed with specific words) in natural languages (see vol. II, § 9.3), which are triggered by a shared social environment, which expresses emotional categories under the form of overt or covert prescriptions, expectations, prohibitions, etc.

This process represents the shift from the individual mind to the cultural group – from the I to the we – and ontogenetically starts around the mid 3 years of age, as the developmental studies on the birth of *perspectival cooperation* and the development of a *theory of mind* shows (vol. I, § 10.1).

Note

1 For Charles Sanders Pierce, unlike deductive reasoning, where conclusions are necessarily true if the premises are true, and inductive reasoning, where conclusions are probabilistically based on the strength of evidence, abductive reasoning involves generating hypotheses to explain observed phenomena. These hypotheses are then evaluated based on their explanatory power and coherence with the available evidence. The relationship between abductions and Jung's theory of the inherently creative transformation of the libido into symbols and analytical amplification is quite clear.

References

de Martino, E. (2023). *The End of the World: Cultural Apocalypse and Transcendence*. Kindle.

Jung, C.G. (1911/1956). Symbols of Transformation. In: *The Collected Works of C.G. Jung*, vol. 5. London: Routledge.

Jung, C.G. (1928). On Psychic Energy. In: *The Collected Works of C.G. Jung*, vol. 8. London: Routledge.

Magnani, L. (2018). Ritual artifacts as symbolic habits. *Open Information Science*, 2, 147–155.

Turner, V. (1967). *The Forest of Symbols*. Ithaca, New York: Cornell University Press.

Chapter 3

Images

So far, I have discussed the often unilateral tendency of the debate on complexes and archetypes to refer to cognitive studies, mostly on infant research, and I have underscored the primacy of affects for psychic life, which are normally not taken into consideration in such studies. My attempt was to show the validity of Jung's hypothesis on the existence of something like an archetype – i.e., a species-specific innate formative complex of images dispositionally triggered and organized by affects.

Throughout this discussion, I highlighted the possibility that the debate on the neotenic nature of humans – which would produce a nonspecific psychological set-up based on a general form of intelligence (the altricial nature of humans) – does not exclude the concurrent existence of precocial, specialized structures, which would function in predetermined modular ways within particular domains. While the altricial cortical structures of the brain would be roughly connected to self-reflective consciousness (the symbolic realm) differentiation and diversity (hence, individuation), i.e., the precocial structures, which Jung correctly imagined as mostly referring to the sub-cortical midline structures and limbic system, would be organized by those collective, unconscious, affectively intelligent "modular" complexes that Jung called archetypes. Therefore, the collective nature of Jung's unconscious would belong to the Darwinian perspective, as this deals with the selective processes and adaptation mechanisms *not of the individual* organism (the Ego) but of the species (the collective unconscious).

Here, there are two points that I would like to highlight.

First, Jung is often criticized for not having understood Darwin. For instance, Roesler writes:

> Jung argues that archetypes are the result of precipitations of experiences of early humans repeated again and again. This is in strong contrast to the insights of modern evolutionary theory, which has found out that the only mechanisms at work in changing the genome are mutation and subsequent selection.
>
> (Roesler, 2022, p. 108)

DOI: 10.4324/9781003586463-3

Roesler argues that Jung was referring not to Darwin but to Jean Baptiste Lamarck. As I wrote in the first volume, these criticisms are not really convincing, as they do not take into consideration the complementary role within the evolutionary dynamics of the organism's top-down causation on the genome (i.e., the organism's triggering genes expressions) that is today studied by systemic biology (Ginsburg & Jablonka, 2022; Levin, 2022) and the definite possibility that at the end of the story, it may be the phenotype that guides genotypic evolution (through the genome's coding) (Müller & Newman, 2003; Callebaut et al., 2007; Pigliucci & Müller, 2010; Müller, 2013).

On a psychological domain, as I wrote in my brief discussion of the innate inferential systems, natural selection may act precisely the way it does because of the innumerable circular interactions of the organism with the environment through time, which produced selective mutations at the level of the phenotype (through its action of genes' expression) because of the latter's survival strategies and which have eventually been passed on to the next generations, i.e., into DNA coding. If those interactions were limited, the probability of their occurrence would decrease and either the mutation would not be selected or its carriers would go extinct.

Secondly, for a *second* biological perspective that today interacts with Darwinian selective evolutionary processes – the so-called "developmental" biology – the organisms' biological principles, together with environmental conditions, constrain the number of possibilities in which the selective process unfolds. As I already said, the evolutionary and the developmental perspectives form the so-called Evo-Devo theory.

Within this perspective, I redefined the archetype not as something *within* the organism – like the genes – but as *something-in-between* the organism and its environment, hence, as an active organizing principle embedded in a co-evolutionary milieu. This hypothesis would fit well with Jung's view of transference as a relational field in which both the altricial conscious and precocial unconscious processes of the participants are involved.

In discussing all these matters, I tried to show the plausible ground of Jung's theory by framing it within the picture of contemporary science.

If under a biological perspective, the environment is conceptualized biologically, and in a psychological perspective it is conceptualized psychologically, what we now need to do is to examine this concept under a *social* perspective – more precisely, under a cultural/anthropological frame.

Since the main issue within this last level of analysis is the symbolic nature of human social life, after having dealt with affects and dispositionality, it is now necessary to discuss the nature of images.

To re-establish a proper homeostatic state in the organism – in our case, a properly balanced dynamic process of individuation – affects dispositionally trigger and organize images, i.e., *representations*. Such representations may a) have a purely individual meaning, hence, they may be valuable for the individual only, and they may not be necessarily meaningfully socially shared; or b) they may be shared in an unstable or temporary way to form a social milieu; or c) they may be stably shared by some others in a stable way to form what we call a "culture".

This discussion on images and representations is meant to show that, once again, also at this level (not only at a biological nor at a purely psychological level), the possibility of universal representations, like Jung's archetypal images, is far from being out of the question.

Therefore, to approach this complex discussion, I will now try to share some thoughts on the nature of images (along with cognitive anthropologists, I will call them also "representations") and on the possibility that there exist universal or quasi-universal images, which would be connected to what Jung called archetypal images.

The realm of images belongs to that of "cognition" because images as representations of affects are by their nature cognitive structures for the apprehension of the subject's inner and outer world. An image focalizes and selects what will be part of itself and what will be its background, hence, offering an essential synthetic form of order and categorization.

Since an image is the reflective transformation and representation of an affect, at the next step of such a Jacob's ladder, the transformation and representation of an image is a thought and a concept. This redescriptive process will eventually lead to *language* as an expression of an emotional meaning through a cognitive content. It is not a surprise that, due to such cognitive proximity of images to cognition, cognitive studies become pivotal at this point, yet bearing in mind the primary underpinning role of affects. In fact, the fundamental themes of the affect and of the psychoid-synchronistic nature of archetypes is never taken into consideration by cognitive anthropology (as it is not in most of infant research), and I also doubt that cognitive anthropologists, whose work is so valuable, would easily follow Jung along this path. Yet in my opinion, this does not necessarily mean that Jung's hypothesis on the psychoid nature of archetypes and synchronicity is not important and valuable; it could also mean that Jung's theory might be more advanced and complete than cognitive anthropology, which may be useful if relativized within its own methodological confines.

On the other hand, I must add, in favor of cognitive anthropology, or of one of its specific subfields – like cognitive studies on religion – that they do not directly deal with the affective roots of representations nor with any issues regarding the transgressive nature of what Jung called archetypes because they are pursuing other more specific goals.

Nevertheless, if a natural sciences' researcher may, and often must, confine the complexity of reality into her laboratory and her well-defined theoretical frame of reference, the psychotherapist cannot and should not. He must empirically welcome everything the patient is and whatever the relationship with him brings forth. Outside the necessary confines of today's scientific research, there may be phenomena, like affects and synchronicity, that the scientist cannot see because he is methodically excluding them from his setting. Therefore, I wish to remind the reader that the scientific support to Jung's ideas that I find in these important branches of science – in this case, cognitive anthropology or evolutionary psychology or cognitive science in general – *do not exhaust the complexity of Jung's vision*, which, therefore, must not be reduced to these theories.

I will now turn to cognition and cognitive studies and, more precisely, focus on cognitive anthropology. I hope that the reader will keep in the back of his mind the fact that any of the images I will discuss are generated and organized like complexes, i.e., by affectivity. I hope that this contribution will be useful to frame in a better-balanced way – even if in a minimal way – the complex and difficult issue of human creative and adaptive imagination.

References

Callebaut, W., Müller, G.B., Newman, S.A. (2007). The Organismic Systems Approach: Evo-Devo and the Streamlining of the Naturalistic Agenda. In: Samson, R.N. (eds) *Integrating Evolution and Development. From Theory to Practice*. Cambridge, MA, London: The MIT Press, pp. 25–92.

Ginsburg, S., Jablonka, E. (2022). *Picturing the Mind. Consciousness Through the Lens of Evolution*. Cambridge, MA, London: The MIT Press.

Levin, M. (2022, March 24). Technological approach to mind everywhere: An experimentally-grounded framework for understanding diverse bodies and minds. *Frontiers in Systems Neuroscience*, 16. https://doi.org/10.3389/fnsys.2022.768201

Müller, G.B. (2013). Le Origini della Novità Morfologica. In: Pinotti, A., Tedesco, S. (eds) *Estetica e Scienze della Vita Morfologia, Biologia Teoretica, Evo-devo*. Milano: Cortina.

Müller, G.B., Newman, S.A. (2003). *Origination of Organismal Form. Beyond the Gene in Developmental and Evolutionary Biology*. Cambridge, MA, London: The MIT Press.

Pigliucci, M., Müller, G.B. (eds) (2010). *Evolution. The Extended Synthesis*. Cambridge, MA, London: The MIT Press.

Roesler, C. (2022). *Development of a Reconceptualization of Archetype Theory. Report to the IAAP*. https://Iaap.Org/Wp-Content/Uploads/2022/04/Report-Archetype-Theory-Roesler-1.Pdf

Chapter 4

Images and neurobiology

If we consider evolutionary history, the functioning of the most archaic organisms was (and is) based on the triggering of reflexes (Tinbergen's fixed action patterns), which produce automatic responses to outer and inner stimuli. In fact, if we imagine something like a mental activity in lower organisms, like the invertebrates, we should interpret their functioning as a fragmented, discontinuous set of reflex-based responses within the continuous flow of their life. The fact that this behavior is produced by pre-set reflexes indicates the endogenous innate predisposition of even the most elementary form of life, which selects the proper response to the relevant stimuli of its co-evolutionary milieu into which it is entangled. Therefore, we witness specific sets of preformed behaviors triggered by specific reflexes and, later, motivational systems, such as foraging, mating, attacking, eating, etc. Such a scenery involves the life and behavior of primitive organisms (even bacteria), i.e., of animals whose nervous system, if present, is essentially made of ganglia. It is important to remember that throughout evolution, nothing that works is lost and that, as McLean argues, the human brain, together with the autonomic system, is the embryological product of a stratification of structures, from the most archaic – the so-called "reptilian" brain – to the most recent ones, the neo-mammalian brain and the neocortex (Maclean, 1985, 1990). I have already referred to McLean when I discussed the double nature of our psychology as made by precocial and altricial structures. I would like to point out that the evolutionarily most archaic structures that are part and parcel of our mental life may be those that form the limbic system, the brainstem, the mesencephalon, the basal ganglia and the reticular formation. Yet these are the structures that are part of our *centralized* nervous system.

At the base of our brain, we find archaic structures, like the solitary nucleus, which is made of a series of sensory nuclei that form a vertical column of gray matter in the medulla oblongata of the brainstem. The solitary nucleus receives general visceral and/or special visceral inputs from the facial nerve, glossopharyngeal nerve and vagus nerve, through which it receives and relays stimuli related to taste and visceral sensation. Therefore, at this level, the central nervous system is connected to the body and, deep down, to the 500 million neurons that make the autonomic system, where the over 100 trillion ancestral microbial cells live and

DOI: 10.4324/9781003586463-4

strive in our microbiome. As I have been trying to argue, *all* organic activity up to self-reflective, conscious mental life is a product of a continuous development from the most archaic anatomical forms and functional organization[1] of life, which acts bottom-up as constraining factors that entangle the organism with its specific ecological niche. In an article, written with Antonio Alcaro (Carta & Alcaro, 2022), I have argued the possibility that the famous dream of Jung's, in which he explores a three-story house (Jung, 1964, pp. 42–44), may be the self-representation of such an embryological evolutionary continuity.

Movement, and, therefore, SEEKING, is one of the crucial factors that underpin all life. Taking into account such a perspective, it is possible that the movement from water to land that took place during the Devonian (450 million years ago) required the reorganization of mental life, from a continuous behavioral activity of SEEKING, typical of fish and organisms that live in water, to a more discrete, "categorized" activity, necessary to minimize oxygen consumption in an environment in which the force of gravity makes movement energetically much more expensive. Such a process of reorganization of the flow of mental life was possible because of the corticalization of the nervous system and the development, from a-noetic consciousness, of a new form of affective consciousness organized in images – *noetic consciousness*.

As Antonio Alcaro argues:

> The process of corticalization [. . .] plays a fundamental function in the construction of an abstract knowledge of reality, in which a dynamic order based on a temporal flow of events is broken into parts and converted into static configurations that can be perceived all at once, crystallized images endowed with a specific spatial extent. So much of this capacity for abstraction results in a polarization of comma experience, in which the subject separates himself from the objects of the external world, perceiving and representing them from the outside.
>
> (Alcaro, 2019, p. 131. My transl.)

Indeed:

> in the absence of noetic consciousness, experiences are affectively integrated within a fluid field of awareness, with no sharp distinction between the organism and the environment. In contrast, the evolution of the noetic mind is accompanied by an inhibition of more immediate affective expression and a conversion of emotional arousal into attentional-cognitive attention that presides over ideational capacities.
>
> (Alcaro, 2024, p. 124. My transl.)

Noetic consciousness implies a process through which the perceptions of the outer world may be interiorized and memorized under the form of representations. While such a process of imaginal interiorization is already present in ectotherm species, like reptiles, it would further develop in homeotherm animals, like birds and mammals, as a much deeper and pervasive form of interiorization through which what was interiorized are the parameters of the "outer" environment's temperature. This freed the organism from its strict dependency from the outer world and increased the autonomy of its inner mental life. In my opinion, these are the phylogenetic conditions for what Lacan calls the *imaginary*.

This evolutionary scenery, in which SEEKING and movement is the essential factor, is the probable scenery for the birth of images and the differentiation between outer perceptions and inner sensations, i.e., conscious phenomenological experiences, through which we, together with many animals, from reptiles to birds, mentally represent our own movement and the outer world and onto which we are entangled *without necessarily spending any energy necessary for bodily activity.*

What we call "perception" informs us of the fact that there is an object "out there". This object may be moving, or I may be moving; it may touch me, I may touch it. In a few words, we are in a situation in which perception is associated with movement; we are dealing with *perceived images*.

Let us imagine four situations. The first is when we see an object and there is no physical contact. The second when someone tickles us. The third when I myself try to tickle myself. The fourth is when I close my eyes to see (like in sleep), and I imagine (like in dreams).

Let's see the first situation. Why is it that when we move our eyes, we do not see the world moving? It has been known for a long time that visual perception tends to degrade if it is not anchored in exploratory eye movements (Yarbus, 1967). In other words, the capacity to see deteriorates if one does not move the eye muscles (see further, vol. II, § 4.1). After all, the situation is not dissimilar to that in which, on the surface of the retina, the excitation produced on the photoreceptors by an external moving stimulus is moved, while the eyes stand still. The reason is that when the extraocular muscles of the eye receive the motor command to contract or release, the same signal in carbon copy reaches a comparator (probably in the cerebellum) that evaluates the sliding signal of the stimulation on the retina. If the sliding is produced by the movement of extraocular muscles, the sensation is cancelled, and I will have a perception of an object outside myself. In fact, if these muscles are blocked pharmacologically, when the brain sends the motor command the patient's very unpleasant sensation is that the environment around him is rotating.

Let's now see the two situations about tickling. The difference between the two conditions is that in one case, I receive the sensory stimulus passively, while in the other, I produce it myself by actively moving. The neurobiological mechanism involved is the same that controls the eye movements. It has been known since the 1950s and was identified by Eric von Holst, a collaborator of Konrad Lorenz, along with one of his students, Horst Mittelstaed (von Holst & Mittelstaedt, 1950). It may be that, when I touch myself, that is, when the brain sends a signal, a motor command, to the muscles, a second signal, which is called *efference copy* and which is, so to speak, a carbon copy of the motor signal, called *corollary discharge*, is also sent to the sensory system itself to alert it to the fact that the stimulation that is shortly to be felt is produced by my own movement. This second signal cancels out the first. Thus, when I move my arm and hands and try to tickle myself, a carbon copy of the motor command is sent also to the somatosensory cortex, and I have a particular sensation without a perception of an object outside myself.

Thus, the mechanism of *efference copy* informs me that what happened was done by myself, and this will prevent me from *feeling* the touch as a tickle. Hence, distinguishing internal sensations from external perceptions – that is, external (extrovert) images from internal (introvert) images – the mechanism of afferent copying could be at the origin of the transformation of perceptions into sensations, i.e., into *subjective experiences*.

I said that the phylogenetic birth of inner images was the condition for what Lacan calls the *imaginary*. The moment in which perceptions and sensations may be properly connected in the fictional unity and identity of the subject is the jubilant recognition of the infant's own image in the mirror in Lacan's mirror stage.[2] Here, the process of perceiving the infant's image aggregates the sensation of his own sense of selfhood. Within this perspective, what we are calling "perception" corresponds to Lacan's "real", or to Bion's beta elements. It is the possibility to commute such perceptions into sensations that makes a perception a truly psychological (imaginal) experience, an experience which is an *image* – somehow a copy – of an original "ectopsychic" perception. The gap between the ectopsychic perception and the imaginal sensation opens an infinite empty space that will activate the infinite symbolic activity of the psyche. Furthermore, it must be recalled that, due to the anticipatory and predictive nature of the processes of the brainmind (vol. 1, §10), this whole perception-sensation cycle seems not to be aimed only at the extroverted analysis of the outer world but also, most of all, at the mind-wandering activity of the teleological self-exploration of the inner psychic world, an exploration at the service of a quasi-stationary equilibrium, a metastable homeostasis.

Let's now look at the fourth situation. You may recall that in dealing with unconscious consciousness, I gave the example of the blind sight of the rhesus monkey Helen, who was cortically, but not perceptually, blind sighted (vol. I, § 5). In her case, we may say that she had perceptions but not sensations. On the other hand, in the case of inner images, we may say that we have sensations without perceptions.

Adopting Winnicott's language, we must underscore that what he called *conceptions* are far from being carbon copies of *perceptions* supposedly represented or stored into the mind as memories. No memories are realistic; as we know, memory is a productive and not a reproductive process, which confirms the dispositional nature of the brainmind. Even when we try to represent the perception in the mind in the most faithful way possible – when we try to remember "by heart" – the inner image that we retrieve will be *radically* different from the original perception because the mind always *intrinsically* transforms perceptions into conceptions. The radical difference of such images does not have anything to do with their being dissimilar from perceptions, like, for instance, when we dream something that has really happened and where the images might be pictorially the same to the original perceived ones. The radically different nature of imagined images – both the recalled ones and the ones that are really imagined – lies on their wholly different origin and function. In fact, these conceptions do not reproduce real perceptions; they (mostly visually) *simulate* them because they borrow their perceptive apparatus not to perceive the outer "factual object" but *to represent affects*, whence their radically different nature. Conceptions do not represent objects but affects. Now, if we remember that the affects are the product of the subjective dynamic homeostatic processes of the living psychoid Self, we may say that *what we are calling conceptions are the imaginal self-reflection of the Self.* I propose that, instead of talking about "perceptions", we might talk about "images". When referring to conceptions – which have to do with sensations – we might resort to use the Latin word *imago/imagines*, which has been a constant reference in the analytical literature. *The purest sensations without perception are the images of the dream.*

Thus, we would have four kinds of representations: 1) images perceived as external, with no subjective movement; 2) images perceived as external data with sensory contact, where through the "afferent copying" mechanism, our sensory apparatus will produce a certain subjective sensation (for example, a person performs a motor act and tickles me, and I feel tickled); 3) images felt as subjective sensations produced by my own movement (I try to tickle myself, but I do not sense it as such, although I feel the touch of my fingers); and 4) imagines *that are not produced by the sensory apparatus but are imagined as representations of subjective emotional* sensations. *These are the introverted images that the psyche self-generates by borrowing the global, fragmented or recomposed (as in the case of many dream* imagines)[3] *forms of objects perceived in the external world, which had once been synthesized* by the infant thanks to his innate cross-modal sensory competence (vol. 1, § 9) according to the specific human *Umwelt* (vol. 1. § 6). The origin of these introverted, symbolic *imagines* is the dispositional human Self, and their foundation is the affects.

As the fundamental homeostatic organizer of all biological life is the affect and the sensation being its precursor, this means also to sink into ancestral, phylogenetic history and into the *archè* of the collective unconscious. It is precisely because I wish to underscore the archaic, primary origin of the introverted *imagines*, and therefore of what Jung called the "collective unconscious", that I am referring to the phylogenetic strata of the psyche-soma and phylogenesis.

Therefore, we may say that those images that we perceive, hence the outcomes of our own empirical experience, do *not* produce what I am calling *imagines*. I argue that the process is exactly reversed. Life is *first* imagined from the ancestral depths of our body-mind, and *then selected and perceived* throughout our empirical experiential life.

If these sensations without perception, these *imagines*, are the endogenous representations of the affects that confer meaning and sense to our life, our "individuation process", their archaic, fundamental core-affective quality is the *numinosum*, which Jung expressly said to be the foundation and at the same time the goal of life and of the individuation process. I agree with him.

Theses *imagines* [. . .] are those introverted, emotionally meaningful *imagines* that have survived throughout time, history and space. Such a selective survival of these *imagines* throughout history indicates that they *ipso facto* have an essential, highly relevant affective meaning. It is an affective meaning that is organized precisely by their imaginal, visual form, and which may be subsequently referred to extroverted, empirically differentiated cultural contexts. Hence, [. . .] "archetypal" images on one side express the phylogenetic ancestral foundation of particular sets of affects and emotions – therefore arché-*typical* meanings – while, on the other, they give historical shape and form to those specific conditions that each human being and every human group has to face in their historical predicaments, hence producing an indefinite number of variable and differentiated cultural meanings.

(Carta, 2024)

I think that Goodwyn would agree with me when he writes:

the mind takes something experienced, and creates an image that has an essence, a predator-prey dimension, an anthropomorphic set of beliefs and intentions, and likely a host of other aspects yet to be uncovered by empirical research. The mind then says "this situation/feeling/impression is like this animal. In other words, the brain uses animals to create symbols.

(Goodwyn, 2012, p. 68)

While all perceived images are relevant insofar as they are affectively salient, these imagined imagines *are pure representations of the affective layer of the psyche.* This is what I mean when I say that salient images are representations of affects.

The *imagines* that belong to 4) are the symbolic, i.e., emotionally and epistemically significant images that show what the mind makes of its own experiences, whether perceived or imagined in the form of memories, projects, desires or predictions.

A last interesting observation is that some schizophrenic can tickle themselves. This may be interpreted as a malfunctioning of the efference copy mechanism, which would explain why the patient can experience positive symptoms and cannot determine which ones are his own thoughts or perceptions and which ones are not (Whitford et al., 2017; Roach et al., 2020).

The subjective space of inner symbolic images – i.e., imbued with affective meanings – differentiated from the outer space of objectual perceptions is the space of the *default mode network*. It is the inner space of the psyche, as it creatively constructs its world.

4.1   The default mode network

Studies of the self-referential DMN activity have radically changed our understanding of the brain. Until the 1990s, research in cognitive psychology and neuroscience was dominated by a task-centric view of mental functioning and emphasized the view of the brainmind as an organ reacting to interoceptive and/or exteroceptive stimuli. However, the massive presence of *endogenous* activity implies a tendency to form self-organized dynamic patterns (Brown, 2002; Llinás, 2002). This also implies that the brainmind does not merely react to stimuli but that it *dispositionally integrates* them within its endogenous "intrinsic" functioning.

Mind wandering has been specifically related to the activity of the medial temporal lobe (MTL), a set of brain areas centered on the hippocampus and the parahippocampal complex that constitute the oldest component of the DMN and whose antecedents have been found in the medial cortex of reptiles (Reiter et al., 2017). The MTL is implicated in navigating through the world (both physically and mentally) and in the formation of complex and abstract representations necessary for spatiotemporal orientation, declarative memory, contextual learning, creative thinking and social behaviors (Reiter et al., 2017). Connected to the default mode network, the MTL is the essence of the imaginative function and constitutes the first form of reflection, where intentions and drives gain a primordial form of conscious (but not yet self-conscious) representation. The endogenous mind wandering has been related to an intrinsic virtual-models generator function, through which the organism forms an inferential knowledge about the structure of its reality, its *Umwelt* (Hobson & Friston, 2012). During REM sleep, this inferential process may be subjectively experienced in the form of perceptual-like images that we call dreams and that express a primordial form of consciousness, or proto-consciousness (Hobson, 2009). During resting wakefulness, it may be subjectively experienced as an internal flow of imagines and thoughts (Carhart-Harris & Friston, 2010; Schacter et al., 2012; Agnati et al., 2016; Fox et al., 2013) that clearly resembles what William James described as the "stream of consciousness" and that Freud used for his "fundamental rule" for the "Psycho-Analytic Procedure" (1904):

> [to advice our patients] whatever comes into their heads, even if they think it unimportant or irrelevant or nonsensical [. . .] or embarrassing or distressing.
>
> (p. 251)

Freud was referring this rule as the "primary process of thinking" described as the instinctual, visual and unstructured mental processing typical in children, in dreams and in those with psychoses. Whereas for Freud, the primary process involves only the cathartic discharge activity of psychosomatic drives, for Jung, it constituted a specific way of "thinking". According to Jung, such processes carry not only an unknowable somatic aspect (Freud's drives) and a fundamental affective content but also a cognitive activity which may be potentially extremely developed, albeit functioning in its specific, imagistic, metaphorical, condensed way.

Recent neuroscientific evidences show that the degree of subjective self-relatedness – i.e., self-integrity – depends on the functioning of a core ventral portion of the DMN (D'Argembeau et al., 2005), which is specifically involved in carrying the emotional-affective ground within internally-oriented mental activity

(Christoff et al., 2016). In other words, it seems that the ventral portion of the DMN "constrains" the imaginative activity within specific orbits of meaning centered on characteristic emotional feelings or moods.

Under a Jungian light, the endogenous mental activity (the Self) is formed by potential psychic organizers that give to outer objects their emotional and cognitive value/meaning. Such organizers derive from endogenous emotional activation *and* the innately constrained production of cognitive schemas that I recalled earlier, which possess a general validity for interpreting the perceived stimuli and which will progressively match with outer experiences and perceptions to form personalized complexes (for a report of this matching in babies from birth – or possibly even before – one foundational study, Trevarthen, 1979).

After Jung, Melanie Klein's unconscious fantasies, or Winnicott's "conceived objects", or Bion's "pre-conceptions" also expressed the idea of endogenous psychological structures that will filter, interpret and match with perceived objects and that are eventually stored under the form of memories belonging to coherent episodes and narratives.

Within the line of research in neurodynamics, for Freeman, these dynamic patterns are not *representations* of stimuli but rather express the *meaning* that the nervous system of us animals attributes to the lived experience (Freeman, 1999). Seen this way, they match Jung's description of the complexes.

Moreover, as Alcaro, Panksepp and I have underlined in a previous contribution,

> the application of "non-linear dynamic theories to neuroscience": (Freeman, 1999; Brown, 2002; Llinás, 2002; Krieger, 2014), shifting the level of neurological analysis from the material-neurochemical to less readily discerned electrical fields, theoretically opens the way to shift from the physics of massive bodies to that of quantum physics, and, therefore, to the level of reality in which synchronistic phenomena may be rationally admissible (Jung, 1985; Bohm, 1980/1981; Penrose, 1989; Brown, 2002).
>
> (Alcaro et al., 2017, p. 7)

Therefore, we find the same element of integration to which I am often referring, now expressed in neurobiological terms under the form of immaterial *attractors* that organize large neuronal populations, or under the concept of *degeneracy* (vol. 1, § 5), in the very heart of subjective consciousness, which, as I have already said, has the peculiar qualities of always being a) *mine*, b) cohesive and d) unitary.

Subjective life emerges when primary affects are ready to be integrated into secondary emotions within ontogenetic evolution, developmental cognition and symbolization. This represents the transformation from procedural to declarative (self-conscious) states of the mind – those elements of the mind that Bion called (emotional) *thoughts*. However, we know that animals, even the simplest species, always modify their behavioral repertoire and adapt their responses contingent upon conditions. In view of this, some contemporary ethologists have concluded that such goal-directed flexibility is understandable only if we postulate the existence of subjective affective states that help in coordinating multiple action patterns in a complex and coherent way (Griffin, 1976). Otherwise, the enormous variability with which most animals adapt to changing environmental situations would necessitate an infinite number of instructions (either genetic or dependent on experiential learning), the problem of combinatorial explosion. Therefore, as direct expressions of internal modes of functioning – of "intentions-in-action" (Panksepp, 1998b) – affects may be viewed as the basic organizers of the mind (Panksepp, 1998a, 1998b; Panksepp & Biven, 2012; Damasio, 1999; Denton, 2006) and express a form of intentionality and rudimentary consciousness (Alcaro & Panksepp, 2014).

Intentionality, as a goal-directed organized process, may be equated to a description of a dynamic patterning process unfolding towards a goal. Consciousness is the process through which the flux of dynamic changes is accompanied by qualitative phenomenal experiences.

The (pre)conscious qualities of emotions are intrinsically related to their intentional character since positive and negative affective feelings always reflect the intention to approach or avoid certain situations. Therefore, we may see emotions as primal forms of intentional dispositions. For example, the SEEKING disposition drives the organism to forage for essential resources (food, water, sex, etc.), the FEAR disposition to avoid a source of danger, etc.

This teleological view, also fundamental in Jung's model of the psyche, considers emotional affects as self-perceptions of internal modes of functioning (the "intentions-in-action") – expressing a form of "a-noetic" consciousness, which is the first primal layer of the brain in which the core-self affectively experiences its own sense of itself.

> The intrinsic self-referential dynamism of the brainmind originated from REM sleep arousal and then evolved in the resting-state activity of the Default Mode Network. From our neuro-ethological perspective, it is sustained by an "introverted" SEEKING activity leading to the subjective exploration of internally constructed virtual scenarios. This "mind wandering" function, implicated in dreaming, fantasy processing, remembering and thinking, is the essence of the imaginative function and constitutes the first form of reflection and image-formation, where intentions and drives gain a primordial form of conscious (but not self-conscious) representation.
>
> (Alcaro & Carta, 2019)

You might remember that mental *conceptual primitives* are derived from a process of perceptual analysis of *moving objects by the moving self*. Such a process is, at the same time, linked with the origin of subjectivity and, hence, of the integrative function of affects. In fact, most investigators may not have even considered the idea that primary process-consciousness is integrally linked to *emotional* action coordinates because they assume that motor responses are mere "outputs" of the brain, and hence, the motor apparatus just governs nonconscious motor reflexes like the knee jerk (this way of thinking has been especially prevalent in areas such as fear-learning).[4]

How could such "mere" outputs of the brain constitute central integrative principles? Perhaps this relationship of "instinctual" (i.e., *constrained*) actions as foundations for consciousness may be easier to picture if we consider well-studied visual functions.

Once again, we must turn to vision. Referring to the role of efference copy, I have mentioned the role of movement while our eyes perceive an object. I already referred to the fact that visual perception tends to degrade if it is not anchored in exploratory eye movements (Yarbus, 1967).

Also, the stability of low-level visual perceptions in the superior colliculi (SC) is dependent on stable eye-movement coordinates. Therefore, eye-movement maps determine where, and presumably how, the SC processes the incoming visual sensory information (Strehler, 1991).

The SC, in addition to their role in vision (i.e., the most superficial layer of the SC), are integrated with hearing and touch in successive neural layers down below – a most interesting evolutionary progression, indeed. Touch preceded hearing (connected to feelings) and hearing preceded vision (connected to images and then concepts). This area – hearing – is a candidate for being a core affective structure of the self (Carta, 2009). For a relationship between language, emotion and hearing, see vol. 2, § 9. In any event, an action system required for visual orientation lies at the very "basal" layer of the SC, which sits right over the periaqueductal gray. In other words, the lowest neuronal layers of the superior colliculi constitute a basic motor orientation system that stabilizes, and perhaps permits, visual perception in self-referential coordinates, which may also interact with primary-process emotional systems just below, in the periaqueductal gray.

What I am trying to describe at a neurobiological level is the relationship between motion and affects for the subsequent formation of image-schemas, which will give phenomenological form to emotional meanings and purposes – in other words, to psychological experiences. Once again, this relationship between motion and affects is profoundly coherent with Jung's motivational theory and with his theory of the libido, which, as we have seen, is precisely rooted in these two factors – motricity and affects.

This bears repeating. When one records from the visual surface of the SC as animals make orienting eye and head movements towards visual stimuli, the neural registrations of the stimuli on the SC change position; they "float around", so to speak, depending on how the animal has just oriented itself. In other words, the same stimulus in visual space (the perception) changes locations on the surface of the SC depending on where the animal has moved its eyes and, hence, its focal attention (Lee et al., 1988). By comparison, the underlying motor map always remains stable and predictable, behaving the same when animals make specific orienting movements. There are good reasons to consider that the functions of the emotional action networks were laid down by evolution in comparably stable ways. Such findings encourage us to suggest that the emotional affective functions of the core-self are fundamentally modelled on the formal map of emotional-driven action systems that we can visually observe in animal behaviors.

In passing, it is interesting to notice that Damasio's idea – that the body schema is built on the motor activity of the sensory organs, like the eye (which are like brain surfaces projected towards the outer environment) – is coherent with Freud's idea of the Ego as a surface projected onto a surface. The fundamental difference is that for Jung, the Ego is not derived situationally – via the reality test with the environment – but by the dispositional nature of the affective core-self, from which such a motor surface is derived. Therefore, the Ego could be represented as a sort of fractal derivative of the Self, which, in turn, is entangled with the world.

From these studies on the endogenous nature and function of affectivity, it seems that Jung's idea might be right and that it is within this disposition that Freud's Ego as a surface interacts with the external world.

In closing this section of the neurobiological relevance of affects for images, we may see affects as internal, *teleological* modes of functioning as "intentions-in-action" (Panksepp), while "*complexes*" are a "readiness to act" (Jung). What is essential is to notice that the integrating element, the glue, for evolving consciousness and psychic integration of the conscious self by the ego-complex is always given by affectivity.

4.2   Images towards consciousness. An evolutionary (archetypal) history

With the formation of images – mental representations – and the development of cognition, emotions emerge. In fact, at this point, the dynamic, endogenous, dispositional and teleological principle of metastable homeostasis had functioned as non-representational, a-noetic affects. Now it is enriched by direct emotional representations, which, at first, are noetic and later become meta-noetic – reflectively conscious. These representations would refer to two critical sets of facts and events: (1) the conditions in the inner world of its own organism and (2) the conditions of its organism's environment.

> The existence of images was not possible before nervous systems grew in complexity. The world of sponges or of cnidarians such as hydras was enriched by the gift of a simple nervous system, but image making is unlikely to have been among its capabilities.
>
> (Damasio, 2021, p. 78)

As I had already mentioned in vol. 1, throughout evolution, the formation of centralized nervous systems enabled fine multisensory perceptions based on the mapping of numerous features. According to Damasio (2021), such mapping made it possible the creation of images for the construction of minds. To Damasio's position, I add the fundamental contribution of what would become the affects (the overall a-noetic metastable dynamic life-process of the organism) and, later on throughout evolution, of affects proper. These images provided synthetic and accurate internal representations, based on the organism's ongoing sensory descriptions of both external and internal events, and were able, among other things, to organize, following such proto-affects and affects, such a-noetic consciousness, and guide movement of a limb or of the whole body with precision towards a goal. It should be clear that such images did not need to be conscious in a self-reflective, autonoetic way; arising from the previous a-noetic state, they were conscious at a noetic way only. At any rate, homeostasis was improved. Differently from Damasio, I think that, already at the point of the noetic formation of inner images, the organism is capable of subjectivity, although not yet at a self-reflective level. Its images could automatically guide the execution of a movement, i.e., which movement would be more precise in terms of its target and better integrated within the evermore complex biological structure of these evolving organisms.

If affective awareness is an a-noetic state characterized by undifferentiated primary-process affects, conscious experiences involve a complex interplay of feelings and cognition, which forms what we call emotions, comprising the emergence of discrete objects of perceptions as well as the distinction between a "Sense of Self" and a "Sense of World" (Edelman, 1989; Alcaro, 2019). Therefore, if awareness has a continuous nature, consciousness introduces a fundamental fracture caused by a cognitive action that cuts specific borders around its objects. A few pages ago, I mentioned this situation and the evolutionary pathway that led to this organization. This dividing movement breaks the integrity of awareness and fixes the experiential flow around mental images, the representational structures that become the objects of experiences.[5]

> If there is no distance between body and brain, if body and brain interact and form an organismic single unit, then feeling is not a perception of the body state in the conventional sense of the term. Here the duality of subject-object, of perceiver-perceived, breaks down. Relative to this part of the process, there is unity instead. Feeling is the mental aspect of that unity.
>
> (Damasio, 2021, p. 126)

I think that through his own perspective, Damasio is describing something quite coherent with Jung's views. In fact, he is describing how the Self primarily comes to know itself through *feeling itself* and how these feelings regulate its homeostasis in a dispositional way, i.e., by triggering the proper responses that integrate the environment (the inner and outer stimuli) within its teleological homeostatic goal. I would also like to point out that this situation of "unity" is related to feelings because they are felt in a global, pervasive form. Phylogenetically and ontogenetically for the first months of life, they precede the mind's possibility to form proper representations, which imply a differentiation between figure and background. Images and then cognition will come later.

> Duality does come back in, however, at a different point of the complex process of brain-body interaction. When images of the body frame and its sensory

portals are formed, and when images of the spatial positions occupied by viscera are referred to that overall frame and placement within it, it becomes possible to generate a mental perspective of the organism, a set of separate images that is distinct from sensory images of the exterior (visual, auditory, tactile) and from the emotions and feelings they provoke. A duality sets in then, images of the "body frame and sensory-portal activity" to one side and, to the other, the rest of the images, those of the exterior and of the interior. That is the duality related to the process of subjectivity.

(Damasio, 2021, p. 126)

In this passage, Damasio is describing the birth of duality, i.e., the differentiation of opposites from an original affective oneness to a twoness described as inside/outside, subject/object. If, as Jung writes, consciousness means differentiation, this is one of the conditions by which consciousness appears ontogenetically. What is important is to emphasize that feelings always represent, express and evaluate the global situation, i.e., are a function of the Self as the union of opposites between self (with small s) and object. I would also like to point out that when Damasio writes, "separate images [. . .] distinct from sensory images of the exterior (visual, auditory, tactile) and from the emotions and feelings they provoke", the verb "provoke" should not imply a situational reading of the process and should be interpreted dispositionally as follows: "from the emotions and feelings whose interpretation they trigger".

Therefore, neural activity, rather than generating sentience, is involved in breaking the experiential continuum, giving rise to fragments of condensed experiences divided by way of actions. However, in affective awareness, these discontinuities are related to instinctive emotional responses directed towards specific goals. That said, the evolution and expansion of the cortex in vertebrates leads to a generalized inhibition of the endogenous emotional dispositions and to the emergence of cognitive-perceptual representations of external entities (images), built upon a mental separation between a subject and an object, that results in an increased capacity to act upon the external world (Bergson, 1896/1991).

More precisely, cognitive consciousness emerges when vigorous and unfocused exploration is inhibited and restricted to specific and detailed features of the environment, hence, imagistic representations. This important step in neuro-evolution happened when vertebrates moved from water to dry land and is related to cortical development and to the coincident reorganization of midbrain reticular nuclei, responsible for focused attention (Edelman et al., 2005).

The corticalization process is evident in reptiles with the evolution of the medial cortex, the first archeocortical formation that in mammals corresponds to the hippocampus and other temporal lobe regions (Reiter et al., 2017). As is well-established in the literature, the temporal lobes perform a special role in building an abstract and virtual knowledge of reality, where a dynamic flux of events is converted into static configurations that may be perceived all at once, crystallized images that have a specific spatial extension (Alcaro & Carta, 2019; Alcaro, 2019).

This is the description that Damasio gives of this phylogenetical development, starting from the ancestral situation in which there were no feelings, no mind and no consciousness but just a kind of homeostatic regulation to maintain and ensure survival and reproduction. A momentous leap in evolution happened with the development of a nervous systema capable of mapping and producing schemas – images. While these schemas – these patterns – were at first integrated maps of the outer world, during the Cambrian explosion, after numerous mutations, some creatures with a nervous system generated not only images of the outer environment but also:

> an imagetic counterpart to the busy process of life regulation that was going on underneath. This would have been the ground for a corresponding mental state, the thematic content of which would have been valenced in tune with the condition of life, at that moment, in that body. The quality of the ongoing life state would have been felt. To begin, even if the rest of the nervous system of such creatures would be very simple, just capable of producing simple maps of varied sensory information, the introduction, in such a mix, of obligate information about the "life-favorable or life-unfavorable" state of the organism would lead to more advantageous behavioral responses than previously available. Creatures equipped with this novel element, a simple qualifier juxtaposed with the image of certain places, or objects, or other creatures, would gain an automated guide as to whether they should approach or avoid those certain places or things or creatures. Life would be better run and possibly last longer, making reproduction more likely.
>
> (Damasio, 2021, pp. 123–124)

Damasio argues that these creatures, equipped with such automatic schemata – which already bear a strong resemblance with the way complexes work – were in a very favorable position to pass on the genes responsible for such a biological innovation and win in the evolutionary selection game.

> We have no way of knowing exactly when and how in evolution the actual emergence of feelings took place. All vertebrates have feelings, and the more I think of social insects, the more I suspect that their nervous systems generate simple minds with early versions of feeling and consciousness. A recent study favors this view. One thing is for certain: the processes that supported feelings after minds emerged had been in place long before and included the mechanisms necessary to generate the hallmark component of feelings – valence. As I see it, then, early life-forms were able to sense and respond and had the undergirding of feelings but not feelings as such, or minds, or consciousness. To arrive at what we call minds, feelings, and consciousness, evolution required a number of critical structural and functional increments that largely occurred within nervous systems. Simpler creatures than we are, including plants, sense and respond to stimuli in their environments. Simpler creatures also fight forcefully to maintain their physical integrity – but not plants, because they largely

lack movement, being encased in cellulose. You can hardly punch back if you are immobile. Sensing, responding, and forceful defenses against all manner of physical threats, however, which are indispensable parts of the great and variegated story of life, are not comparable to the mental phenomena we call minds, feelings, and consciousness.

(ivi)

Noetic, imagistic knowledge:

arises when refined attentional capacities permit a clear distinction and categorization of specific features of the environment which, with enough neo-cortex, allows animals to reflect[6] upon and elaborate their behavior in response.

Indeed, when specific aspects of events become the focus of attention, explicit object-related reflective awareness comes into the fore, while semantic (conceptual) memory helps to analyze and categorize the situation (Tulving, 1983). This is the form of consciousness that Edelman called "primary consciousness" and that he related to the activity of reentrant thalamic-cortical brain circuits (Edelman, 1989). Indirect evidence suggest that noetic consciousness is present across mammals, birds and perhaps also in reptiles (Edelman et al., 2005) and that human babies, born comparatively immature, start to manifest it after the 3rd month of development (Alcaro et al., 2017, p. 10).

This evolutionary change affords organisms a tremendous manipulative power over their environment, a power to build upon a dissociation of the subject from the representations of external objects of perception. Thus, the organism gains the ability to manipulate and adapt to its surrounding reality. At the same time, however, the effect of this awareness constitutes a fundamental threat, the risk of a loss of immediacy and integration between the organism and its environment, a hardening or fragmentation of the boundary between the subjective and the objective. However, recent experimental findings have shown that in parallel with the development of the medial archeocortex, vertebrates in general exhibit electrophysiological activity during sleep, which has been compared to the REM phase of sleep in mammals (Naumann et al., 2015). This evidence suggests that waking cognitive consciousness is accompanied by a dream consciousness in sleep, through which the animal can create or imagine internal scenarios and objects that are not present in the external perceptual world.

Interestingly, during the REM phase, endothermic animals lose their thermoregulatory capacity, so the body is left without its usual metabolic controls, while the brain instead becomes metabolically hyperactive, especially in certain MTL regions (Cerri et al., 2017). The "regression" to a metabolic pattern similar to the ectothermic state supports the view that dreams represent an evolutionary, archaic, imaginal mode of functioning of the brainmind (Panksepp, 1998b) and express a primary form of consciousness, or proto-consciousness (Hobson, 2009). Such a view also fits with the fact that the brainstem nuclei controlling the REM phase are evolutionarily older than those controlling slow wave sleep and active wakefulness (Panksepp, 1998b). Moreover, neurodevelopmental studies show that REM sleep appears before non-REM sleep and active waking in the human embryos and that REM sleep is largely preponderant in the last trimester of pregnancy, decreasing progressively after birth (Birnholz, 1981).

From our neuro-ethological perspective, dreaming is sustained by an "introverted" SEEKING activity leading to the subjective exploration of internally constructed virtual scenarios (Alcaro & Carta, 2019), integrating the other primary affects, such as PLAY. As we have seen, this "mind-wandering" function originated from REM-arousal and then evolved in waking resting-state activity implicated in fantasy processing, remembering and thinking.

In a recent article published with Antonio Alcaro, we presented the hypothesis that dream and resting-state imaginative activity evolved to reorganize the set of cognitive memories accumulated during the day,[7] starting from a primary exploratory mode, no longer based on focused attention but rather on a kind of mental wandering (Alcaro & Carta, 2019) – a kind of erratic dance, seemingly disorderly and illogical, but its origins are the expression of an affective dimension. A similar hypothesis to ours was put forward more than 30 years ago by Micheal Jouvet, who considered dreams a form of neurogenetic programming, where the experiences lived in contact with external reality are assimilated and reorganized starting from one's primary psycho-biological identity (Jouvet, 1975). Yet this re-collection and reorganization of the daily occurrences in dream would have the function to reintegrate Ego-experiences – therefore, the Ego itself – within the perspective of the Self. Refining gold from vile metal, the dream saves and transforms those everyday experiences through which the numinous gold of universality will shine.

I just referred to the level of the brainmind functioning in which a-noetic affects represent themselves into "images". One of the most frequent criticisms of Jung's theory of the archetypes regards the "archetypal images" because it is believed that such complex contents cannot be possibly inherited. To clear the way from any possible misunderstanding, I wish to make clear that I wholly agree on these words written by Jean Knox, which I have already quoted:

> The central theme here is that of self-organization of the human brain and the recognition that genes do not encode complex mental imagery and processes, but instead act as initial catalysts for developmental processes out of which early psychic structures reliably emerge. A developmental account of archetype lends considerable scientific support to the key role archetypes play in psychic functioning and as a crucial source of symbolic imagery, but at the same time identifies archetypes as emergent structures resulting from a developmental interaction between genes and environment that is unique for each person. Archetypes are not "hard-wired" collections of universal imagery waiting to be released by the right environmental trigger, a model which would lead straight

into the trap of categorizing them as innate ideas, a concept demolished by Locke long before anyone had ever heard of genes.

(Knox, 2004, p. 4)

Nevertheless, in the same article, Knox writes:

An alternative model is offered by this international collaborative research group who state that: "some innate predispositions . . . channel the infant's attention to certain aspects of the environment over others. Our view is that these predispositions play different roles at different levels, and that as far as representation-specific predispositions are concerned, they may only be specified at the subcortical level as little more than attention grabbers so that the organism ensures itself of a massive experience of certain inputs prior to subsequent learning . . . at the cortical level, representations are not pre-specified: at the psychological level representations emerge from the complex interactions of brain and environment and brain systems among themselves.

(Knox, 2004, p. 5)

I do not agree with this view, as it seems to be referring to an idea of the psyche as something built to respond to the environment, without taking into consideration the dispositional nature of biological life, for which, as I have already said, homeostasis is a principle that refers to the organism's *inner* balance. Yet the whole question might be put in a different way. In fact, as I already wrote, I think that we must *not* consider these *imagines* as "contents" but as *representations* of the interplay between a core affect, or more often, of a secondary emotion (also depending on the development of the subject's personality) formed through the same mechanism that Annette Karmiloff-Smith called representational redescription, integrated into cognitive schema and developed within a co-evolutionary, relational field. As I already pointed out, these inner images are of a very different nature from perceptions of outer objects; they are subjective emotional sensations represented *as* perceptions.

In this perspective, the *imagines* are spontaneous representations of endogenous emotional action patterns that connect the subject with her inner and outer environment which *use* the perceptual structures to acquire a form, a pattern under the form of visual images. They are symbolic. We have seen how important is to be able to distinguish perceptions from sensations (remember the issue of schizophrenia). In this perspective, it means to be able *not to conflate factual information with our creative capability to find a subjective "gnostic" meaning from experience.*

These action-patterns, represented as schemas, would be *functional* structures and not "contents", perhaps corresponding at a neuro-anatomical level to modularized neural networks (in which the principle of degeneracy would play a key role). They would be equated to verbs produced by emotional qualities (adjectives) and not to nouns. In fact, the noun would be the end product of a cognitive process of categorization and abstraction of the ongoing flow of a relational process.

Therefore, as I already wrote, what would be "inherited" (and this process needs a differentiated analysis) would not be the complex "archetypal" image[8] but the following: a) some core-triggering affects which work towards the re-establishment of a psychosomatic homeostasis and b) the representational redescriptive (transcendent) *process* itself, something that seems postulated by Annette Karmiloff-Smith for cognition and generally accepted as plausible. These inner, "mental" conditions would always take place within a co-evolutionary milieu.

Together with Antonio Alcaro, I wrote:

Most scholars today consider subjectivity (personal experience) the result of an individual historical process and, therefore, as an acquisition of human development. In particular, the emergence of a mental life and of a sense of "self" have been associated with emotional and cognitive skills that permit the child to reflect upon his/her experience.

Such an essential function, called "mentalization" or "reflective function", is usually considered a product of the attachment relationship (Stern, 1985; Schore, 1994; Fonagy & Target, 1997; Fonagy et al., 2002). Cognitive psychologists, psychoanalysts and neuroscientists are in agreement that the child *learns* to have a subjective mental life and to recognize it as his own by internalizing experiences and aspects of the attachment relationship, which are dependent on the self-reflective capacity of the caregiver (Bowlby, 1969, 1978; Bretherton & Munholland, 1999).

While recognizing the importance of such theories, we think that strict developmental views fail to consider that newborns are provided with an innate potential endogenous mental activity where the intersubjective environment is subjectively experienced and represented. Indeed, newborns are provided with functional "core-Self" subcortical midline brain structures (SCMS) implicated in the emergence of a primary form of "a-noetic" affective consciousness, characterized by moods, somato-visceral states and basic emotional feelings, which constitute the first form of self-orientation in the world (Panksepp, 1998b; Damasio, 1999; Solms & Panksepp, 2012; Alcaro et al., 2017). Moreover, neurodevelopmental studies have shown that human embryos already possess an intrinsic brain dynamism typical of REM sleep, that appears before non-REM sleep and active waking and that is largely preponderant in the last trimester of pregnancy (Birnholz, 1981). On the base of the relation between REM sleep and dreaming, it has been proposed that the "noetic" form of consciousness implicated in the representation of the external world may have developed from a dream-like imaginative function, already active at birth, that interprets objectual experiences on the base of internally generated phantasies (or virtual models of reality) (Hobson, 2009; Hobson & Friston, 2012). Therefore, following such neuroscientific paths and in accordance with Jung's Analytical psychology (Jung, 1937), we believe that the so-called "reflective function" is grafted in an embryonic form of mental activity, characterized by the ancestral "instinctual" pre-disposition to imagine and dream. Flowing from this instinct for reflection, the intrinsic drives of the living organism turn inwards and rather than expressing themselves in actions (motor or physiological) they fit back upon themselves and eventually establish a noetic subjective psychic dimension (Jung, 1937; Shamdasani, 2003). In humans and other endothermic animals, the product of this reflective instinct is a pouring out of images that, like jets of clear water from the rocks of a mountain's stream, are born in a borderland between the unconscious and the conscious, between the body and the mind, whose substratum is that of raw emotions.

(Alcaro & Carta, 2019, pp. 1–2)

My hypothesis is that Jung's reflection could, therefore, act not just to transform perceptions into proto-concepts (as in Jean Mandler's theory, through perceptual analysis and Karmiloff-Smith's representational redescription) but also act on the other evolutionary, "archaic" level of the brainmind – the primary affects, which are progressively transformed and differentiated into qualitatively different and diverse affects (the word "love" means many more things for Shakespeare than for an average child or, for that matter, an average human being) and into secondary emotions.

Karmiloff-Smith's *implicit* level of representational redescription would, therefore, produce a schematic representation from sensory-motor data (which, in this case, has a *cognitive* nature) and in so doing would express just a portion of the more encompassing activity of reflectivity and the transcendent function, which would redescribe and represent an implicit schematic representation emerging from a-noetic affects into noetic *emotional* images (as in dreams, in which, according to Jung, every image is a visual representation of a complex, which we may define as an "intentional emotional action pattern").

As symbolic images are the emergent product of the transformation of affects structured by sensory-motor patterns, they may be thought of as cognitive organizations of the motivational affects. Further abstraction will lead to declarative knowledge and, eventually, culture and language.

Notes

1 A telling example is the fact that, although placed in different parts of the brains, there is a striking similarity of the functional architecture of working memory between humans and birds, although their common ancestor is around 400 million years ago. This is the case of the avian nidopallium caudolaterale, a key brain region for guiding goal-directed behavior, which is believed to be analogous to the mammalian prefrontal cortex (Divac et al., 1985; Güntürkün, 2005).
2 Although he never quoted him, Lacan derived this idea directly from the French psychologist Henri Paul Wallon (1931, 1954). The mirror stage is as famous as it is controversial for many reasons (Tallis, 1988; Webster, 2002). Lacan explicitly refers to a visual perceptual mirroring experience, although one cannot not notice that this would be highly improbable, due to the scarcity, if not complete absence, of decent mirroring until a very short time ago. I might be wrong, but I do not see how the infant in front of the mirror that Lacan describes would have ever occurred, if not in this imaginary situation of a child

in a bourgeois apartment in Paris, held by a walker (Lacan's "*trotte-bébé*"). Lacan could have referred to touch *in coordination* with vision, *but not just vision*, and to the relationship between perceptions and sensations. Therefore, I wonder whether he should instead be talking about the principle of reflectivity, perhaps in terms of efference copying. In so doing, perhaps his theory might be simplified in his extraordinarily complex deductions (such as the infant's jubilance), all gravitating from narcissism and its discontents.

3 Hillman (1975) very appropriately cites the "tortured images" described by Frances Yates in her seminal *The Art of Memory* (1966).

As the Neoplatonists, from Proclus and Porphyrius to Marsilio Ficino's Renaissance and Giulio Camillo's "Theater of Memory", had perfectly understood, memory is the opposite of a reproductive process of factual perceptual matter.

As usual, even now, alchemy comes to our rescue with its metaphors: the perceptual *prima materia* (*alas!* what is nowadays called "evidence-based" experience) is tortured "psychopathically" (Hillman) in the *athanor* of the mind and undergoes a process of *mortificatio*.

As I tried to say earlier referring to the analyst's not-knowing, it is through the *nigredo* of this perceptual-factual matter (i.e., produced by the perceptual apparatus of the Ego) that the mind imagines and, therefore, symbolically apprehends itself and, through itself (through, Kant would say, the conditions of its own knowing), knows the world.

As artists, mystics and scientists know in the moment of discovering and not of proving, for the human species, the true origin of knowledge is imagination, and this proceeds, in wonder, awe and gratitude, from "God".

4 In fact, the contemporary discussion *does not* consider reflexes to be emo*tions*, like the startling response (see: Ekman et al., 1985).

5 This issue is discussed regarding the relationship between the acoustic (and music) *vs.* the visual (images), where the center of the complex is not representational/imaginative but affective/acoustic vs. the visual (Carta, 2009).

6 Here, "reflect" describes a process of transformation/transcription that mirrors affects into images.

7 Far from being a flat temporal surface, this day that precedes the dream contains, as Husserl argues, the past of the present, the present of the present and the future of the present.

8 Therefore, these are symbolic images produced by an affect that belong to the subjective world of sensations and not to the world of perceived objects.

References

Agnati, L.F., Guidolin, D., Battistin, L., Pagnoni, G., Fuxe, K. (2016). The neurobiology of imagination: Possible role of interaction-dominant dynamics and default mode network. *Frontiers in Psychology*, 4, 296.

Alcaro, A. (2019). Il Soffio della Consapevolezza e Il Taglio della Coscienza. *Rivista Di Psicologia Analitica*, 48(100), 119–237.

Alcaro, A. (2024). *La Mente Affettiva*. Roma: Astrolabio.

Alcaro, A., Carta, S. (2019). The "instinct" of imagination. A neuro-ethological approach to the evolution of the reflective mind and its application to psychotherapy. *Frontiers in Human Neuroscience*, 12, 422481.

Alcaro, A., Carta, S., Panksepp, J. (2017). The affective core of the self: A neuro-archetypical perspective on the foundations of human (and animal) subjectivity. *Frontiers in Psychology*, 8, 1424.

Alcaro, A., Panksepp, J. (2014). Le radici affettive e immaginative del Sé. Un'indagine neuroetologica sulle origini della soggettività. In: Nortoff, G., Farinelli, M., Chattat, R., Baldoni, F. (eds) *La Plasticità del Sé. Una Prospettiva Neuropsicodinamica*. Bologna: Il Mulino.

Bergson, H. (1896/1991). *Matter and Memory*. New York, NY: Zone Books.

Birnholz, J.C. (1981). The development of human fetal eye movement patterns. *Science*, 213(4508), 679–681.

Bohm, D. (1980/1981). *Wholeness and the Implicate Order*. London, New York: Routledge.

Bowlby, J. (1969). *Attachment and Loss, Vol. 1: Attachment. Attachment and Loss*. New York, NY: Basic Books.

Bowlby, J. (1978). *Attachment and Loss, Vol 2: Separation: Anxiety and Anger*. London: Penguin Books.

Bretherton, I., Munholland, K A. (1999). Internal Working Models in Attachment Relationships: A Construct Revisited. In: Cassidy J., Shaver P.R. (eds) *Handbook of Attachment: Theory, Research, and Clinical Applications*. New York, NY: The Guilford Press, pp. 89–111.

Brown, J.W. (2002). *The Self-Embodying Mind. Process, Brain Dynamics and the Conscious Present*. New York, NY: Barrytown.

Carhart-Harris, R., Friston, K. (2010). The default-mode, ego-functions and free-energy: A neurobiological account of freudian ideas. *Brain*, 133, 1265–1283.

Carta, S. (2009). Music in dreams and the emergence of the self. *Journal of Analytical Psychology*, 54(1).

Carta, S. (2024). *What Images of What? Sensations and Perceptions as the Foundation of Image Creation*, in press.

Carta, S., Alcaro, A. (2022). Una Casa Di 3 Piani + 1. Il Sogn Di Jung e Le Omologie Archetipiche Cervello-Mente in una Prospettiva Evolutive. *Studi Junghiani*, 28(1).

Cerri, M., Luppi, M., Tupone, D., Zamboni, G., Amici, R. (2017). REM sleep and endotherm: Potential sites and mechanism of a reciprocal interference. *Frontiers in Physiology*, 8, 624.

Christoff, K. et al. (2016). Mind-wandering as spontaneous thought: A dynamic framework. *Nature Reviews Neuroscience*, 17, 718–731.

Damasio, A. (2021). The *Strange Order of Things: Life, Feeling and the Making of Cultures*. New York: Pantheon Book.

Damasio, A.R. (1999). How the brain creates the mind. *Scientific American*, 281(6), 112–117.

D'Argembeau, A., Collette, F., Van Der Linden, M., Laureys, S. (2005). Self-referential reflective activity and its relationship with rest: A PET study. *Neuroimage*, 25(2), 616–624.

Denton, D.A. (2006). *The Primordial Emotions: The Dawning of Consciousness*. New York, NY: Oxford University Press.

Divac, I., Mogensen, J., Bjorklund, A. (1985). The prefrontal "cortex" in the Pigeon. Biochemical evidence. *Brain Research*, 332, 365–368.

Edelman, D.B., Baars, B.J., Seth, A.K. (2005). Identifying hallmarks of consciousness in non-mammalian species. *Consciousness and Cognition*, 14, 169–187.

Edelman, G.M. (1989). *The Remembered Present: A Biological Theory of Consciousness*. New York, NY: Basic Books.

Ekman, P., Friesen, W.V., Simons, R.C. (1985). Is the startling reaction an emotion? *Journal of Personality and Social Psychology*, 49(5), 1416–1426.

Fonagy, P., Gergely, G., Jurist, E.L., Target, M. (2002). *Affect Regulation, Mentalization, and the Development of the Self*. New York, NY: Other Press.

Fonagy, P., Target, M. (1997). Attachment and reflective function: Their role in self-organization. *Development and Psychopathology*, 9(4), 679–700.

Fox, K.C. et al. (2013). Dreaming as mind wandering: Evidence from functional neuroimaging and first-person content reports. *Frontiers in Human Neuroscience*, (7), 412.

Freeman, W.J. (1999). *How Brains Make Up Their Minds*. London: Weidenfeld and Nicolson.

Freud, S. (1904). *Freud's Psycho-Analytic Procedure. SE*, vol. 7. London: Hogart Press, pp. 247–254.

Goodwyn, E. (2012). *The Neurobiology of the Gods. How Brain Physiology Shapes the Recurrent Imagery of Myths and Dreams*. London, New York: Routledge.

Griffin, D.R. (1976). *The Question of Animal Awareness. Evolutionary Continuity of Mental Experience*. New York, NY: Rockfeller University Press.

Güntürkün, O. (2005). The avian "prefrontal cortex" and cognition. *Current Opinion in Neurobiology*, 15(6), 686–693.

Hillman, J. (1975). *Re-Visioning Psychology*. New York: Harper & Row.

Hobson, J.A. (2009). REM sleep and dreaming: Towards a theory of protoconsciousness. *Nature Reviews. Neuroscience*, 10(11), 803–813.

Hobson, J.A., Friston, K.J. (2012). Waking and dreaming consciousness: Neurobiological and functional considerations. *Neurobiology*, 98(1), 82–98.

Jouvet, M. (1975). The Function of Dreaming. A Neurophysiologist's Point of View. In: Gazzaniga, M.S., Blackemore, C. (eds) *Handbok of Psychology*. New York, NY: University Press.

Jung, C. G. (1937). *Psychological factors determining human behaviour, in The Collected Works of C.G. Jung*, vol 8. R.F.C. Hull (Trans.), eds H. Read, M. Fordham, G. Adler and W. McGuire (Princeton, NJ: Princeton University Press), 114–128

Jung, C. (1964). *Man and His Symbols*. New York: Dell Publishing.

Jung, C.G. (1985). Synchronicity: An Acausal Connecting Principle. In: *Collected Works*, vol. 8. London, New York, NY: Routledge.

Knox, J.M. (2004). From archetypes to reflective function. *Journal of Analytical Psychology*, 49(1), 1–19.

Krieger, N.M. (2014). *Bridges to Consciousness. Complexes and Complexity*. New York, NY: Routledge.

Lee, C., Rohrer, W., Sparks, D. (1988). Population coding of saccadic eye movements by neurons in the superior colliculus. *Nature*, 332, 357–360.

Llinás, R. (2002). *I of the Vortex: From Neurons to Self*. Cambridge, MA: MIT Press.

Maclean, P.D. (1985). Brain evolution relating to family, play, and the separation call. *Archives of General Psychiatry*, 42(4), 405–417.

Maclean, P.D. (1990). *The Triune Brain in Evolution: Role in Paleocerebral Functions*. New York: Plenum Press.

Naumann, K.N., Ondracek, J.M, Reiter, S., Shein-Idelson, M., Tosches, M.A., Yamawaki, T.M., Laurent, G. (2015). The reptilian brain. *Current Biology*, 25(8).

Panksepp, J. (1998a). The periconscious substrates of consciousness: Affective states and the evolutionary origins of the SELF. *Journal of Consciousness Studies*, 5, 566–582.

Panksepp, J. (1998b). *Affective Neuroscience: The Foundations of Human and Animal Emotions*. New York, NY: Oxford University Press.

Panksepp, J., Biven, L. (2012). The *Archaeology of Mind: Neuroevolutionary Origins of Human Emotion*. New York, NY: W.W. Norton & Company.

Penrose, R. (1989). *The Emperor's New Mind*. New York, NY: Oxford University Press.

Reiter, S., Liaw, H.P., Yamawaki, T.M., Naumann, R.K., Laurent, G. (2017). On the value of reptilian brains to map the evolution of the hippocampal formation. *Brain, Behavior and Evolution*, 90(1).

Roach, B.R., Ford, J.M., Biagianti, B., Hamilton, H.K., Ramsay, I.S., Fishe, M., Loewy, R., Vinogradov, D., Mathalon, D.H. (2020). Efference copy/corollary discharge function and targeted cognitive training in patients with schizophrenia. *International Journal of Psychophysiology*, 145, 91–98.

Schacter, D.L. et al. (2012). The future of memory: Remembering, imagining, and the brain. *Neuron*, 76(4), 677–694.

Schore, A.N. (1994). *Affect Regulation and the Origin of the Self: The Neurobiology of Emotional Development*. Mahwah, NJ: Lawrence Erlbaum Associates, Inc.

Shamdasani, S. (2003). *Body and Soul, Jung and the Making of Modern Psychology: The Dream of Science*, Vol. 254. Cambridge, MA: Cambridge University Press.

Solms, M., and Panksepp, J. (2012). The "id" knows more than the "ego" admits: neuropsy-choanalytic and primal consciousness perspectives on the interface between affective and cognitive neuroscience. *Brain Sci.* 2, 147–175. doi: 10.3390/brainsci2020147

Stern, D.N. (1985). *The Interpersonal World of the Infant: A View from Psychoanalysis and Developmental Psychology.* London: Karnac Books.

Strehler, B.L. (1991). Where is the self? A neuroanatomical theory of consciousness. *Synapse*, 7(1).

Tallis, R. (1988). *Not Saussure: A Critique of Post-Saussurean Literary Theory.* London: Macmillan.

Trevarthen, C. (1979). Communication and Cooperation in Early Infancy. A Description of Primary Intersubjectivity. In: Bullowa, M. (ed) *Before Speech: The Beginning of Human Communication.* London: Cambridge University Press, pp. 321–347.

Tulving, E. (1983). *Elements of Episodic Memory.* Oxford: Clarendon Press.

von Holst, E., Mittelstaedt, H. (1950). Das Reafferenzprinzip. *Naturwissenschaften*, 37, 464–476.

Wallon, H. (1931/1967). Come si Sviluppa la Nozione del Proprio Corpo nel Bambino. In: *Sviluppo Della Coscienza e Formazione Del Carattere.* Firenze: La Nuova Italia, pp. 35–78.

Wallon, H. (1954/1967). Cinestesia e Immagine Visuale Del Proprio Corpo nel Bambino. In: *Psicologia Ed Educazione Del Bambino.* Firenze: La Nuova Italia, pp. 59–76.

Webster, R. (2002). The *Cult of Lacan: Freud, Lacan and the Mirror Stage*. http://www.Richardwebster.Net/Thecultoflacan.Html

Whitford, T.J., Mitchell, A.M., Mannion, D.J. (2017, July). The ability to tickle oneself is associated with level of psychometric schizotypy in non-clinical individuals. *Consciousness and Cognition*, 52, 93–103.

Yarbus, A.L. (1967). Eye Movements during Perception of Complex Objects. In: *Eye Movements and Vision.* Boston, MA: Springer.

Yates, F.A. (1966). *The Art of Memory.* London: Routledge.

Chapter 5

Culture and representations

Throughout these two volumes, I have referred to the role of constraints, out of which "modules" emerge as biological, morphological and functional structures within the realm of biology. In the psychological realm, another important developmentalist, Annette Karmiloff-Smith, whose theory I have taken as an important model, disagrees with the sometimes too-strict modular theory of some evolutionary psychologists (like Jerry Fodor), presupposing the existence of psychological constraints from which specific cognitive learning domains would eventually emerge. In this light, I wrote that the notion of a cognitive "g factor" (i.e., the existence of a general form of intelligence which should be able to learn and adapt free of constraints) seems to be untenable, if not as an altricial *more flexible* form of intelligence metaphorized from a precocial layer. Hence, the notions of psychological constraints and attractors seem to be generally accepted; what is still under discussion is their role and pervasiveness – whether they stretch into and how much they determine symbolic and cultural formations.

This discussion has important consequences for the radical culturalists who, following Durkheim's perspective, exclude from their analysis any reference to bio-psychological constraints and to Darwin, as if humans were not bound by Darwinian's evolution but that were, once again as in pre-Darwinian times, *special, unique and radically different animals.*

This release of what is thought to be typically human – the symbolic world of "culture" – from "nature" refers to the debate between "altricial" and "precocial" species that I discussed in vol. I, § 7.2. and to the consequences of the indisputable, yet perhaps not wholly de-specialized, nature of *Homo sapiens*.

> In human evolution, natural selection removed "genetically determined" systems of behavior and replaced them with general-purpose learning mechanisms or content-independent cognitive processes. Supposedly, these more general systems were favored by evolution because they did not constrain human behavior to be maladaptively inflexible (e.g., Geertz, 1973; Harris, 1979; Montagu, 1964). Neurobiology is the account of how these general mechanisms are instantiated in our nervous system.
>
> (Barkow et al., 1992, p. 30)

DOI: 10.4324/9781003586463-5

Once again, I should recall Jung's position, for which the pervasive de-specialized nature of human psychology has to do with consciousness, whereas the unconscious would maintain a level of evolutionary ancestral, modularized (complexual) specialization.

Durkheim's principle allows for sociological factors to be explained sociologically, which is acceptable if it is meant to be a provisional, fictional, analytical strategy. However, if this means, as it does, the expulsion, or rather, the denial, of other levels of human reality, such as the psychological and the biological, it sounds much more like a religious ideology.

> But one would be strangely mistaken about our thought if, from the foregoing, he drew the conclusion that sociology, according to us, must, or even can, make an abstraction of man and his faculties. It is clear, on the contrary, that the general characteristics of human nature participate in the work of elaboration from which social life results. But they are not the cause of it, nor do they give it its special form; they only make it possible. Collective representations, sensations, emotions, and tendencies are caused not by certain states of the consciousnesses of individuals but by the conditions in which the social group, in its totality, is placed. Such actions can, of course materialize only if the individual natures are not resistant to them; but these individual natures are merely the indeterminate material that the social factor molds and transforms. Their contributions consist exclusively in a very general attitudes, in vague and consequently plastic predispositions which, by themselves, if other agents did not intervene, could not take on the definite and complex forms which characterize social phenomena.
>
> (Durkheim, 1895/1962)

The complicated point is *how to connect the various levels of reality without explaining away – therefore, "reducing" – one to the other*. This implies the search for the "missing, transformational links" between levels of reality or, better said, the levels of analysis.

If we really want to be epistemologically parsimonious and produce heuristic statements about the nature of things, whenever we have a paradigm or a theory that could be able to *connect* levels of reality, instead of declaring the metaphysical autonomy and/or supremacy of any one of them from the others, *we must endorse it*. Therefore, the problem is *how* to connect ecology, biology, psychology and anthropology/sociology to pursue a harmonic picture of that amazing complexity that is human life – the complexity that the psychotherapist must deal with every patient.

Together with Durkheim, neither Kroeber (with his notion of culture as something "superorganic") nor Lowie agrees with this perspective:

> Culture is a thing sui generis which can be explained only in terms of itself. . . . Omnis cultura ex cultura.
>
> (Lowie, 1917/1966, pp. 25–26)

The only antecedents of historical phenomena are historical phenomena.

(Kroeber, 1917)

I do not agree with this metaphysical, irreducible gap between biology, psychology and anthropology (or sociology) or with a radical split between explanation and experience. I argue that within the co-evolutionary scenario, attractors and constraints appear *at least already* within the biological (evolutionary) perspective, if not in the physical domains, and reveal their influence within anthropology *through psychology*. For this perspective, behavior evolves just as structure evolves, and the two are intimately linked.

According to Fox:

> even if species shed its dependence on instincts, it still has to do the same things the instincts were designed to do. As Bergson saw so clearly, culture has to do the same job that instinct had been doing. This is another paradox, I suppose, but an intriguing one, because to get culture to do the same job that instinct had been doing, had been made in many ways, like instinctive behavior. It had to be unconscious so that it did not require thoughts for its operation; it had to be automatic so that certain stimuli would immediately produce it; it had to be common to all members of the population.

(Fox, 1973, p. 260)

In fact, within a speculative fiction for which Adam and Eve would be re-created:

> They would eventually produce society. It would be likely to have laws about property, its inheritance and exchange; rules about incest and marriage; customs of taboo and avoidance; methods of settling disputes with the minimum of a bloodshed; beliefs about the supernatural in practises relating to it men women were excluded; courtship practises, including the adornment of females; gambling of some kind; a tool – and the weapon making – industry; myths and legends; dancing; adultery; homicide; kinship groups; schizophrenia; psychosis and neurosis, and various practitioners to take advantage of or cure these (depending on how they are viewed).

(Fox, 1973, p. 252)

For Dan Sperber and cognitive anthropology, culture is *not* the "thing sui generis" that Lowie imagined but is a property of some general, social communication of shared representations that are in the mind of each individual that participates in the social exchange. From a cognitive point of view, it is fruitful to think of culture as a stabilized ensemble of representations (classifications, schemas, models, competences), the possession of which makes an individual a member of a social group. This view of culture refers to the concept of the "missing link" between biology and anthropology that connote Wilson's reductionist sociobiology discussed by Tooby and Cosmides. The missing link would be precisely such psychic "representations", which, in modern terms, represent Ficino's notion of *anima copula mundi.*

What kinds of objects are we talking about when we speak of representations? According to Sperber, we can talk of representations both as internal mental formations and as external concrete, physical objects located in time and space. At this concrete level, we must distinguish two kinds of representations: there are mental representations, internal to the subject, and there are representations external to the subject, which can process as inputs – i.e., public representations.

As Sperber maintains, such representations become cultural – one may say make a culture – only when they become "stabilized" within a social group through time. Hence, a central question becomes, for Sperber, why some representations are stabilized and some are not.

Differently from Sperber, I wish to point out again that, in my view, such cognitive representations are abstractions from those "embodied thoughts" that we normally call emotions. Hence, when Sperber mentions external and internal representations, we should remember that the connecting nature of emotions (and not their reification into "things", substances) that I have already mentioned, starting from the notion of the archetype as an operator-between, is twofold: emotions are stable socially connecting factors between individuals which create social institutions and social artifacts, while, at the same time, connect and give meaning to the relationship of the subjective, *inner* experiences of the group's members.

> After deconstruction, emotion retains value as a way of talking about the intensely meaningful as that is culturally defined, socially enacted, and personally articulated. It retains value also as a category more open than others to use as a link between the mental and the physical, and between the ideal or desired world and the actual world. [. . .]
>
> Although we may experience emotion as something that rises and falls within the boundaries of our bodies, the decidedly social origins of our understandings of the self, the other, the world, and experience draw our attention to the interpersonal processes by which something called emotion or some things like joy, anger, or fear come to be ascribed to and experienced by us. [. . .] the use of emotion concepts, as elements of local ideological practice, involves negotiation over the meaning of events, over rights and morality, over control of resources-in short, involves struggles over the entire range of issues that concern human groups.
>
> (Lutz, 1988, p. 5)

In early cognitive anthropology, culture was often compared to a language, with a copy of it in the mind of every culturally competent member of the group. Since then, it has been generally recognized that cultures are much less integrated than languages and tolerate a much greater degree of interindividual variation. Moreover, with the recent insistence on the role of artifacts, it has become common to acknowledge the cultural character of these artifacts: culture is not just in the mind. Still, in a standard cognitive anthropological perspective, culture is first and foremost something in the mind of every individual. The fact that culture is a population-scale phenomenon is, of course, acknowledged but plays only a trivial role in explanation.

This perspective is very interesting, as it fundamentally criticizes the very idea of culture as an organic social something. In fact, this idea of culture as a unitary corpus may well be a product of a Western colonial perspective, in which the nation-state is conceived as a unitary, homogeneous entity, while it should be re-conceptualized as a dynamic flow of an exceedingly complex number of individual emotional-cognitive representations – may they be social, economic, ethical, relational, religious, etc. – dynamically shared by a certain number of people.

5.1   What is a susceptibility?

Framed in this way, the notion of representation brings us to the last step of our hierarchical ladder, in which biological constraints, after producing emergent psychological constraints, become psycho-social *susceptibilities*. Hence, now the issue is to explain how some individual representations are socially shared and some are not and how some of them stabilize through time into a common specific culture.

In anthropology, the term "susceptibility" can have various meanings depending on the context. Here are a few possible interpretations:

- Cultural susceptibility: Anthropologists may study the susceptibility of a particular culture to external influences, such as globalization, technological change or cultural diffusion. This involves examining how a culture responds or adapts to new ideas, practices or technologies.
- Social susceptibility: Anthropologists might also investigate the susceptibility of social groups to particular behaviors, norms or social changes. For example, they might study how different communities respond to economic shifts, political events or changes in social structures.
- Environmental susceptibility: Anthropologists studying environmental anthropology might examine the susceptibility of human societies to environmental changes. This could include investigating how different cultures adapt to or are impacted by changes in climate, ecosystems or natural resources.
- Health susceptibility: In medical anthropology, researchers might focus on the susceptibility of populations to health issues, diseases or medical interventions. This involves understanding how cultural, social and environmental factors contribute to health outcomes.

"Susceptibility", therefore, typically refers to the vulnerability or responsiveness of individuals or groups to various external or internal factors, whether cultural, social, environmental, health-related or cognitive. This last meaning of the words is the one that most interests us – the cognitive meaning of susceptibility – *if we put cognition in its proper place, as something triggered, organized and directed by "susceptible affects".*

- Cognitive susceptibility refers to the perspective adopted by those anthropologists interested in cognitive anthropology. Within this perspective, this word indicates the susceptibility of human minds to certain cognitive processes, beliefs or cultural ideas. Such susceptibilities refer to the cultural domain, as they selectively produce, maintain or eliminate by decay symbolic, cultural and social structures and contents. In so doing, they determine what is internal and characteristic of a social/cultural group and, therefore, *belong to the cultural domain* as peculiar forms of constraints which derive from underlying constraints of a psychological nature – i.e., internal to the mind of each individual that participates to the social group.

The study of susceptibilities involves studying how individuals acquire and internalize cultural knowledge and how and to what extent and at what level cultural knowledge is specific to the culture to which it belongs or whether its constraints also determine a level in which it has a universal, "archetypal" nature.

The concept of susceptibility is directly connected with that of ontological category, which acts towards the centrifugal production of virtually infinite more concrete inferences and concepts in a centripetal way, thereby constraining and organizing such concepts in a manner similar to that of the variation on a theme.

To approach the crucial issue of susceptibilities, we must, therefore, take a step back and look at its antecedents: the biological and the psychological constraints.

Human genetically determined cognitive abilities are the outcome of a process of natural selection. We are entitled to assume that they are adaptive, i.e., that such abilities helped the species survive and spread. This is not to say that all their effects are adaptive. Some of the effects of our genetic endowment can be described as dispositions, others as susceptibilities, even though the distinction is not always easy to draw. Dispositions have been positively selected in the process of biological evolution; susceptibilities are side-effects of dispositions. Susceptibilities which have strong adverse effects on adaptation get eliminated with the susceptible organisms. Susceptibilities which have strong positive effects may, over time, be positively selected and become, therefore, indistinguishable from dispositions. Most susceptibilities, though, have only marginal effects on adaptation; they owe their existence to the selective pressure that has weighed, not on them, but on the disposition of which they are a side-effect.

(Sperber, 1985, pp. 80–81)

In my perspective, we refer the affective/cognitive concept of susceptibility to that of the *Umwelt*. The susceptibilities should be thought of as homologous to the relationship between the biological organism and its natural or social environments.

Referring to the works by the entomologist Jean-Henri Casimir Fabre in his "Wie sehen wir die Natur und wie sieht sie sich selber?" [How do we see nature and how does it see itself?] (1922), J. von Uexküll writes:

> Fabre's excellent works can serve as a starting point for us to derive a representation of insect environments in particular. If we observe a burrowing wasp (a non-social, but solitary species), intent on building its burrow on the edge of a sand mound, we will first imagine the "soap bubble" surrounding the wasp's horizon, placing it at a distance of 10–15 meters from the animal; then, we will try to transform everything in the bubble into a "wasp-thing". Sand, with all its properties – fineness of granules, moisture, heat, comma and its yellowish glow – seems to belong to the "wasp-thing", since only certain properties can enable the construction of the burrow, and sand must be able to be recognized even from a distance.
>
> (von Uexküll, 2013, p. 46. My transl.)

We should remember that von Uexküll often describes his *Umwelt* as the inner and outer space that envelops the organism like a "soap bubble". Let's pay attention to his notion of the specific biological relationship between the organism's receptors and the percepts that it is dispositionally apt to detect and transform into its specific sensations. Von Uexküll is telling us that everything a wasp can experience must be a "wasp-thing" because the wasp is surrounded by a its own wasp-Umwelt (vol. I, § 7).

As I see a continuity in the wonderful thread of nature, *it seems to me that these "things" that each organism presupposes by its own perceptual and motor apparatus are homologous to those representations that the human mind is supposedly good-to-think – what Sperber calls "susceptibilities".* The specific kind of homology I am referring to is Alan Love's *functional homology*, which we may describe as the specific relational structure that is activated by a modularized constellation of a specific biological form (Love, 2007).

You might recall that in agreement with Sahlins, I criticized the central hypothesis of sociobiology, for which the Darwinian concept of biological fitness for selection and reproduction applies *directly* also to social and cultural structures. Now I can explain why I wrote "directly" in italics. While such a direct application of the biological Darwinian constraint – fitness for reproduction – is untenable (is "folk biology"), what we witness is a process of top-down exploitation of those bottom-up constrains. In fact, after all, a social group culturally stably organized must ensure that its members survive (not necessarily as individuals but as those "selected" to belong to that group, obviously mostly by social, economic or cultural mechanisms), even if through culturally and symbolically based institutions.

For the fact that we are now at a cultural, symbolic level of reality, survival and reproduction will not (necessarily) involve the biological reproduction of the individual carriers of genome (as it happens in nature) but the reproduction of those symbolic forms of organization and of those institutions that are most *symbolically* and *socially* "fit" in a given cultural environment. A model of this may be found in Pierre Bourdieu's analysis of symbolic violence and its reproduction (1933a, 1933b, 1976, 1977, 1976).

In relation with this issue, I argue that Warburg's "survivals" of antiquity (vol. I, § 7.2) throughout the whole development of Western art and, generally speaking, Western representations might be evidence of the fact that art as such is art exactly insofar it insists on the general pool of the human mind's susceptibilities, historically selected by a certain culture. With a certain degree of freedom, it uses those lower constrains in a top-down manner to metaphorize new meanings. This would be one possible explanation for the survival of certain figurative patterns for millennia (Warburg, 2021). In this case, Warburg's images – cultural images, indeed – may still be brought back to archetypal formative principles, provided the cultural nature of their expression, stabilized through time by the mind's susceptibilities which, on their part, are a transformation of biological, bodily, ancestral susceptibilities common to our species.

An interesting evidence of such ancestral susceptibilities, which involve the biological sphere of sensory organization and the symbolic realm of culture at the same time, may be Genevieve von Petzinger's paleontological findings (2017).

Barring a handful of outliers, there are only 32 geometric signs across a 30,000-year time span (Table 5.1.) and the entire content of Europe. That is a very small number. Now, if these were random doodles or decorations, we would expect to see a lot more variation. But instead, what we find are the same signs repeating across both space and time – things like lines, rectangles, triangles, ovals and circles. And while certain signs span thousands of kilometers, other signs have much more restricted distribution patterns, with some being limited to a single territory, like these divided rectangles that are only found in northern Spain and which some researchers have speculated could be some sort of family or clan signs. There is a surprising degree of similarity in the earliest rock art found all the way from France and Spain to Indonesia and Australia. With many of the same signs appearing in such far-flung places, especially in that 30,000- to 40,000-year range, it's starting to seem increasingly likely that this invention actually traces back to a common point of origin in Africa.

(Von Petzinger, 2022)

Using uranium decay rate calculations in three caves in Spain, von Petzinger claims that some of these geometric signs may actually be around 65,000 years old and that they may have been done not just by *Homo sapiens* but also by Neanderthals, therefore, showing possible common features that date to an age that precedes the differentiations between these two groups of the species *Homo*, around 600–800,000 years ago. These signs are related to the so-called "entoptic forms" that Haule discusses (2011, vol. 1) in relation to the states of trance induced by the sensory-deprived experience of entering and spending time in a cave by the Paleolithic humans – a fully numinous, religious experience.

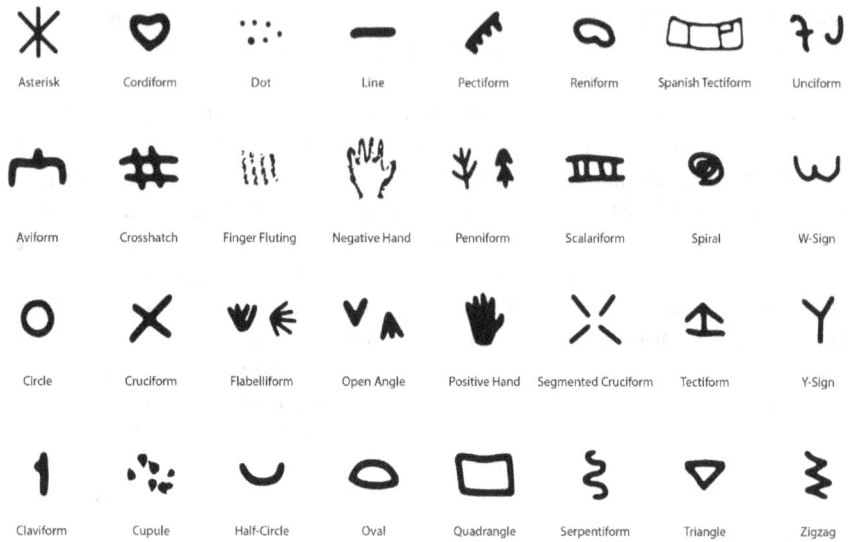

| Asterisk | Cordiform | Dot | Line | Pectiform | Reniform | Spanish Tectiform | Unciform |

| Aviform | Crosshatch | Finger Fluting | Negative Hand | Penniform | Scalariform | Spiral | W-Sign |

| Circle | Cruciform | Flabelliform | Open Angle | Positive Hand | Segmented Cruciform | Tectiform | Y-Sign |

| Claviform | Cupule | Half-Circle | Oval | Quadrangle | Serpentiform | Triangle | Zigzag |

Figure 5.1 Von Petzinger's 32 graphic signs.

Quoting Jean Clottes and David Lewis-Williams (1998), Haule describes these three stages of trance, the first one being that of experiencing abstract geometric forms, called "phosphenes", or "entoptic forms". Such spontaneous visual formations are produced endogenously by the brain and, therefore, seem to be something like the perceptual projection of the brain's visual architecture. During trance, "In other words, people in this condition are seeing the structure of their own brains" (Lewis-Williams, 2002, p. 127, in: Haule, 2011, vol. 1, p. 53).

Through the next two stages, the Paleolithic man might have experienced a further imaginal elaboration of such elementary endogenous perceptual visual patterns that ended into the wonderful images that we can still admire – hunters, animals, monsters, etc. – which do not represent the objects perceived by the waking mind (no art does) but numinous imaginal presentations arising from the collective unconscious, *from whom* the perceived objects acquired their meaning.

What I am trying to argue is that the social level of reality emerges from the interaction between more elementary bio-psychological constraints *through psychology*. As psychological, mentalized representations are more abstract than sensory information, cultural representations and models of organization are more abstract than the latter, so much so that *what will be reproduced will not be the Darwinian individuals that carry a certain genome but images, ideas, values and institutions that represent their own cultural form of organization*. This process of further transmission of constraints from one level to another via a reflective process of progressive abstraction and differentiation from the realm of psychological representations to the cultural one is what Sperber calls "susceptibility".

My hypothesis is that this process of abstraction and further differentiation may explain how, from archaic, simple, bottom-up, biologically based constraints, we may get to those extremely complex symbolic formations that Jung called arche-typal images. The part of such images that derives from the progressive transforma-tion of the original constraints will represent the archetypal side of the archetypal image, whereas the part that expresses a particular variation stably shared by a social group will express what we call cultural complexes.

To describe more precisely what I have in mind, we must refer once again to the level of Mandler's *conceptual primitives* and to ontological categories. You will remember that they are psychological ideas that emerge from the biological work-ings of the perceptual-motor system via what Mandler calls perceptual analysis. At this point in my discussion, we may refer to such conceptual primitives, as they are strictly related to the hypothesis that cultural and symbolic contents represent the result of a progressive diversification and abstraction. The hypothesis, therefore, is that these concepts, which seem to be universal and foundational to human cogni-tion, are shared across cultures and languages, providing a common ground for understanding and communication. Such a common ground would not involve just the cognitive level but would be triggered by underlying affects.

> Consider a human group. That group hosts a much larger population of repre-sentations. Some of these representations are entertained by only one individual for but a few seconds. Other representations inhabit the whole group over sev-eral generations. Between these two extremes, one finds representations with narrower or wider distributions. Widely distributed, long-lasting representations are what we are primarily referring to when we talk of culture. There exists, however, no threshold, no boundary with cultural representations on one side, and individual ones on the other. Representations are more or less widely and lastingly distributed, and hence more or less cultural. So, to explain culture is to answer the following question: why are some representations more successful in a human population, more contagious, more "catching" than others? And, in order to answer this question, the distribution of representations in general has to be considered. I see, then, the causal explanation of cultural facts as necessar-ily embedded in a kind of epidemiology of representations.
>
> (Sperber, 1985, p. 74)

A key area within the cultural domain is that of religion. From a Jungian perspec-tive, this is obvious, insofar as it is in this area that what is activated is the feeling of numinosum to which I already referred in vol. 1. Now we may integrate this area and take into consideration a fruitful anthropological approach to the study of religion called *cognitive science of religion.*

The term "cognitive science of religion (CSR)" came into use gradually after the publication of Lawson and McCauley's *Rethinking Religion* (1990) and Boyer's *The Naturalness of Religious Ideas* (1994). Cognitive scientists of religion have been less interested in the old issue of the origin of religion (see Anttonen, 2002); the focus is rather on how the human mental architecture (Anderson, 1996) "cana-lizes" the spread of religious traditions (Atran, 2002). The idea of religious trans-mission was first introduced in anthropology by Sperber (1975, 1985) and Atran

(1987). As we have seen, Sperber (1975) seeks to replace symbolist anthropology and semiotic approaches to cultural and artistic symbolism with cognitive explanations of the mental mechanisms that make symbolic interpretation possible in the first place. Sperber (1985) then introduces the idea of an "epidemiology of beliefs", which is a research program that focuses on how and why certain kinds of mental representations easily become widespread in human populations (Sperber, 1996).

According to this approach, cultural facts are not mental facts but *distributions* of causally linked mental and public facts in a human population. More specifically, chains of interaction – of communication in particular – may distribute similar mental representations and similar public productions (such as behaviors and artifacts) throughout a population. Types of mental representations and public productions that are stabilized through such causal chains are, in fact, what we recognize as cultural.

For cognitive anthropology, the nature of human cognition explains why certain kinds of mental representations become "attractors" in a statistical sense.

(I)n a given space of possibilities, transformation probabilities form a certain pattern: they tend to be biased so as to favour transformations in the direction of some specific point, and therefore cluster at and around that point" (Sperber, 1996, p. 112). We find recurrent patterns in concepts and beliefs within and across cultures because some ideas are more appealing to the human mind than some others.

(Sperber, 1996, p. 112)

An important feature of such concepts and beliefs is that they are "contagious" (Claidière & Sperber, 2007, 2010). As we noticed, this is a feature that Jung refers to archetypal contents, which derives from their emotional (numinous) and impersonal nature (Bion had the same opinion).

Following Sperber, Boyer (1994) picks up the ideas of epidemiology and cognitive constraints in developing a strictly cognitive "catalogue of the supernatural" and a cognitive explanation of why certain kinds of supernatural beliefs are "contagious". As I wrote, this anthropological issue is consistent with Jung's description of the empirical experience of archetypal (religious) formations.

Such beliefs correspond to our intuitive ways of thinking *while yet including one minimal violation of intuitive expectations that make them attention-grabbing.* These violations are counterintuitive in the sense that they are at odds with an intuitive ontology consisting of the categories of solid objects, living kinds, and agents together with three types of explanations: mechanical, biological and intentional

(see Boyer, 2001; Pyysiäinen, 2009, pp. 22–28)

This idea of an intuitive ontology traces back to Keil's (1979, 1996/1989) work in developmental psychology.

(Pyysiäinen, 2012, p. 7)

Therefore, according to these studies, the crucial issue at stake regarding the possibility of universal images would not be their existence but their extent – the depth and complexity of their meaningfulness, together with the extent of such an *intuitive ontology*, which produces beliefs and "folk theories".

Following the approach of cognitive anthropology, I am underscoring the suceptibilies' representational component, their "images". What needs to be pointed out is that this approach analyzes these matters at the noetic level of neuro-psychological organization. Yet we know that this level emerges from a deeper, more fundamental a-noetic one, in which affects are still devoid of representations. Therefore, it is once again important to reiterate that the noetic/cognitive level is *not* the original level at which human susceptibilities appear. Like with Tomasello's work on the perspectival mind, which seems cognitive but whose logical core is, at least in my opinion, emotional, also in this case, instead of representations, we should first refer to *intersubjective values* that imbue with meaning and salience such representations.

Therefore, although the representations to which Sperber and, generally, cognitive anthropologists refer are susceptible to be represented for cognitive reasons, they are represented and retrieved from memory on the ground of their *emotional* salience, their *emotional* meaning. Hence, I interpret Sperber's representations as those thoughts abstracted from emotions that Rosaldo calls "embodied thoughts" (1980). In my view, the building blocks of cultural contents are not the cognitive representations but their underlying emotions that glue, connect and organize into social groups the *inner* phenomenological experience of their participants – what von Uexküll called *Umwelt*.

This fundamentally emotional level of human interactions, the level of values, is rightly put at its proper place by Ernesto de Martino. In the following quote, he describes the "apocalyptic" consequences (for both the subject and his cultural community) of the collapse of such a fundamental level of the sharing of common "ethical" principles between humans, which, like Sperber's representations, may be susceptible to be produced by the human psyche.

The *Weltuntergangserlebnis*, the experience of the end of the world, is an alteration in the form and structure of the *Dasein* in its entirety. As Wetzel says, the experience of the end of the world is immersed in the "instantiation of an *Unheimlichkeitstimmung*": that is, a humoral disposition of an ominous non-domesticity in which a total, decisive threat moves in a hidden and inexpressible way. The single delusional images can be understood starting with this fundamental experience (Storch & Kulenkampff, 1950, p. 102). In the experience of the end of the world, being is manifested as "an at least partial, yet radical 'detachment' from the shared world and into a private world".

Here we cannot better express the experience of the end of the world as an experience of losing the intersubjectivity of values that make a world possible as a human world. The inner sign of worldhood, what makes up its fundamental character of normality, is its projectable intersubjectivity based on a practicability that is socially and culturally conditioned. And it is no coincidence that the most pertinent term for designating the normality of the world comes from associational life, where the normal world is domestic, familiar, mine, in that it is communicable to "others" (even if it is only a group of socially and culturally conditioned others: to those others who are with us in the same house, who live in the same landscape, who live in the same village, the same homeland, who participate in the same group, who speak the same language or dialect, who share our memories, institutions, customs, perceptions, aversions).

(de Martino, 2023, pp. 19–20)

An essential element of de Martino's thought is that the loss of any world's "normality" corresponds to the loss of its historical nature, a regression from what he calls "the public" to "the private", meaning with "private", not the intimate, introverted space of the soul but what Eugen Bleuler called "autism", one of his four fundamental symptoms of schizophrenia.

The loss of the world's "normality" is a loss of its historicity, its exit from the path that leads from the "private" to the "public". This happens because what is "private", intimate, extremely personal has an embodied meaning when it is opened up to the public realm, when it is inserted as a moment in a dynamic of intersubjective valorization, when it sooner or later becomes a word and communicating gesture. The idolization of incommunicability takes on an almost morbid character unless it becomes a polemic against the rigidification of socialized and commonly accepted values and when it is a sign of a new effort of recovery of the human in view of a more profound communication. This idolization of incommunicability assumes the morbid dimension of a manifest egotism, of a collapse of the ethos of presence, and an abdicating love that retreats from its inexhaustible worldly task. And we are not amiss in looking suspiciously or with dismay or pity on all those who spend their days exalting the ineffable that they carry within, the treasure they hide in their chest, of which they are usually miserly for others, except when they break their silence and offer highly enigmatic products on written pages, colored canvases, and plied materials.

In the experience of the end of the world, the loss of the ordinary world reflects the loss of presentification, the reversal of the movement that leads from the private to the public, a collapse in the capacity to transcend the situation of value, the reduction of leeway for value attribution along the whole gamut of possible situations of valorization. This in turn implies the collapse of the everyday process of worlding that is constantly taking place, being preserved and reshaped thanks to humanity's primordial "communitarian" impulse.

(*ivi*)

As I said, this spreading of the representations *endowed with shared emotional, intersubjective values* through people's minds is analogous to Jung's idea of the contagious nature of unconscious, collective, numinous contents. Such contagious situations take place whenever an archetypal image expresses, in diversified ways, similar underlying constrained psychological structures for different individuals. I would like to emphasize this point of contact between cognitive susceptibilities and psychological emotional contagion, as they both refer to collective phenomena.

If the images and constructs of religion studied by cognitive science of religion belong to an intuitive ontology and have a contagious nature, we must acknowledge the fact that we are *already* dealing with the most profound, paradoxical, enigmatic *emotional* contents of *any* culture. We are getting close to Jung.

References

Anderson, J.R. (1996). *The Architecture of Cognition*. York: Psychology Press.

Anttonen, V. (2002). Identifying the Generative Mechanisms of Religion: The Issue of Origin Revisited. In: Pyysiäinen, I., Anttonen, V. (eds) *Current Approaches in the Cognitive Science of Religion*. London: Continuum, pp. 14–37.

Atran, S. (1987). Ordinary constraints on the semantics of living kinds. *Mind and Language*, 2, 271–295.

Atran, S. (2002). *In Gods We Trust: The Evolutionary Landscape of Religion*. Oxford: Oxford University Press.

Barkow, J., Cosmides, L., Tooby, J. (eds) (1992). *The Adapted Mind: Evolutionary Psychology and the Generation of Culture*. Oxford, New York, Toronto: Oxford University Press.

Bourdieu, P. (1976). Les modes de domination. *Actes de la Recherche en Sciences Sociale*, 2, 2–3.

Bourdieu, P. (1977). *Outline of a Theory of Practice*. Cambridge: Cambridge University Press.

Bourdieu, P. (1993a). Stratégies de reproduction et modes de domination. *Bulletin d'information de la Mission Historique Française en Allemagne*, 26–27, 125–141.

Bourdieu, P. (1993b). Esprits d'État. *Actes de la Recherche en Sciences Sociales*, 19, 96–97.

Bourdieu, P. (2019). *Habitus and Field: General Sociology, Volume 2 (1982–1983)*. Cambridge, Oxford, Boston, MA, New York, NY: Polity Press.

Boyer, P. (1994). *The Naturalness of Religious Ideas: A Cognitive Theory of Religion*. Oakland: University of California.

Boyer, P. (2001). *Religion Explained: The Evolutionary Origins of Religious Thought*. New York, NY: Basic Books.

Claidière, N., Sperber, D. (2007). The role of attraction in cultural evolution: Reply to J. Henrich and R. Boyd, 'On modelling cognition and culture'. *Journal of Cognition and Culture*, 7(1–2), 89–111.

Claidière, N., Sperber, D. (2010). Imitation explains the propagation, not the stability of animal culture. *Proceedings of the Royal Society B: Biological Sciences*, 277(1681), 651–659.

Clottes, J., Lewis-Williams, D. (1998). *The Shamans of Prehistory: Trance and Magic in the Painted Caves*. New York: Harry N. Abrams.

De Martino, E. (2023). *La fine del Mondo: Contributo all'nAalisi delle Apocalissi Culturali* Milano: Einaudi.

Durkheim, E.P. (1895/1962). *The Rules of the Sociological Method*. Glencoe, IL: Free Press.

Fox, R. (1973). *Encounters with Anthropology*. Harmondsworth: Penguin.

Geertz, C. (1973). *The Interpretation of Cultures*. New York, NY: Basic Books.

Harris, M. (1979). *Cultural Materialism: The Struggle for a Science of Culture*. New York, NY: Random House.

Haule, J.R. (2011). *Jung in the 21st Century*. London, New York: Routledge.

Keil, F.C. (1979). *Semantic and Conceptual Development: An Ontological Perspective*. Cambridge, MA: Harvard University Press.

Keil, F.C. (1996/1989). *Concepts, Kinds, and Cognitive Development*. Cambridge, MA: MIT Press.

Kroeber, A. (1917). The superorganic. *American Anthropologist*, 19, 163–213.

Lawson, E.T., McCauley, R.N. (1990). *Rethinking Religion: Connecting Cognition and Culture*. Cambridge: Cambridge University Press.

Lewis-Williams, D. (2002). *The Mind in the Cave*. London: Thames & Hudson.

Love, A. (2007). Functional homology and homology of function: Biological concepts and philosophical consequences. *Biology and Philosophy*, 22(5), 691–708.

Lowie, R.H. (1917/1966). *Culture and Ethnology*. New York: Basic Books.

Lutz, C. (1988). *Unnatural Emotions: Everyday Sentiments on a Micronesian Atoll and their Challenge to Western Theory*. Chicago: University of Chicago Press.

Montagu, M.F.A. (1964). *Culture: Man's Adaptive Dimension*. Chicago, IL: University of Chicago Press.

Pyysiäinen, I. (2009). *Supernatural Agents: Why We Believe in Souls, Gods, and Buddhas*. New York, NY: Oxford University Press.

Pyysiäinen, I. (2012). *Cognitive Science of Religion: State-of-the-Art*. Sheffield: Equinox Publishing Ltd.

Sperber, D. (1975). *Rethinking Symbolism*. Cambridge: Cambridge University Press.

Sperber, D. (1985). Anthropology and psychology: Towards an epidemiology of representations. Malinowski memorial lecture 1984. *Man (New Series)*, 20(1), 73–89.

Sperber, D. (1996). *Explaining Culture: A Naturalistic Approach*. Oxford: Blackwell.

Storch, A. & Kulenkampff, C. (1950). Zum Verständnis des Weltuntergangs bei den Schizophrenen, in *Der Nervenarzt*, 21, 1950.

Von Petzinger, G. (2017). *The First Signs: Unlocking the Mysteries of the World's Oldest Symbols*. New York: Atria Books.

Von Petzinger, G. (2022). Why are these 32 symbols found in ancient caves all over Europe? *TED talk*. www.ted.com/talks/genevieve_von_petzinger_why_are_these_32_symbols_found_in_ancient_caves_all_over_europe?utm_campaign=tedspread&utm_medium=referral&utm_source=tedcomshare.

von Uexküll, J. (2013). Come Vediamo la Natura e Come la Natura Vede Se Stessa? In: Pinotti, A., Tedesco, S. (eds) *Estetica e Scienze della Vita Morfologia, Biologia Teoretica, Evo-devo*. Milano: Cortina.

Warburg, A. (2021). *Fra antropologia e storia dell'arte. Saggi, conferenze, frammenti*. Torino: Einaudi.

Chapter 6

Stabilization

As I already said, both constraints and attractors are innate and hereditary, and therefore, they are supposed to biologically shape, through a process of metaphorization, the possible forms that human psychological representations and, quite possibly, human *cultures* take. In fact, from innate constraints, new complex formations may emerge, which will act, like a wonderful helix, as potential modifiers of their own constraints, and hence, constraints for further processes.[1] At the same time, at the other end of the spectrum, the more interacting elements will be present; the more "adjacent possible" functions (vol. I, § 2.2) may emerge. Therefore, if at one end you have an increase of constraints, with the emergence of new forms (for instance, at a social level, new values, institutions, habits, etc.), diversity may also increase because those new conditions may be used for potential adjacent purposes (for example, a social code that determines private property obviously has a constraining function, yet it may give rise to an indefinite number of responses for, against or just about it). Constraints (i.e., universals) and diversity do not exclude each other.

If we want to deal with the issue of the possible existence of recurrent/universal "images", the question that the anthropologist Robin Fox poses becomes paramount:

> If we do not really know what biological universe is, how can we study the cultural differentials? How can we study the variables without the constants?
>
> (Fox, 1973, p. 246)

First, it must be understood that neither constraints nor attractors correspond to representations or behaviors. As Fox writes:

> What the flexible learning ability of man allows him to do is extended the range of his behavior, but only within well defined limits. His genetic behavioral inheritance lays down for him a limited number of things to do, but he can vary enormously the ways in which does them.
>
> For example, as with other animals, man prefaces the formation of stable mating arrangement with some form of courting activity. The form of this

DOI: 10.4324/9781003586463-6

activity, however, can be extremely varied, and consists of great many postures, gestures and, sounds that are traditional rather than genetic. The black-headed gull can look away and do a few other things, but it cannot write sonnets, dance the frug, or wear an engagement ring. *The difference can perhaps be expressed in a metaphor: animal behavior is like filling in a form; in some animals there are a lot of instructions on the form but only a limited space for answers, while in other animals there is the same number of instructions but the space for answers is large and the range of possible answers is wide. It is not that animals have instincts while man does not, but that man can do more things about his instincts than other animals.*

(Fox, 1973, p. 44. My italics)

Here, Fox refers to "instincts" – as we have already seen, a debatable and controversial word, indeed. Once again, like Jung and, for example, Bowlby, *Fox also does not refer to instincts as "fixed action patterns"* (FAP) but as a trigger within a *potential state of readiness for a response.*

For Sperber, cultural phenomena (as a special kind of social phenomena) are "ecological patterns of psychological phenomena". They do not belong to an autonomous level of reality but are *stabilized* patterns of individual representations shared between the members of the same group. Sperber characterizes social and cultural contents as representations shared by the members of the same group and *psychologically* linked by what Sperber calls "*Cognitive Causal Chains*" (CCC).

What makes this chain *cognitive* is, roughly, the fact that to each of the *causal* links in the chain, there corresponds a *semantic* or *content* relationship.

> Why then characterize social and cultural causal chains in term of their psychological links rather than in term of their environmental links? To begin with I would like to stress that psychological links are themselves a sub-category of environmental links. They are links located in brains and bodies which are themselves part of the environment. So, to recognize a special place to psychological links in a social CCC [cognitive causal chain] is just to highlight one type of ecological factor. The reason for giving a defining role to psychological links is that the other, non-psychological links in a social CCC can be indefinitely varied: sounds of speech, gunshots, images, paths, dances, foods, clothes, machines, and so on. No sub-category of these environmental links is either necessary or sufficient for the causal chain in which they occur to be thereby a social chain. What makes a causal chain social is the cognitive linking of different individual minds. What makes a social chain cultural is the stabilisation of representations. It does not follow, however, that the psychological ingredients of the social are more interesting than its non-psychological ingredients. Interest is a pragmatic matter.
>
> (Sperber, 2001, pp. 297–317)

To help explain why some items stabilize and become cultural (when the vast majority of mental representations and public productions have no recognizable descendants), it is suggested that evolved domain-specific dispositions act as receptors and tend to fix specific kinds of contents. Many cultural representations stabilize because they resonate with domain-specific principles.

Because such representations tend to be rapidly and solidly acquired, they are relatively inured to disruptions in the process of their transmission.

Such a process directly involves some of the developmental issues that we discussed in vol. 1. In fact, at this point:

> the epidemiological approach to culture dovetails with evolutionary psychology (see Cosmides & Tooby, 1992) and with much recent work in developmental psychology, which has highlighted the role of innate preparedness and domain-specificity in learning (Hirschfeld & Gelman, 1994; Sperber et al., 1995).
>
> Children are not just the passive receptors of cultural forms. Given their cognitive dispositions, they spontaneously adopt certain cultural representations and accept others only through institutional support such as that provided by schools. The greater the dependence on institutional support, the greater the cultural lability and variability. Other inputs, children reject or transform. A compelling example is provided by the case of CREOLES. When colonial, commercial, and other forces bring populations together in linguistically unfamiliar contexts a common result is the emergence of a pidgin, a cobbled language of which no individual is a native speaker. Sometimes, children are raised in a pidgin. When pidgin utterances are the input of the language acquisition process, a creole, that is a natural and fully elaborated language, is the output. Children literally transform the contingent and incomplete cultural form into a noncontingent and fully articulated form. This happens because children are equipped with an evolved device for acquiring language (Bickerton, 1990).
>
> (Sperber & Hirschfeld, 1999, pp. cxi–cxxxii)

> Cultural forms stabilize because they are attention-grabbing, memorable, and sustainable with respect to relevant domain-specific devices. Of course, representations are also selected for in virtue of being present in any particular cultural environment. Domain-specific devices cannot attend to, act on, or elaborate representations that the organism does not come into contact with. For the development of culture, a cultural environment, a product of human history, is as necessary as a cognitive equipment, a product of biological evolution.
>
> (Sperber & Hirschfeld, 1999, p. cxxii)

One of the tasks of anthropology should be to identify the type of factors that may be involved in such stabilization or changes and to explain how these factors work by affecting people's minds and people's environments. This happens via such Cognitive Causal Chains.

As I anticipated at the beginning of the first volume, it seems to me that such a relationship between causes and semantic contents calls for avoiding the term and the principle of "cause", to refer instead to that of "reason". Human behavior, therefore, should not be thought anymore as the result of causes but of reasons.

When a CCC extends over several individuals, Sperber calls it a "social CCC". Social CCCs may involve just two individuals, or a few, or they may extend indefinitely over social time and social space. Most social CCCs are short, yet some social CCCs are long and lasting and involve a great many individuals over time, while exhibiting no discontinuity of content. These long and lasting social CCC have the effect of stabilizing mental representations and public productions in a population and its environment. Mental representations and public productions (practices or artifacts) that are stabilized by such extended social CCCs correspond to what we call "cultural" (hence, Cultural CCC – CCCC). Sperber proposes to call social CCCs those that do so stabilize cultural representations and productions (Sperber, 2001, p. 305).

Social CCCs link together mental and public things. Some of these public things, for instance, are physical artifacts. If they carry a symbolic meaning, they will tend to stabilize as cultural artifacts because they represent the "disembodiments" of the preconscious psychological contents of the culture's participants – in many cases, precisely those "contents" that have a potential fundamental value for the "collective", "arché-types".

For Sperber, a Cognitive Causal Chain (CCC) is a causal chain where each causal link instantiates a semantic relationship, a Social Cognitive Causal Chain (Social CCC) is a CCC that extends over several individuals, and a Cultural Cognitive Causal Chain (CCCC) is a Social CCC that stabilizes mental representations and public productions in a population and its environment (Sperber, 2001, pp. 297–317).

When we build an external cultural artifact like the one I am describing using Sperber's model of the susceptibility and CCCs, we are transforming a natural niche into a "cognitive niche" (Laland et al., 2000) and defining the border of a semiosphere (Lotman), thanks to the psychic activity of both human consciousness and unconscious. As I have been pointing out, such CCCCs are stable and reliable because of their constraint origin, but now I may add: also because they are stabilized by their external existence – so they can overcome the puzzling status of evanescent subjective thoughts and representations and the structural impossibility for one to decide if one's idea is really accountable or not in the absence of any social mirroring – if it really *exists*.

One important consequence of such a disembodiment of the collective unconscious into cultural "things" is discussed by Lorenzo Magnani:

> They [the external artifacts such as the Wachandi ritual of the Earth/Vagina fertilization as interpreted by Jung] can relatively easily promote abductions in the minds of individuals that pay attention to them, [. . .] favoring the knowledge of the acts of cultivation. Jung also stressed that – analogously to the case of the Wachandi – symbols are important in that case of diagnostic reasoning that is at play in the psychoanalytic treatment. The analysand's abductive cognition is enhanced thanks to artifacts (drawings, sketches, icons, etc.) made by the

analysand herself during the treatment, as tools that are not merely a product of consciousness but also of the unconscious. Furthermore, these symbols share various aspects with the ones produced during the history of humanity as archetypes still present in the so-called collective unconscious, Jung obviously adds: they favor that abductive cognition of the analysand which has to detect aspects hidden to her consciousness.

(Magnani, 2018, p. 151)

These comments support Jung's paradigm of the transformation of the libido into symbolic forms in an interesting way, also because it elegantly connects imagination, cognition, creativity, the practical techniques for the transformation of nature into cultural artifacts[2] and, overall, into "culture", and in so doing, it emphasizes the extreme abductive power of Jung's transcendent function.[3] The mental contents involved are mental representations and processes, whose susceptibilities determine their own nature and make some representations more probable and stable than others.

These representations may produce behaviors, and these behaviors may produce consequences that are directly perceptible and become stimuli for further cognitive processes.

The consequences Sperber refers to derive from the following:

a) The direct perception of those behaviors, when, for instance, a mental representation makes a person say something, move her body in a certain way, gesture some gestures, regulate his proxemic behavior, etc.

All these perceived behaviors are stimuli for other further mental representations.

b) Perceptible states of the environment on which those behaviors might have had an impact. For instance, building a building, walking on a certain path until it becomes visible in the forest, producing artifacts, writings, etc.

Sperber calls such perceptible behaviors and effects of behavior "*public productions*". Some public productions – for instance, utterances, signals or pictures – are produced for the purpose of being perceived and causing mental representations. Therefore, social CCCs are characterized by an alternation, along the causal chain, of mental representations and public productions (including public representations). Hence, we have an alternation of very different sets of stimuli. Some are conducts – like a ritual practice, or a particular conduct. Some are public productions.

CCC events cannot be explained just by saying that they conform to a cultural pattern or norm. On the contrary, a pattern is cultural when it is recurrent, and it is a pattern because relatively idiosyncratic causal factors tend, in a variety of circumstances, to converge on similar courses of action.

An important feature of these mental processes is that they exhibit cross-individual regularities, and *some of these regularities have to do with basic cognitive and emotional dispositions that are part of the biologically evolved psychological make-up of humans*. In this perspective, the anthropologist's real goal is not to explain individual cases but recurring patterns. These regularities are those determined by the constrained susceptibilities of the human mind. Such susceptibilities do not determine precise consequences and responses but define the limit within which these may occur. Within these limits, there is an indefinite number of regularities that are contingent on historical and local circumstances.

According to Sperber, Boyer, Atran and other cognitive anthropologists, and coherently with the Jungian tradition, only some mental representations, such as folktales, mythological patterns and images, and some public productions, like sacrificial rites and rites of passage, or "artistic" representations, like the mandalas, exhibit great resilience and are stabilized by CCCCs. That is, they remain recognizably similar to antecedent representations or productions in the chain. Therefore, those representations that are psychologically "easy to think", because they "parametrized" (Sloman, 2021) by their original emotional constraints, tend to be selected to become CCC and, if stabilized, CCCC. This process of stabilization now becomes fully cultural (i.e., specific and diverse) yet still being funded by the original blueprints of those constraints that make those cultural representations *easy to think in a specific cultural environment*.

In my perspective, it is important to recall that such easy-to-think nature of the representations rests on a deeper emotional quality for which they must be *worth*-to-think and *worth*-to-be-retrieved from memory. Without this emotional salience, minds and groups would be parasited by an indefinite number of equivalent contents.

We are now contiguous to the sphere of *cultural complexes*.

This process of further stabilization through social relations or to their variation or decay is described through many examples. One is the example of a diviner who, when "reading" the entrails, produces a version of past diagnoses adjusted to the particulars of the situation.

Each particular type of diagnosis is maintained by a specific cultural chain. In choosing a particular diagnosis, the diviners are contributing to the persistence of one of these cultural chains. Each time a type of diagnosis is chosen, it gains in saliency and in likelihood of being considered on future occasions. If a particular type of diagnosis becomes more and more popular with the enteromancers, its cultural importance will grow, and so will the likelihood that sub-variety of this diagnosis will become distinguished, leading to a split of the underlying CCCC into several new CCCCs. On the other hand, if a type of diagnosis becomes less and less reproduced, its CCCC will lose momentum and may eventually come to an end.

[. . .]

In elaborating on the diviners' diagnosis, consultants contribute to the way the diviners themselves understand and mentally exemplify their somewhat cryptic diagnoses such as "*gomé* of mother's insult", or "*gomé* of honey".

[. . .]

It is likely that, without their awareness, the interpretive preferences of the ent-eromancers determine the evolution of the rules of interpretation.

like the Dorzé at the time of my visit, almost exclusively resort to explana-tions in terms of transgression and sanction. The relative place given to these two types of explanations results from a series of micro-decisions and behaviors along cultural causal chains.

(Sperber, 2001, p. 304)

It seems to me that this notion of cultural phenomena may be in accord with my proposal of the archetype as the entangling "something in between", i.e., the particular emotional and later on the cognitive bond that organizes the relationship between an organism (a person) and its co-evolutionary environment.

An epidemiology of representations is a study of the causal chains in which these mental and public representations are involved: the construction or retrieval of mental representations may cause individuals to modify their physical environ-ment, for instance to produce a public representation. These modifications of the environment may cause other individuals to construct mental representa-tions of their own; these new representations may be stored and later retrieved, and, in turn, cause the individuals who hold them to modify the environment, and so on. There are, then, two classes of processes relevant to an epidemiol-ogy of representations: intra-subjective processes of thought and memory, and inter-subjective processes whereby the representations of one subject affect those of other subjects through modifications of their common physical envi-ronment. Intra-subjective processes are purely psychological. Inter-subjective processes have to do with the input and output of the brain, that is, with the interface between the brain and its environment; they are partly psychological, partly ecological.

(Sperber, 2001, p. 77)

Jung's position on the relationship between subjective and objective representa-tions seems like Sperber's:

the term "subjective" also means an argument coming from the subject, but nonetheless an object. In every person there are certain collective ideas – such, for example, as the Darwinian theory – which are quite objective. They in no sense belong to the subject simply because they are to be found in his mind. Again, there are certain unconscious products which people like to think of as establishing forever the uniqueness of their individualities., but which in reality are shared by all and are, by reason of this collective quality, objects vis à vis the subject's mind.

(Jung, 1925, p. 58)

6.1 Intuitive beliefs, folk theories and cultural complexes

As we have seen from some previous quotes from contemporary cognitive science of religion, the activation of "intuitive beliefs" produces "intuitive cosmologies". I would like to highlight the fact that, for the cognitive science of religion, what Boyer calls the psychological "primary process" – out of which "folk theories" develop – has a constrained nature and an *intuitive* character. These two features seem in line with Jung's idea of intuition as the "unconscious kind of thinking" (Jung, 1911/1956). This shows the intrinsic, epistemic, cognitive nature of Jung's affective preconscious, in which the non-focused, nonlinear kind of thinking that Jung describes in *Symbols of Transformation* is not confined to the realm of raw primary drives, as it is in Freud's primary process, and produces Miss Miller's representations and narratives – although in this case, not just at a "folk" level but at a "mythical" or psychotic one. In fact, for Jung, the obsolete construct of "drive" was substituted from the beginning of his work with Bleuler by the constellating affect – a position fully in line with scientific literature.[4]

Jung writes:

> [Intuition] is that psychological function which transmits perceptions in an unconscious way. Everything, whether outer or inner objects or their associations, can be the object of this perception. Intuition has this peculiar quality: it is neither sensation, nor feeling, nor intellectual conclusion, although it may appear in any of these forms.
>
> (Jung, 1921)

Under a non-psychopathological frame of reference, like in the case of Miss Miller but within an anthropological domain, the products of these intuitive ontologies would be not-idiosyncratic personal contents but *numinous folk theories* culturally (i.e., stably) shared by the members of a social group. We may describe one of the main features of psychotherapy as that of making the most thorough sense of both the patient's idiosyncratic *and* folk theories – to look for the latter's motivational (i.e., affective) roots and to find the patient's own best narrative about the reasons and the intrinsic goal, the symbolic sense, of his folk theories by interpreting them as autonomous products of the unconscious.

Let's imagine that a patient's theory – in this case, a folk theory shared by his social group – is that all mothers are nice and good and that, therefore, her own mother is also *obviously* so. In cases like these, we may – and often should – highlight the subjective aspect of these theories and the fact that they might not correspond to "reality" since perhaps the patient's mother was not good *while* the socially shared belief of the goodness of all mothers is also untrue. The task of a psychotherapist is not that of analyzing the patient's inferential error for which his mother must be good because all mothers are defined so. This would be the task of a social psychologist, who studies inferential errors. The task of a psychotherapist is to include the patient's feeling of his mother's goodness in a reality – in a context – in which an alternative reality becomes thinkable, a reality in which not all mothers are good and in which, perhaps, his own mother was also not good after all.

We will do this because, as I recalled at the opening vol. I, what is real is what is affectively effective. In this case, the patient may emotionally feel two contrasting realities: one, false, shared by his social group; the other, true, that will define a new subjective attitude and the belonging to a different social group (in this case, the group of those who are such "bad" children to think that their mothers are not always good). After all, according to Tobie Nathan, the affiliation to a new symbolic social group is one of the aims of every non-Western psychotherapeutic practice. (Nathan, 1996)

Sperber's epidemiological approach insists on the fact that the causal chains of cultural distribution are complex cognitive and ecological processes that extend over time and across populations.

> The basic idea that people have intuitive ontological ideas that then canalize the cultural transmission of concepts and beliefs (epidemiology) is an important step forward in the study of culture.
>
> (Pyysiäinen, 2012, p. 8)

Although such intuitive ontologies, like folk theories, are studied by cognitive science of religion as cognitive phenomena, they are the cognitive descriptions of more complex and encompassing psychological processes that cannot be just reduced to cognition. Such processes are poetically described by Hillman (after Keats) as *soulmaking* and involve affects, perceptions, images, thoughts, language and action. This is an important point because it lets us keep the same attitude that I took before cognitive sciences and infant research and refer to cognitive studies also within an anthropological domain, whose importance is also indisputable, without reducing the complexity of human psychology to cognition and reinstating the role of affects as its primary movers and organizers.

Such "folk theories", therefore, represent *the product of the collective unconscious way in which reality is apprehended through an archetypal (constrained) emotionally based cognitive process; this emerges within cultural and personal complexes*. For these features, folk theories have an intuitive, self-evident, unreflective nature. From a Jungian perspective, I should add that the primary kind of thinking (the primary process) is not only based on the psychological function of intuition but also on primary *sensation*, which seems to be quite coherent with the foundation of the psyche together with affects – the sensory-motor part of the unconscious original psyche. Nevertheless, if constraints are perceived by sensation, they always involve attractors. In Jung's entelechial psychology, since causes exist for the realization of potential goals, preexisting constraints (sensations) always exist in relation to affective attractors that the mind apprehends through *intuition*.

Both the sensation and intuition functions are *irrational* functions, i.e., they are fundamentally just-so-factually self-evident. This characteristic makes them good to embody and express the affective experience emerging from the bodily Self. We all know that words may lie but not the body. What the emotional body conveys is always ontologically subjectively/objectively real and true.

You will recall our discussion on the default mode network and its relations to dreams. This is the way the psyche works out and through the emerging emotional experiences that from the primary process are to be integrated in the secondary process and possibly creatively modify the psyche's own contents. In line with Jung's two kinds of thinking, contemporary research maintains that humans have two different reasoning strategies that have been variously labeled as "intuitive" and "reflective", "spontaneous" and rational", systems 1 and 2 and so forth. These two systems can be differentiated on the bases on the neural processes and cognitive mechanisms involved and the kinds of contents processed (Evans, 2008). The two systems or strategies can be distinguished by such criteria as their relative speed, amount of emotion involved, type of motivation, type of information consulted, the form of reasoning employed and the amount of "extracranial" scaffolding needed.

> The intuitive system is responsible for fast (Kahneman), associative and emotionally colored thinking with purely practical goals, using "innate" information together with information derived from the environment through analogical reasoning. It operates reflexively, not reflectively, drawing inferences and making predictions on the basis of temporal relations and similarity. It employs knowledge derived from personal experience, concrete and generic concepts, images, stereotypes, feature sets, and associative relations, relying on similarity-based generalization and automatic processing. It serves such cognitive functions as intuition, fantasy, creativity, imagination, visual recognition, and associative memory. Some authors also argue that it is a sub-symbolic pattern-recognition system that relies on connectionist, parallel distributed processing.
>
> The intuitive thinking system proceeds from the immediate experience of individuals; aims at short-term, practical efficacy, not at creating general theories; seeks evidence and not counter evidence; makes use of individual cases as evidence; personalizes values and ideals; makes use of abductive inference and presents arguments in the form of narratives. The reflective system serves such cognitive functions as deliberation, explanation, formal analysis, and verification. It seeks logical, hierarchical, and causal-mechanical structure in its environment, using information from language, culture, and formal systems. It is a rule-based system capable of encoding any information with a well-specified formal structure and relies heavily on external memory stores such as books and pictorial representations (see also Sperber, 1975).
>
> (Pyysiäinen, 2012, p. 9)

These are the words of a contemporary cognitive scientist. They are strikingly in line with Jung's ideas of the distinction between the two kinds of thinking, the "rational" being that of ego-consciousness and the "intuitive" being that of the unconscious part of the Self.

As I already wrote, the Ego kind of conscious thinking is triggered by primary dispositional affects organized and constrained by the sensory motor apparatus, which make it possible, through the relationship between the Ego and the environment to develop into secondary and tertiary emotions expressed by complex imagery. Such a conscious process has typical altricial characteristics and transforms its original precocial, collective, unconscious theme into an indefinite number of variations. At the same time, the unconscious Self's form of thinking is imagistic, synthetic and – for obvious reasons, being affects the center of the core-self – dispositionally affective.

As we have seen, the core of the cognitive approach to religious contents, images and rituals refers to a "intuitive" ontologies. Such ontologies follow the pre-set boundaries of inherited constrains and further acquired susceptibilities, together with teleological developmental affective attractors (in analytical terms, their individuative path). Such attractors belong, first of all, to the bio-psychological level and regulate and determine the boundaries of individual psychology and its representations.

As I said, once a CCC is stabilized and shared, it becomes a cultural CCC (a CCCC), which will receive from and transmit representations (obviously explicit and implicit) to the minds of those that participate in that culture. This means that the social and the cultural are co-extensive, the latter being the stabilized form of the socially shared representations or of productions – may they be artifacts or behaviors – that express or derive from those representations. Once a culture has coalesced by a stabilized shared number of individual representations, culture itself will polarize many possible individual variations by setting an implicit expectation or prescription about how to do what one does. In this case, culture itself will act as an attractor and an organizer of the individual, diverse representations.

Sperber's theory offers an interesting model by which we can connect psychology and its constraints with culture and with psychology's relatively specific status and autonomy. In fact, once stabilized, the socially shared CCCs deriving from the individuals' minds form a cultural context of reference which will polarize future behaviors and interpretations of the culture's members. If, let's say, an individual behavior differs from the cultural norm, the CCCC will be weakened – even if in a minimal form. If on the contrary, the individual behavior conforms to the stabilized cultural CCCC, it will contribute to confirm and stabilize it further. I find Sperber's view applicable also within Gadamer's hermeneutics, especially in reference to his concepts of (historical and cultural) "horizon" and to the "hermeneutic circle" between understanding and presuppositions (Gadamer, 1990).[5]

We could say that what we call "cultural values" are such attractors – affective in their core – around which socially shared individual CCCs coalesce to form a culture. In fact, we must remember that, from the start, the *prima materia* – the representations – that tends to become thinkable, rememberable and intuitively understandable by an individual mind follows and ultimately emerges from original affective bio-psychological constraints. These representations and only these will have the greater rate of CCCC stability through historical time. Hence, some will last for a very long time – all the way to satisfy archetypal conditions – and will have a greater possibility to emerge in many social groups, while others may have more localized features and a shorter life.

I think that we may extend the notion of folk theories (as sets of compelling intuitive – i.e., not (yet) rationally and emotionally scrutinized – beliefs) to Thomas Singer and Samuel L. Kimbles' theory of *cultural complexes* (2004). In fact, a cultural complex might represent a shared and stabilized folk theory, derived by CCCCs formed by highly meaningful – i.e., dispositionally emotionally charged – constraints. A cultural complex would represent the direct, untransformed emergence of the individuals' highly charged CCCCs shared within the social realm.

Such shared CCCCs, due to their charged nature and their intense function of attractors and organizers for the minds that participate in the social group, are not only preconscious, like most cultural structures, but also *tend to stay so* since any conscious scrutiny would menace their convincing intuitive power and, therefore, their function as emotional and ideological organizers of the identity of the cultural group. These CCCCs, as such cultural complexes, may have a variable degree of emotional charge. The more intense a charge is, the more *numinous* the implicit folk theory will be; and therefore, the stronger the social defenses about possible conscious scrutiny. In particular cases, such cultural complexes may structure a culture held together as a polarized/polarizing religious system. On the contrary, if the emotional charge of the CCCCs that forms a folk theory is not too intense, there is the possibility to shift from an intuitive, emotionally compelling and self-evident, absolute and undifferentiated ontology to a conscious one.

Therefore, cultural folk theories become cultural complexes to the extent that they are *directly* informed by individuals' CCCs that are archetypally – i.e., emotionally – compulsively constrained. On the contrary, if it is possible to uplift such "folk theories", such intuitively compelling beliefs, into consciousness, their self-evident (in a way, delusional) polarized nature will be transformed, and from a religious kind of culture, we would experience a "secular" – differentiated – form of cultural organization.

In fact, if consciousness means differentiation, the shift from a compelling intuitive ideology to a conscious one would mean to shift from the feeling of the absolute nature of such a largely implicit folk theory into its real *relative* value. It would mean a transformation from a state of absolute purity to one of impurity (with all the dangers that the impure carries with itself (Douglas, 1966; Jankélévitch, 2014) – from total undifferentiated simplification to complexity (Papadopoulos, 2018, 2021). This shift would be made possible by the intrinsic nature of consciousness as a *critical* attitude towards its objects, whereas the unconscious constrained activity may tend to assimilate (make similar) differences or actively negate their existence and their specific value.

The tension between the religious and the secular nature of social groups, cultures and political systems is constantly under our eyes. An important reference may be Bion's analysis of the group's unconscious dynamics that he describes as being organized by three well-known constraints, which he calls "basic assumptions" of "dependency", "flight-fight" and "pairing" (Bion, 1968). In his own words, Bion is describing three archetypal (constrained) forms of emotional apprehension, which emerge straight out from the dispositional level of primary a-noetic affects and operate within the co-evolutionary environment of the group as archetypes-in-between persons. As Bion shows, their unconscious, compelling activation transforms the social group into a "religious", "encapsulated", undifferentiated archaic whole dominated by a numinous, totalizing, implicit "group culture".

Examples of the activation of true cultural complexes and the religious functioning of large social and political groups are everywhere. As soon as a group – meaning a number of persons whose CCCs are stably shared with the others – enters in a highly charged conflict or in a stressful situation, the "natural" path (for the idea of religious thinking and folk theorizing as "natural", see: Boyer, 1994) is to activate or regress to "religious" forms of thinking and behaving, i.e., by dramatically reducing any complexity, polarizing, scapegoating, de-humanizing and acting out unclear, wrongly generalized emotional responses.[6]

The depth and the degree of such a fall into unconscious archaic, undifferentiated emotional and cognitive unilaterality may vary from the presence of engrained value-sets *subjectively* felt as undisputable to a pervasive organization of *social* life around undisputable and often literally non-thinkable values and principles that refer to absolute "self-evident" truths. Such regressions may be triggered by conflictual or stressful situations that collide with the dominant structural narratives and value-sets, therefore, exposing the members of a cultural group to the effect of something like a collective trauma. Hence, collective traumas may be described as produced by situations whose emotional and cognitive representations cannot be contained and expressed by representations already available. This kind of void may produce a regression into the numinous state, in which the normal functioning becomes dramatically radicalized, or into the spontaneous activation of latent representations arising from primary affects – Jung's *archetypes*.

Under this perspective, a development within the social, cultural and political realm is also, like the individual one, a true *opus contra naturam*. It is the irruption of what we may call the social and political Shadow. Within the social realm, becoming conscious means letting go of the illusion to know and to be necessarily right through a relativization of the value and truthfulness of the representations shared within the common culture. In fact, while cultural complexes – these preconscious CCCCs – have a compelling and dangerous side because *they are highly charged due to a critical or enduring state of explicit or implicit social tension or alarm*, in situations of relatively enduring social stability, folk theories will not be emotionally overcharged, and social change will occur slowly and imperceptibly through them. It is when there is an actual or possible structural fracture within the social group that the CCCCs will develop true cultural complexes, which may manifest all the negative features I have described, like the circular radicalization of the cultural members' radicalized minds. Nevertheless, in such critical predicaments, when the cultural complexes are emotionally highly charged, the transformation that is needed will rarely happen, if not through a religious activation of a new complex. In fact, cultural complexes are often also the only way through which a new, truly creative paradigm may change a social group in a moment of crisis. In my opinion, deep cultural transformations and cultural revolutions always have an underpinning religious nature. Once again, in all of its manifestation, the collective unconscious may save or damn.

In discussing the need to take into consideration cultural differences *and* recurrencies (all the way to universals), Paden writes:

> If the study of "world religions" separated religious material into systems defined by different sets of beliefs, and if Eliadean-style typologies elaborated patterns of symbolic meanings,[7] a more anthropologically inclined comparativism might differentiate religious data according to behavioral types, sets, and subsets. Identifying these domains and diverse functions also allows us then to more effectively get behind the clumsy, entified term "religion" in order to see what is taking place on the ground, and in turn, the study of such ground patterns may affect theoretic consilience with the wider work of the social sciences. There is then both a theoretic program "upward" toward explaining the contextual variables of cultural difference, and "downward" toward the realm of broader, connective, infrastructural generalizations and explanations of human behavior (2001, p. 288).
>
> (Paden, 2001, pp. 87–88)

Paden's view is useful, as it lets us connect the highly complex, symbolic nature of archetypal images (which *tend* to have a numinous feeling-tone) with the building blocks that constricted them bottom-up – the building blocks I have been examining in this book, like the way innate inferential systems work. Therefore, in a bottom-up perspective, starting from the assumption that we have an innate disposition to develop concepts according to certain schemas, we would have different schemas for different domains. From this, Sperber argues:

> our concepts of living kinds tend to be taxonomic; our concepts of artefacts tend to be characterised in terms of function; our concepts of color tend to be centred on focal hues; etc. Concepts which conform to these schemas are easily internalised and remembered. Let us call them basic concepts. A large body of basic concepts is found in every language.[8] Of course, basic concepts differ from one language to the next, but they do not differ very much. The basic concepts of another language tend to be comparatively easy to grasp, learn and translate. There is a growing body of research on basic concepts both in psychology and in anthropology, with more collaboration between the two disciplines in this domain than in any other. This work tends to show that individual concept formation, and therefore cultural variability, are indeed governed by innate schemas and dispositions. This has been shown, of course, only for a few semantic domains. Could it be generalised? Are all concepts formed according

to fairly specific innate schemas? I doubt it very much. First, there is no a priori reason to assume that concept formation is always achieved in the same way and falls therefore under a single model. Second, while some concepts are easily acquired with very little prompting, which suggests that there is a readiness for their acquisition, the formation of other concepts, say scientific or religious ones, takes a great amount of time, interaction and even formal teaching. These elaborate concepts are acquired within the framework of complex representations of the world. These representations and, therefore, the concepts which are characteristic of them, are based as much or more on susceptibilities than on dispositions.

(Sperber, 1985, p. 82)

The point that Sperber is making is important. Following Boyer's idea that "religion is natural, science is not" (Boyer, 1994), Sperber is differentiating those concepts that directly emerge from psychological constraints from those other "second-degree" concepts that emerge from those susceptibilities that arise from those constraints. These susceptibilities will guide the process of metaphorization further and, therefore, of the multiplication of concepts that belong to a cultural-symbolic domain and that may form an image as condensed and complex as an archetypal image. This image will express, at the same time, the essential nature of the species-specific mind from which it emerged (the fundamental constrained themes) and the culturally-specific variations that metaphorize its contents (the variations of the theme).

Everyday empirical knowledge is developed under strong constraints: conceptual, logical and perceptual. As a result, such knowledge tends to be empirically adequate and consistent. But, on the other hand, it applies only to some cognitive domains and does so rather rigidly. Other forms of mental representations are developed with greater flexibility and weaker filtering mechanisms. They involve other cognitive abilities, in particular that of forming representations of representations. Humans can mentally represent not just environmental and somatic facts, but also some of their own mental states, representations and processes. The human internal representation system – the language of thought, to use Jerry Fodor's expression can serve as its own meta-language.

(Sperber, 1985, p. 83)

In my opinion, when Sperber refers to "representations of representations", he is emphasizing the same mechanism of reflection and abstraction that we find in Jung's motivational theory and in Karmiloff-Smith's process of representational redescription. In so doing, he is indicating the leap from a psychological individual constraint to a cultural, social susceptibility which not only implies such reflective, abstracting and redescripting process (which is encompassed by Jung's transcendent function) but also the metaphorization into multiple forms and specific meaning of the original content.

I already mentioned that one feature that seems to me to be particularly relevant is that, within the field of cognitive studies of religion, what Sperber refers to as "representations" are also narratives that tend to stabilize in time – therefore, that tend to become "cultural" contents – precisely because the individual minds think them "easily" and remembers them. This is, of course, the case of oral narratives. What is interesting is that these anthropologists notice that these narratives often have the form of myths and fairy tales, therefore, in line with the Jungian established perspective on the productions of the collective unconscious.

> What is it that makes some representations harder to internalise, remember or externalise than others? We might be tempted to answer, "their complexity", and to understand "complexity" as an abstract property of representations. This answer will not do.
>
> (Sperber, 1985, p. 80)

According to Paden, while some representations are difficult to understand (like, for instance, Godel theorem), others may be difficult to remember (like long strings of numbers or letters or words), and therefore, transmit to others. This is not true for all representations. Paden refers to some representations like, for example, the story of Little Red Riding Hood or a popular tune (this is a classic example by Sperber), which we cannot help remembering, even though we might wish to forget them (see: Paden, 2001, pp. 276–289).

Hence, in line with the studies by Johnson, Mandler or Lakoff on conceptual primitives that I quoted earlier, for the cognitive science of religion:

> We use minimal cues to intuitively place a perceived or an imagined entity into an ontological category: if an entity can cry, for example, it must be an agent with the default properties of an agent; if it is being fixed, it must be an artifact (a solid object), and so on and so forth. Thus, all information need not be culturally transmitted; much of our knowledge and presuppositions come from non-conscious and automatic inferences based on intuitive ontology. Yet we are also capable of forming counterintuitive ideas by either deleting a default property or adding a property that violates intuitive expectations. An agent without a physical body exemplifies the first case, while a solid object that hears prayers is an example of the latter (Boyer, 1994, pp. 91–124; 2001, pp. 40–202, 2003). A combination of naturalness and minimal counterintuitiveness (cognitive optimality) makes a representation salient and yet easy to process in mind; by the same token such representations will become widespread in human populations.
>
> (Pyysiäinen, 2012, p. 7)

Once again, along with Atran or Sperber, we are back at the notion of constraints and attractors, i.e., implicit rules that govern the contents of the (human) mind. And once again, we are mostly dealing with references to their sensory-motor origin as the fundamental format that give form and shape to affects. I am once again going back to these issues because at this point, we are far beyond the study of the individual mind, as we are dealing with the cultural, social and anthropological level, i.e., with what may have to do with Jung's collective unconscious' cultural productions (the archetypes) and with the cultural complexes. Therefore, in this model, even low-level effects like primordial fears (I will mention the case of snakes) are not just set up as automatic preformed (rigidly modularized) responses but develop out of interactions between:

> *prepotentials* for discriminating certain environmental conditions, a preparedness to fast learning, and actual environmental inputs. In general, domain-specific competencies emerge only after the competence's initial state comes into contact with a specific environment, and, in some cases, with displays of the competence by older conspecifics. As the environmental inputs vary so does the outcome (within certain limits, of course). This is obviously the case with higher-level conceptual dispositions: It goes without saying, for instance, that even if there is a domain-specific disposition to classify animals in the same way, local faunas differ, and so does people's involvement with this fauna.
>
> (Sperber & Hirschfeld, 1999, pp. cxi–cxxxii)

Here, I must emphasize two elements. First, the accordance of the relationship between such prepotentials and environmental conditions with Jung's definition of the complex as a *readiness to act*. It is such a specific readiness – something like a particular gravitational field – that transforms empty archetypical dynamic attractors and constraints into personal and cultural complexes.

Second, at the same time, if we take an analytical perspective, we should redefine the concept of "environment". In fact, if we underscore the primary role of the dispositional nature of the psyche, which is coherent with the concept of co-evolution as an *active* process initiated by an organism, we must realize that the responsible element for the activation of the "prepotential" is the environment – the stimulus – through the organism's sensory apparatus. Yet this is a stimulus that the organism has been looking for and attentively selecting (see my discussion on co-evolution at vol. I, § 7). This precisely fits Winnicott's description of the object presenting. In fact, in Jung's perspective, it would be the psyche that actively looks for and selects the proper environment to "survive" and "evolve". If the organism could not find a good-enough environment, it would have to either act on his environment to change it, or merely adapt by developing a Persona or, in a Winnicottian perspective, a False Self, Jung's Persona.

In the social domain, the Persona is indispensable (Carta, 2017); it is a fundamental relational and dialectical structure that joins the individual prepotentials with the possible conditions for their entering into existence. As we know, if the balance is not good enough, we would have either a hyper-adapted result or, at the opposite end, "archetypal" fantasies looking for their embodiment – negatively ranging from delusions and hallucination all the way to, positively, art and religious experiences.

Every time we deal with the hypothesis of something universal – i.e., something belonging to the precocial evolutionary level – the issue of the human's stunning cultural and historical diversity arises. It is the same with the existence of thousands of present, or dead, natural languages.

According to Sperber and Hirschfeld:

> There is another and deeper reason why domain-specific abilities are not just compatible with cultural diversity, but may even contribute to explaining it (see Sperber, 1996, chap. 6). A domain-specific competence processes information that meets specific input conditions. Normally, these input conditions are satisfied by information belonging to the proper domain of the competence. For instance, the face recognition mechanism accepts as inputs visual patterns that in a natural environment are almost exclusively produced by actual faces. Humans, however, are not just receivers of information, they are also massive producers of information that they use (or seek to use) to influence one another in many ways, and for many different purposes. *A reliable way to get the attention of others is to produce information that meets the input conditions of their domain-specific competencies.* For instance, in a human cultural environment, the face recognition mechanism is stimulated not just by natural faces, but also by pictures of faces, by masks, and by actual faces with their features highlighted or hidden by means of make-up. The effectiveness of these typically cultural artifacts is in part to be explained by the fact that they rely on and exploit a natural disposition. Although the natural inputs of a natural cognitive disposition may not vary greatly across environments, different cultures may produce widely different artificial inputs that, nevertheless, meet the input conditions of the same natural competence. Hence not all societies have cosmetic make-up, pictures of faces, or masks, and those that do exhibit a remarkable level of diversity in these artifacts.
>
> (Sperber & Hirschfeld, 1999, p. cxxxiii)

I would like to draw your attention to the process of transformation "from faces to masks" that in Sperber's anthropological theory transforms biologically constrained patterns (face structure, recognition and functions) into cultural artifacts which, while being culturally and historically different and specific, are still shaped by *susceptibilities*. In fact, I see a striking analogy between such a transformation from faces to masks (or from constraints to susceptibilities) in Jung's theory when he makes the example of the Wachandi that I have already recalled:

> Just as man has succeeded in inventing a turbine, and, by conducting a flow of water to it, in transforming the latter's kinetic energy into electricity capable of manifold applications, so he has succeeded, with the help of a psychic mechanism, in converting natural instincts, which would otherwise follow their gradient without performing work, into other dynamic forms that are productive of work.
>
> [. . .]

The transformation of instinctual energy is achieved by its canalization into an analog of the object of instinct. Just as a power station imitates a waterfall and thereby gains possession of its energy, so the psychic mechanism imitates the instinct and is thereby enabled to apply its energy for special purposes. A good example of this is the spring ceremony performed by the Wachandi, of Australia. They dig a hole in the ground, oval in shape, and set about with bushes so that it looks like a woman's genitals. Then they dance around this hole, holding their spears in front of them in imitation of an erect penis. [. . .] By means of the whole, the Wachandi make an analogue of the female genitals, the object of natural instinct.

(Jung, 1928, §82–3, my italics)

The new symbolic form that the libido acquires in its dynamic flow is an equivalent of the previous one. It seems to me that when Jung discusses the principle of symbolic equivalence of the transformations of the libido, he is pointing exactly at the same mechanism (Jung, 1911/1956) that Sperber is theorizing – a mechanism of transformation from biological constraints to symbolic cultural artifacts. This process of transformation will produce a potentially infinite number of *variations on a theme*, which is an example of abductive reasoning.

From a functionalist point of view, Paden argues:

the common functions in fact contain endless transformations and varieties of cultural, historical and environmental contents relative to their default possibilities. Identifying comparable forms of behavior is then a pivot point for finding and examining the differential variations, contrasts, and cultural workings and reworkings of those common behaviors. In other words comparative religion focuses on how religious cultures construct pasts, defend identities, negotiate reciprocities, distinguish kin and nonkin, endow objects with prestige, mark significant times, discipline the mind, experiment with consciousness, engage linguistic objects as though they were entities, and map their universes. As with the case of language, "behavior" obviously has an illimitable and richly interesting history, developed from common, often unassuming grammatical possibilities and types. Thus, comparative perspective here moves back and forth between the continuity of common functions and the contrastable differentials of historical specificity and context.

(Paden, 2001, p. 285)

Before this quote, I referred to this process of transformation from constraints to susceptibilities as a "variation on the theme" through equivalent formations. You will recall that I mentioned Daniel Stern's vitality affects and cross-modal perceptions as the two modularized foundations for the progressive development of the infant's mind. In fact, a variation of a theme is not always a repetition but is also a means for a developmental step forward.

The elegance of Stern's description of this process is given by the role that he recognizes precisely as belonging to such a structural "theme with variations", which seems to me, once again, coherent with Jung's quote.

According to Stern:

> These basic self-experiences [agency, coherence, affectivity, continuity] seem to be reasonable choices from a clinical point of view as well as from a developmental point of view, in that they are necessary for adult psychological health. It is only in major psychosis that we see a significant absence of any of these four self-experiences. Absence of agency can be manifest in catatonia, hysterical paralysis, derealization, and some paranoid states in which authorship of action is taken over. Absence of coherence can be manifest in depersonalization, fragmentation, and psychotic experiences of merger or fusion. Absence of affectivity can be seen in the anhedonia of some schizophrenias, and absence of continuity can be seen in fugue and other disassociative states.
>
> A sense of a core self results from the integration of these four basic self-experiences into a social subjective perspective. Each of these self-experiences can be seen as self-invariant. An invariant is that which does not change in the face of all the things that do change.
>
> (Stern, 1985, 1252–1260)

Then speaking about "The Natural Opportunities for Identifying Self-Invariants", Stern asks himself how the interpersonal interactions between the caregiver and the infant are mutually constructed, especially during the first six months of life, when the infant is social at the maximum degree, so that the infant is in a position to identify those invariants (what Stern calls "islands of consistency") that will come to specify a core-self and a core other.

> Given this honeymoon period of intense sociability [i.e., from three to six months], how are the interpersonal interactions mutually constructed so that the infant is in a position to identify the invariants ("islands of consistency") that will come to specify a core self and a core other? This has been discussed in greater detail elsewhere (Stern et al., 1977), but the highlights for our purposes are as follows: First, the caregivers' social behaviors elicited by the infant are generally exaggerated and moderately stereotypic. "Baby talk", the example par excellence, is marked by raised pitch, simplified syntax, reduced rate, and exaggerated pitch contours. [. . .] "Baby faces" (the often odd but effective faces made automatically by adults towards infants) are marked by exaggeration in fullness of display, longer duration, and slower composition and decomposition of the display (Stern et al., 1977). Similarly, gaze behaviors are exaggerated. [. . .] The social presence of an infant elicits variations in adult behavior that are best suited to the infant's innate perceptual biases [. . .] The result is that the adult's behavior is maximally attended by the infant. Ultimately, it is these same

caregiver behaviors that are the stimuli from which the infant must pick out the many invariants that specify an other. The matching of caregiver behavioral variations and infant predelictions gives the infant the optimal opportunity to perceive those behavioral invariants that identify self or other. Caregivers typically perform these exaggerated behaviors in a theme and variation format.

(Stern, 1985, pp. 1274–1292)

Stern argues that there are good reasons why caregivers engage with their infants in this repetitive way, to which variations are interspersed. The first reason is to keep the infant's attention aroused and focused since, without variations, habituation would rapidly intervene because infants are extremely quick in differentiating stimuli and determining whether they are novel and interesting or just old boring stuff. We may say that the caregiver must constantly change to keep the infant where he is – an elegant example of metastability. At the same time, if the variation would be too much, if the variations would not be on a theme, this would infringe one of the most fundamental principles of how the mind works: the search for similarities, recurrences, invariants and, therefore, for categorization.

A format in which each successive variation is both familiar (the part that is repeated) and novel (the part that is new) is ideally suited to teach infants to identify interpersonal invariants. They get to see a complex behavior and observe which parts of it, so to speak, can be deleted and which parts must remain for it to be the same. They are getting lessons in identifying the invariant features of interpersonal behavior. The use of exaggerated infant-elicited behaviors and their organization into a theme-and-variation format are not done by caregivers to teach the infant about interpersonal invariants. That is a byproduct. They are done to help regulate the infant's level of arousal and excitation within a tolerable range (and to keep the parents from getting bored).

(Stern, 1985, 1297–1305)

The elegance of the structure of the "theme with variations" is due to the fact that it regulates and makes possible all the several developmental steps, like the formation of what Stern calls "tunings", which will lead to the possibility of the infant to develop a theory of how the other's mind works, all the way up to the emergence of verbal language and declarative knowledge. If one carefully reads Stern's account, the structuring, pivotal role of such a theme with variations is made quite clear.

Obviously, Stern, who did not know Jung almost at all,[9] would have never used the adjective "archetypal", but he would have probably used "universal". What may be of interest here is the similarity between Sperber's theory of invariants and the role of the theme with variations. Sperber's example of the relationship of the similarity/difference between the face and the mask and the transformation of biological constraints into susceptibilities and Jung's idea about the equivalence principle of the transformation of the libido seem to converge on the same fundamental principle.

The representations I have been discussing so far are not just ideas and images; they are also expressed and stabilized linguistically. In fact, the idea behind conceptual primitives and ontological categories is that these basic concepts are shared across cultures through behaviors and natural languages, providing a common ground for understanding and communication. As we have seen, the transformation from a psychological primitive to a cultural formation (a symbol, a concept, a value, etc.) rests on the notion of susceptibility. In vol. II, 9.3, I will discuss how such susceptibilities involve the domain of language and semantics, where it seems possible to identify a limited number of words that express the same foundational concepts in all the languages that were empirically tested.

Notes

1 See vol. 1. §7.
2 The physical transformation, through specific techniques, of nature into cultural objects and physical institutions is a crucial aspect in which the creative movement of the libido expresses itself – in this case, such material objects. Henri Leroi-Gouran (2018) sees the starting base for the stunning development of "cultural" tools as metaphorizations of the fundamental physiological gestures of the human hand. I this case, the hand seems to play the role of the constrainer and, at the same time, the driving force behind an indefinite number and variety of new forms.
3 "What I call maximization of abducibility is obviously related to the fact that this kind of reasoning is extremely 'eco-cognitive-sensitive'. To better explain this effect of maximization it is necessary to illustrate the general aspects that influence the abductive force of human beings. First there is the so-called 1) optimization of situatedness that directly concerns our example: to favor the solution of the abductive problem at stake, the forms of exosomatization (or externalization of human bodily activities) of our Wachandi example make available a setting that presents data which are 'optimally positioned' to favor the cognitive abductive processes of both the people that invent the ritual and of the ones that later on are attending it. Also other aspects that characterize the maximization of abducibility have to be quoted, even if not present in our present case: 2) maximization of changeability of the various data of the eco-cognitive situation to enrich the information and knowledge available, and so the openness to the variability of them; 3) the importance of the attention to this continuous flux of information: in particular to the constant flux of new information available but also the new information that is cyclically inferentially generated during the various stages of the abductive process itself; 4) multimodality: the inferential abductive processes are strongly multimodal and are favored by the availability of various kinds of cognitive devices (not only propositions, but also diagrams, visualizations, simulations, artifacts, etc.). [. . .] also in the case of 'framing' effects, for instance, individuals react to something they do not deliberately consider and that in this light we can interpret framing in terms of 'symbols that maximize abducibility'" (Magnani, 2018, pp. 152–153).
4 As I have tried to show, this primary dispositional affect in normal conditions (i.e., in non-schizophrenics) is expressed in a structured way by an image whose material (for instance, its visual or acoustic nature [Bucci, 1997]) is exapted from the bodily sensory-motor patterns. In Jung, the fact that the dream means what it shows, or the notion of the symbol as something that does not conceal but expresses in the best way possible a latent, potential meaning, derives from such an originary coupling of affect and representation – a complex – which substitutes Freud's idea of the purely energetic, non-representational, non-cognitive drive. In Jung, energy and structure are always coupled.

5 As Jean Grondin argues (2017, p. 299): "The hermeneutical circle is one of the most fundamental and contentious doctrines of hermeneutical theory. In its most basic form in contemporary hermeneutics, it is the idea that we always understand or interpret out of some presuppositions. In a slightly different reading, which goes back to ancient rhetoric and hermeneutics, the circle is that of the whole and its parts: we can only understand the parts of a text, or any body of meaning, out of a general idea of its whole, yet we can only gain this understanding of the whole by understanding its parts. In both versions, the basic idea is the same, namely that there is no such thing as an understanding without presuppositions".

6 This view goes back to Jung's association experiments on the disturbances produced by affectivity on cognition.

7 As did Jung.

8 See my discussion in vol. II, §. 9.3.

9 This is what he told me in a private conversation, in which I pointed out to him the perfect similarity of his idea of "readiness for" and Jung's idea of the complex. He then honestly said he did not actually know Jung and asked me to send him some material. This increases my great respect for him.

References

Bickerton, D. (1990). *Language and Species*. Chicago, IL: University of Chicago Press.

Bion, W.R. (1968). *Experiences in Groups*. London: Routledge.

Boyer, P. (1994). *The Naturalness of Religious Ideas: A Cognitive Theory of Religion*. Oakland: University of California.

Boyer, P. (2001). *Religion Explained: the Evolutionary Origins of Religious Thought*. New York, NY: Basic Books.

Boyer, P. (2003). "Religious thought and behaviour as by-products of brain function." Trends in Cognitive Sciences 7(3): 119–124. http://dx.doi.org/10.1016/S1364-6613(03)00031-7.

Bucci, W. (1997). *Psychoanalysis and Cognitive Science: A Multiple Code Theory*. New York: The Guilford Press.

Carta, S. (2017). Ideas for an Ecstatic Politics. In: Carta, S. et al., *The Analyst in the Polis*. StreetLib.

Cosmides, L., Tooby, J. (1992). Cognitive Adaptations for Social Exchange. In: Barkow, J., Cosmides, L., Tooby, J. (eds) *The Adapted Mind: Evolutionary Psychology and the Generation of Culture*. New York, NY: Oxford University Press.

Douglas, M. (1966). *Purity and Danger: An Analysis of the Concepts of Pollution and Taboo* (1st ed.). Routledge & Kegan Paul.

Evans, J.S.B. (2008). Dual-processing accounts of reasoning, judgment, and social cognition. *Annual Review of Psychology*, 59, 255–278.

Fox, R. (1973). *Encounters with Anthropology*. Harmondsworth: Penguin.

Gadamer, H.-G. (1990). *Truth and Method* (2nd rev. ed.). New York: Crossroad.

Grondin, J. (2017). What is the Hermeneutical Circle? Revised Version. In: Keane, N., Lawn, C. (eds) *The Blackwell Companion to Hermeneutics*. Oxford: Blackwell.

Hirschfeld, L.A., Gelman, S.A. (eds) (1994). *Mapping the Mind. Domain Specificity in Cognition and Culture*. Cambridge: Cambridge University Press.

Jankélévitch, V. (1978). *Le pur et l'impur*. Paris: Flammarion.

Jankélévitch, V. (2014). *Il Puro e l'Impuro*. Milano: Einaudi.

Jung, C.G. (1911/1956). Symbols of Transformation. In: *The Collected Works of C.G. Jung*, vol. 5. London: Routledge.

Jung, C.G. (1921). Psychological Types. In: *The Collected Works of C.G. Jung*, vol. 6. London: Routledge.

Jung, C.G. (1925). *Analytical Psychology. Notes of the Seminar Given in 1925*. Princeton: Princeton University Press.

Jung, C.G. (1928). On Psychic Energy. In: *The Collected Works of C.G. Jung*, vol. 8. London: Routledge.

Laland, K.N., Odling-Smee, F.J., Feldman, M.W. (2000). Niche construction, biological evolution, and cultural change. *Behavioral and Brain Sciences*, 23(1), 131–175.

Leroi-Gouran, A. (2018). *Gestures and Speech*. Cambridge, MA: The MIT Press.

Magnani, L. (2018). Ritual artifacts as symbolic habits. *Open Information Science*, 2, 147–155.

Nathan, T. (1996). *Principi di etnopsicoanalisi*. Torino: Boringhieri.

Paden, W.E. (2001). Universals revisited: Human behaviors and cultural variations. *Numen*, 48(3), 276–289.

Papadopoulos, R.K. (2018). *Therapeutic Care for Refugees: No Place Like Home* (Tavistock Clinic Series). London: Routledge.

Papadopoulos, R.K. (2021). *Involuntary Dislocation: Home, Trauma, Resilience, and Adversity-Activated Development*. London: Routledge.

Pyysiäinen, I. (2012). *Cognitive Science of Religion: State-of-the-Art*. Sheffield: Equinox Publishing Ltd.

Singer, T., Kimble, S.L. (2004). *The Cultural Complex: Contemporary Jungian Perspectives on Psyche and Society*. London: Routledge.

Sloman, A. (2021). Biological Evolution's Use of Representational Redescriptions. In: Thomas, M.C., Mareschal, D., Knowland, V.C.P. (eds) *Taking Development Seriously: A Festschrift for Annette-Karmiloff-Smith*. London: Routledge.

Sperber, D. (1975). *Rethinking Symbolism*. Cambridge: Cambridge University Press.

Sperber, D. (1985). Anthropology and psychology: Towards an epidemiology of representations. Malinowski memorial lecture 1984. *Man (New Series)*, 20(1), 73–89.

Sperber, D. (1996). *Explaining Culture: A Naturalistic Approach*. Oxford: Blackwell.

Sperber, S. (2001). Conceptual tools for a natural science of society and culture (Radcliffe-Brown lecture in social anthropology 1999). *Proceedings of the British Academy*, 111, 297–317.

Sperber, D., Hirschfeld, L. (1999). *Culture, Cognition, and Evolution*. Cambridge, MA: MIT Encyclopedia of the Cognitive Sciences (MIT Press), pp. cxi–cxxxii.

Sperber, D., Premack, D., Premack, A.J. (eds) (1995). *Causal Cognition: A Multidisciplinary Debate*. Clarendon Press/Oxford University Press.

Stern, D.N. (1985). *The Interpersonal World of the Infant: A View from Psychoanalysis and Developmental Psychology* (English ed.). Karnac Books. Kindle.

Stern, D.N., Beebe, B., Jaffe, J., Bennett, S.L. (1977). The Infant's Stimulus World During Social Interaction: A Study of Caregiver Behaviors with Particular Reference to Repetition and Timing. In: Schaffer, H.R. (ed) *Studies in Mother-Infant Interaction*. London: Academic Press.

Chapter 7

On rituals from representations to behavior

Besides images as representations, numinous experiences also involve behaviors, i.e., what people actually do within their respective cultures. To approach this issue, we must interpret behaviors under their pragmatic aspect for which emotional, relational and, if explicated, conceptual meanings are conveyed and expressed by an action.

We should notice that here, "meaning" (along with language) can and should be understood as behavior. Meaning is something the mind is always doing, always making, just as thinking, imagining and speaking. Speaking itself may have a performative character (Austin, 1962). In fact, one of the contributions of postmodern scholarship has been to draw attention to the way thought, discourse and myth constitute forms of social practice.

In this chapter, I will try to argue that rituals are an example of the existence of archetypal structures (in fact, in this case, these archetypal formations are not visual images but mostly behaviors) and, as all psychological activity, are based on affects – more precisely on the *numinosum*.

William Paden lists some possible universal behaviors:[1]

1. Social behaviors

   - Forming bonds and loyalties with a kinship group
   - Distinguishing between kin and nonkin. Ranking people within a group
   - Learning reciprocities and etiquettes of cooperative relationships (or social give-and-take exchange)
   - Making and following rules
   - Defending/protecting group order
   - Punishing or resolving infractions of order
   - Socializing and initiating the young
   - Recognizing authority and social power
   - Communicating with others; asking, petitioning

2. Sociocultural behaviors

   - Passing on *cultural prototypes for imitation as guidelines for behavior*
   - Endowing certain objects and persons with superhuman status, prestige, authority, inviolability, charisma

DOI: 10.4324/9781003586463-7

- Constructing pasts and reciting sacred histories
- Regenerating social values by performing periodic rites and festivals
- Marking and dignifying important occasions and roles with ritual behavior and special objects

3. Conceptual behaviors

- Creating linguistic objects that have no visible existence and acting towards them as though they were real and efficacious.
- Classifying and mapping the universe, including time and space
- Worldmaking
- Attributing significance (including causation) to events and objects, whether mental or physical

4. Self-modification behaviors

- Experimenting with alternative forms of consciousness, trance, disassociation
- Disciplining the mind and body and forming constraining regimens of behavior to effect certain results and kinds of fitness; using ideas to guide behavior and sort out behavioral options
- Reflecting on perceived errors of thought and behavior
- Reinventing selfhood

(Paden, 2001, pp. 201–202)

The items in the list are at an "emic" level and describe what may be called "reductions" of culturally specific, differential, "etic" behaviors.[2]
Paden writes:

While the behaviors on the list are reductions, they do not as such cancel out what their cultural versions mean to participants, any more than the reduction "water" or H^20 cancels out the significance of swimming or boating to the swimmer or boater. The reductions are neutral with regard to varying cultural and individual meanings. Religious or cultural associations to the insider are thus acknowledged as irreducible and to that extent conserved.

Concepts about universal behaviors are themselves empty of meaning (like the word "water") unless they are connected to other outside networks of theoretic significance. The behaviors on the list bear not only on religious histories but to rich bodies of socio-scientific theory. Thus, the behavior, "passing on cultural prototypes for imitation, as guidelines for behavior", affords a linkage with studies of the importance of imitation and cultural transmission. Or the study of renewal-rites behaviors may bear on theories of the role of emotional loadings in the long-term memory process. Kin sociality and nonkin reciprocity behaviors obviously relate to and are illumined by strong research traditions in both biology and bio-anthropology.

(Paden, 2001, p. 283)

The general formal structure of rituals – all rituals, including ritualizations such as obsessive-compulsive behaviors – has three different features: rigidity, repetition and redundancy.

1. *Rigidity*. Ritual actions must always be performed in the same way (the right way). Fidelity is crucial; deviations from the script are not acceptable. Muslims must face Mecca during the five daily prayers, and a Jew must precisely place items of the Seder table setting at Passover. Likewise, when even the smallest detail is omitted during the ritualistic slaughter of animals (common to Islamic and Judaic traditions), the performer may abandon the ritual altogether as it has failed to achieve the intended purpose.

   Such rigid nature of rituals may be thought of as a procedure whose elements – gestures, positions, words, etc. – are firmly associated together. If we look at this feature of rituals from a psychological perspective, they seem to be like a voluntary or compulsive (in cases of psychopathology) building of an *episode*. In fact, in the context of general psychology, an "episode" is the basic unit of episodic memory (Tulving, 1972, 1983). For the overall scope of our discussion, it is necessary to remember that what holds together or disrupt the different stored memories into a coherent script are the affects. Once again, at the base of a cognitive construct – an episode – we find the activity of affects.

The basic memorial unit is the episode, a small but coherent chunk of lived experiences. The exact dimensions of an episode cannot be specified here; they represent an ongoing problem in the field. There is agreement, however, that an episode is made of smaller elements or attributes. These attributes are sensations, perceptions, actions, thoughts, affects, and goals, which occur in some temporal, physical, and causal relationship so that they constitute a coherent episode of experience. Depending on how one defines episodes, there are no lived experiences that do not clump to form episodes, because there are rarely, if ever, perceptions or sensations without accompanying affects and cognitions and/or actions. There are never emotions without a perceptual context. There are never cognitions without some affect fluctuations, even if only of interest. An episode occurs within one single physical, motivational setting; events are processed in time and causality is inferred, or at least expectations are set up.

An episode appears to enter into memory as an indivisable unit. The different pieces, the attributes of experience that make up an episode, such as perceptions, affects, and actions, can be isolated from the entire episode of which they are attributes. But in general, the episode stands as a whole.

(Stern, 1985, 1647–1654)

Generalized episodes are called "scripts" (Schank & Abelson, 1977). A script is a memory structure that refers to stereotypical knowledge related to sequences of actions. Scripts allow people to make inferences necessary for understanding by inserting missing information.

The script is structured in such a way as to simplify reasoning in all similar situations, i.e., to have the feeling to understand and safely respond to them. In each of those situations, the mind does not need to perform the complex logical reasoning that would be cognitively necessary but simply executes the relevant script.

A script contains two types of knowledge, which assimilate it to rituals: a sequence of actions and a set of roles. Once a situation is recognized and the corresponding script is found, the found sequence of actions enables the understanding of the context and an "anticipatory" processing of events.

The main idea of Schank and Abelson's so-called *Conceptual Dependence Theory* is that all conceptualizations can be represented in terms of a small number of primitive acts performed by an actor on an object. In my opinion, *the role of such primitives is quite similar to the constrained/constraining primitives that* we *have previously discussed.*

I would like to emphasize that episodic memory is also called *autobiographical memory*, which means that the integrity and stability of the self (here with a small s) is guaranteed by the fundamental capacity of the mind to associate contents in a coherent way – i.e., in images that may then form a narrative – in this case, an autobiographical story. This process does not need language; it is preverbal. In fact, it is distinguished from *semantic memory*.[3]

In the original theory, scripts originate from the social phenomenon of sharing knowledge of stereotypical actions with other human beings. I would extend its meaning to the intrapsychic level as the psyche's own social representation and realization of how the psyche itself works. Hence, rituals resemble (or are) the intrapsychic fabric of the mind in its social aspect. In fact, *this is the same process through which the psyche forms its fundamental blocks – the feeling-toned complexes.* Therefore, rituals might be "archetypally" built and perform the same functions as complexes do since their representations are *actions and performative words.* What in the intrapsychic world we call associations and constellations (as in the constellated representations of a complex), in the intersubjective and in the social world we call "relationships". Thus, the mind extends itself into the social world.

Rituals might be a social representation of the individual mind's workings – the individual mind that extends itself to the social and cultural world.

The homology of rituals and complexes as outcomes of the associative workings of the mind triggered by affects involves two other characteristics:

2. *Repetition.* The Catholic liturgy is strictly predetermined; French people kiss three times; every practicing Muslim, from the age of puberty, performs five ritual prayers every day (salāh). To begin the prayer, he must perform ritual ablution (wudū') in the prescribed form; if the Aztec sacrificial ritual to the fifth sun reborn after the apocalypse Tonatiuh was not performed properly, a last, final apocalypse would occur. In addition to this internal repetition, in most cases, the ritual itself is reproduced regularly. Soldiers raise and lower the flag daily, and we tend to sit at the same place at the table and sleep on the same side of the bed.

An ethnographic study carried out at the homes of three German families and three Japanese families, showed how family members in both countries create contentment and happiness by repeating their Christmas and New Year's rituals (Wulf et al., 2011).

My interpretation of repetition diverges from Max Scheler (2009), Helmuth Plessner (1970, 1980–1985) and Arnold Gehlen (1988), the main representatives of philosophical anthropology, who tried to define what is specific to human beings (Wulf, 2013, § 2). For them, in contrast to non-human primates, human beings have an environment that is not exclusively determined by instincts. Thus, the objects of resistance which the human organism perceives in the outside world are transformed into mere factual objects. Therefore, for these authors, we learn as we engage with the world – a process in which repetition and the embodiment to which it leads play a central role. This theory is convincing for all altricial, conscious forms of repetition but *not for rituals*, in which repetition is compulsory. As for repetition, there seems to be something analogous (not necessarily identical) to the instinctual pattern of behavior.

3. *Redundancy*. Rituals are often performed to produce a result, but when the outcome is not produced, people seldom stop performing the rituals in the future. This situation is in stark contrast to ordinary behaviors, where people would stop doing something if it failed to produce the outcome they expected, like pressing the power button a limited number of times when the computer fails to start.

In fact, *rituals are causally opaque*: there is no obvious causal connection between the specific actions they involve and their purported end goal. Many rituals, as Boyer noticed, are also *goal-demoted*. It seems that the real goal is the performing of the rite itself, but even if the end goal of a ritual is known, its content cannot be inferred or predicted based on that goal. This feature seems to me to be the way the symbol works – as something unclear, enigmatic, yet compelling and irreplaceable. Furthermore, this feature of rituals contributes to Sahlins' distinction between ritual logic and causal logic.

The three features of rigidity, repetition and redundancy complete the homology between rituals and complexes so that I can now redefine rituals as follows: *Rituals have the same structure and pursue the same functions as unconscious complexes.*

While the rituals' structure is always "archetypal" (it is everywhere the same ([Lawson & McCauley, 1990]), its contents may not be. They may be as follows:

• Purely personal (like in cases of "plus or minus" obsessive-compulsive expressions [they are not necessarily symptoms]).
• Collective and culturally determined.
• (Quasi) universal (see vol. II, § 8).

This means that rituals are made by automatic and compelling behaviors and thoughts, which (try to) express symbolic meanings, i.e., emotional meanings that are not directly understandable because they belong to the unconscious or, better said, to the *Unbewußt* – literally the "not-known". In fact, as Jung argues in *Symbols of Transformation*, direct understanding of those emotional symbolic meanings would transform the unconscious feature of the ritual into a conscious, individual, nonautomatic and *directed* set of actions and into a non-performative, purely semantic language. This would simply mean that the ritual itself would disappear, vanishing like thoughts burnt to ashes.

The fact is that the unconscious nature of a ritual is bound to the affect that activates it, which cannot be fully and freely represented. This means that such affect has the typical features of the angst/numinosum – i.e., of an affect still devoid of a representation clearly graspable by the Ego, an affect without a semantic, fully conscious referential meaning.

For Jung:

> ritual actions bring about a spiritual preparation to direct libido towards the unconscious to compel it to intervene.
>
> (1911/1956, §450)

As it is in the case of the Wachandi ritual that I have mentioned before, the rite compels the libido to be channelled towards specific constrained, archetypal struc-tures – in the case of the Wachandi, towards the earth and the efforts needed to farm it. Therefore, for Jung, rituals always have a religious nature. But this does not mean that they are religious in a canonical sense, as the ethnoarchaeologist Brian Hayden thinks when he doubts:

> that religious monuments requiring huge amounts of labour such as Stonehenge or the pyramid of the sun Mexico were built because of religious fervour.
>
> (Hayden, 2003, p. 18, in: Haule, 2011, p. 186)

In fact, rituals are not performed *because of* religious fervor, meaning that its aims are religious, but, as Jung thinks, they are *caused* by an induction, through an *abaissement du niveau mental* (a trance) of numinous *religio* – i.e., libido – as a way to harness psychic energy still not at the disposal for the aims and intentions of the Ego of the participants to the social group.

Jung's interpretation is based on energetic considerations, convergent with those that I tried to emphasize throughout this book – i.e., that all psychological activity is based on affects, feelings and emotions. Now we are dealing with the hypothesis that rituals are triggered by a particular emotional state of mind that may be also called *stress* (although this is a somehow simplified word for what I am describing). In my discus-sion, I tried to support the idea that what confers psychological, *gnostic* meaning is at the core an emotional factor represented in images and possibly conceptualized and finally organized and expressed through language. Therefore, what rituals try to deal with are emergent, highly emotionally charged meanings. Hence, we may think of *rituals as behavioral symbols-producers, symbols-organizers and symbols savers.*

Now, a relevant observation is that if somebody interprets an act or a sequence of actions as if he is looking at a ritual – an act not related with clear instrumental and causal goals – his perception will work differently from if he approaches it as an ordinary act. In fact, in a ritualized action, behavior is partitioned into the smallest sub-actions which do not seem to have any immediate instrumental goals (the aforementioned "*goal demotion*": Boyer, 2001; Boyer & Liénard, 2006; Liénard & Boyer, 2006; Boyer & Bergstrom, 2008). Like any response to the activation of anxiety, the activation of (for example) a *hazard precaution system* leads to an arousal and a feeling that *something* must be done, although one does not know why and what exactly.

As Pyysiäinen summarizes:

In the aroused state, attention is focused on low-level properties of action which thus is parsed in smaller units than normally. Such upper-level categories as "walking" are replaced by such lower-level categories as "walking-in-this-or-that-specific-manner". This manifests a "just right" syndrome: everything must be done very carefully, and yet one can never be sure that a goal has been reached. As the relationship of the low-level actions with the more general goal of the ritual comes close to a mystery, repetition of action follows as there is no satiety signal that would stop the repetition.

(Pyysiäinen, 2012, p. 12)

When non-instrumental (ritualistic) behaviors are observed, each step is treated as a unique action and the behavioral flow – or better said, the flow of perception – is parsed in small units, as if there is no need to establish any causal logic nor any consequence of the actions that are performed.

Studies of perception show that when people are presented with ritualized behaviors, they see a greater number of distinct actions taking place (Nielbo & Sørensen, 2011). This means that when something is perceived *or defined* as ritual, all its molecular aspects are considered with extreme care and are felt to be intrinsically, individually special (Kapitány & Nielsen, 2015). This form of perception, related to the activation of the emotional, numinous feeling that something *special* is happening, triggers a special cognitive activity[4] that researchers call *ritual stance* to distinguish it from the *instrumental stance* (Herrmann et al., 2013).

Using the instrumental stance is what allows us to recognise and interpret actions that rely on physical causation to achieve specific goals, such as using a broom to clean the floor, chopping vegetables to make a meal or working together to build a boat. The ritual stance, on the other hand, allows us to recognise and assimilate cultural conventions, such as burning incense to purify a room, chopping fruit to make a sacrifice or coming together to perform a collective prayer.

(Xygalatas, 2022, p. 96)

Here, Xygalatas refers to "social conventions", but this definition should not mislead us. In fact, the conventional aspect of the elements that the ritual is organizing and that the subject is assimilating has to do with the cultural variability through which different cultural groups cope with *the same fundamental recurring issues*. If we look at this situation from one divergent angle, it looks culturally relative; if you look at it from another convergent angle, it looks like a universal, archetypal situation.[5]

The homology between unconscious complexes and rituals demands the following:

a) That the latter are *not* rare occurrences nor that they are confined to the world of religious practices.
b) That all rituals, religious or not, symbolic or symptomatic, social or asocial are connected to a form of activation that, at one end, is just "anxiety" (in this case, the ritual would be connected to personal complexes), while, at the other end, it is connected to the potent irruption of the numinosum – and in this case, they would have a fully religious nature.

I will try to show that both these conditions are satisfied. In fact, the homology between rituals and complexes is even more striking if we take into consideration the fact that the three formal features of rituals (rigidity, repetition and redundancy) are *compelling*. For the feature of rigidity, if the ritual contains a mistake, a wrong step, *the consequence is catastrophic* since the whole ritual must start all over again. In other words, it is as if a whole world must be rebuilt from its origin because the ritual has been radically destroyed.

The dramatic nature of this consequence becomes understandable if we equate the good functioning of the ritual with the good functioning or the psyche in its fundamental activity of complex-formation. In fact, in this case, the collapse of the ritual would represent the analogue of the extremely numinous feeling of *Wahnstimmung* (the "delusion of cosmic catastrophe") in a psychotic breakdown.

Previously, I wrote: When something is perceived or defined as ritual, all its molecular aspects are considered with extreme care – are felt to be intrinsically, individually special. I think it is worth considering that this peculiar form of experience (the intrinsic, numinous quality of cognitively parsed representations disjointed from the system to which they belong, hence, also from causal links and predictability) *is typical of schizophrenic thinking*.

What I am describing is the catastrophic condition that Blankenburg calls "loss of natural self-evidence" (*Natürlichen Selbstverständlichkeit*) (Blankenburg, 1971/1991), which refers to an intersubjective interpretation of schizophrenia (hence, social, cultural), i.e., a predicament related to the collapse of the *Dasein*, the Being-in-the-world. For Blankenburg, the schizophrenic perceives and feels his objects as ontological enigmatic absolutes which will stir what we call *schizophrenic perplexity*.

I think that what happens in the schizophrenic patient has a direct explanation as the limit-experience of the loss of the human *Umwelt*, for which the patient's innate "natural structure" starts to decay, leaving what Melanie Klein and Bion called "bizarre objects", i.e., fragments of representations, thoughts and even sensations that are losing their intimate connection. The undoing of the *Umwelt* in schizophrenia might look like the experience in which nothing *makes any sense*, from sensations to abstract representations and concepts. What the phenomenologist calls *Wahnstimmung* is a literal experience of a cosmic catastrophe, inasmuch as what von Uexküll called *Umwelt* is precisely the ontological "soap bubble" of the human animal, for which the psyche, brain and world are normally entangled in a dynamic, evolving, unbreakable unity.

This interpretation must be integrated with Tatossian's insight for which the schizophrenic situation is interpreted from an *intra-subjective* understanding (Tatossian, 1979/2002).

> Tatossian proposes to consider the schizophrenic alterations of experience, and in particular schizophrenic autism, as resulting from a split in the heart of transcendental life, which is characterized by the simultaneity of the phenomenological onlooker and the constituting consciousness.
>
> (Guardascione, 2023)

Hence, Tatossian interprets the schizophrenic predicament through an introverted perspective as a breakdown of the Self, similar to Husserl's *Ich-Spaltung*.

I think that these two interpretations describe well the perimeter in which the human psyche lives: the double mirror of the inner world that in some conditions may risk the schizophrenic collapse as an image of the intrapsychic collapse of the inner world (Tatossian) and the intersubjective, "social" catastrophe described by Blankenburg.

Seen in this integrated way, we may say not only that the ritual is a mirror of the inner psychological world but it also realizes its integrity at the social and cultural level, with the goal to ritually hold together the intrinsically enigmatic nature of the human experience.[6]

> A patient of mine came for her first session. Her eyes were spirited. She was in a state of agitation and panic. Her life seemed normal. She worked as a writer, had two children and was very well adapted. Yet she gave me the impression that she was about to break down, to break into multiple pieces all alive and all filled and pulsating with angst.
>
> She was crying and in tears she told me of her *terrifying nightmare* she had the night before:
>
> I see a line hanging in mid-air in my garden. My usual pots and pans are hanging from it.
>
> She was in severe danger of a psychotic breakdown. This dream alerted her and saved her life.

In a way, all rituals are ontological attempts to maintain the meaningfulness and understandability of the world/psyche together and, hence, perform activities to guarantee the stability of the (psychological and social) universe. The more intense the activation, the more religious and collective the ritual will be because it will be activated by more and more unconscious complexes all the way down to those that Jung calls archetypes, which *must* be socialized and expressed as shared rituals because archetypes are *between* the subject and its environment.

Rituals are relational functions. In fact, an essential feature of many rituals is their highly intensified emotional climate in which the specific and different individualities merge and are assimilated by the same feelings and thoughts.

As I already noticed, this intense form of regressive *contagion* is not only typical of large group dynamics but also of those special groups that are held together by some deeply seated unconscious affect. Once again, not only does Bion's groups (Bion, 1968) come to mind but also, most importantly, it is the very fabric of *transference*.

The regressive element of such an emotionally highly charged situations like transference and rituals corresponds to the goal of many religious rituals – a *regression* ad primam naturam *to reconnect to the origins and guarantee a symbolic rebirth and integrity of experience*. Therefore, the first question is about the frequency and nature of rituals. In fact, if we now consider the ritual features that I just discussed, the first question is whether we can really distinguish religious rituals and nonreligious rituals.

Often, religious rituals are considered an important subset of cultural behaviors. While I agree on the fact that some rituals overtly involve the religious domain, as they refer to transcendent beings and/or realities, nevertheless, I think that *all* rituals are intrinsically "religious", as they are all organized in the same specific formats and held together by some sort of compellingly motivational force that we may equate to the *numinosum*.

Let me explain why I hold this position for which all rituals may be equated to religious practices, even if they do not directly involve the supernatural.

The etymological meaning of "religion" is to be found in the pair of Latin terms "religere"/"relegere", understood as "to gather again", "to reread", to observe "with scrupulousness and conscientiousness the performance of an act" (Filoramo, 2004, pp. 81–82). Following this etymology, my rhetorical question is this: Given the three formal features that structure all rituals – rigidity, repetition and redundancy – what embodies the definition of "religious" more than any conduct than *any* ritual?

The legitimacy to expand the religious/numinous character to all rituals is important to assess how pervasive the typical ritual behaviors are in everyday life.

As Xigalas writes:

Anthropologists have long been aware that even rituals that seem very different and that take place in entirely unrelated domains can still have remarkable similarities. It's not just that they involve causally opaque actions with no obvious relation to a specific outcome. The daily routines of little children, the superstitions enacted by gamblers and athletes, the prayers directed at various deities, religious and secular collective rituals, and even the pathological hyper-ritualisation of those who suffer from Obsessive – Compulsive Disorder, all seem to share some key structural elements.

(Xygalatas, 2022, p. 66)

Everyone agrees on the fact that human psychology is more complex than that of other animals (although the offensive vagueness of the word "animals" – which groups bacteria and bonobos – should not pass unnoticed [Derrida, 2008]).

As we have seen, the most common theory (which is far too undifferentiated) is that humans are altricial and de-specialized, and the rest of the zoological realm is precocial and guided by instinctive behaviors, *plus or minus* encapsulated in fixed behavioral modules. The sociological claim that social organizations exist and can be understood referring only to sociological principles is based on this claim which, as we have seen, is psychologically based on the idea of the pervasive general form of de-specialized and hyperflexible intelligence. As I tried to show previously, this picture is oversimplified. It may reassure sociologists and makes purely interpretive anthropologists feel comfortable, but in my opinion, it is just not enough.

I previously discussed Jung's idea of the presence in the human brainmind (and surely, in many other animals) of both precocial and altricial competences, which would be necessary to theorize the existence of both (precocial) archetypes and (altricial) personal complexes. As we have seen, the issue of the absence of such patterns of behaviors between humans is well-known, and it has led to the expulsion of this theory. In fact, it is true that we do not find overt rigidly patterned behaviors within humans . . . *except for* rituals and psychopathological ritualizations, which are both universally distributed in time and space. Actually, the point should not be why rituals exist but how it happens that habits, all the way to rituals, may turn into more flexible behaviors.

Whereas religious rituals have a social, shared meaning, psychopathological ritualizations are idiosyncratic. Both are repetitive and rigid, if not stereotypical. Only the ritualized psychopathologies are clearly and *overtly* (i.e., socially) non-instrumental, but in psychotherapy they may reveal their hidden instrumental nature. An example is the use of rituals as a defense from an unconscious feeling of psychological impurity or guilt of the obsessive-compulsive patient. In this last case, the social meaning of the ritualized behavior is expressed through that sort of underdeveloped, ill-formed symbol that we call symptom.

At any rate, the questions are as follows: What are such behaviors? Where do they emerge from? And what is their function?

The fact that we exclude the existence of instinctive patterns of behavior from the human domain *n'empêche pas d'exister* (it does not preclude the existence of, as Charcot once said) such extraordinarily important human phenomena as rituals.

As I already mentioned, an important model connected to the issue of patterns of behavior is the so-called *hazard precaution theory* of ritualized behavior, proposed by Boyer and Liénard (2006). For this theory, all ritualized behavior is triggered by a *hazard precaution system* geared to the detection of and reaction to diverse kind of threats. Given the unclear nature of these threats, such a hazard precaution system is also triggered within a situation in which there will be no clear feedback demonstrating that the threat has been removed.

In my opinion, a shortcoming of this model is that to interpret rituals, it resorts to what is known as "evolutionary mismatch" for which rituals are a product of some sort of an adaptive glitch. The archaic human brain, developed during the Pleistocene, mistakes contemporary stimuli for ancestral ones and performs ritual(istic) behaviors that were adaptive thence but are maladaptive today. The problem with this model, which is elegantly construed and persuasive in many aspects, is that it is not epistemologically parsimonious because it rests upon the hypothesis of an anomaly (the glitch), which sounds like an *ad hoc* explanation.

For the alternative model that I quoted, everyday rituals happen as people get more stressed. When this happens, their movements become more repetitive (like for instance, tapping, waving, scratching, etc.), rigid (following predictable action patterns) and redundant (lasting longer than necessary). This model is interesting because it does not consider rituals as a glitch, a wrong survival vestige of a gone past, but sees them as normal and very common responses in the face of stressful – all the way to numinous – experiences.

According to Malinowski's ethnography of the Trobriand inhabitants:

> [rituals] enables man to carry out with confidence his important tasks, to maintain his poise and his mental integrity in fits of anger, in the throes of hate, of unrequited love, of despair and anxiety. The function of magic is to ritualise man's optimism, to enhance his faith in the victory of hope over fear. Magic expresses the greater value for man of confidence over doubt, of steadfastness over vacillation, of optimism over pessimism.
>
> (Malinowski, 1922, p. 70)

Ritual behaviors are accompanied by what James Frazier called "sympathetic magic" (Frazer, 1890), for which actions rest on two main principles: similarity and contagion. The law of similarity is the idea that "like causes like", or that physical resemblance also implies similar functions. The law of contagion, which I have now mentioned several times already, in this case is the idea that things carry immutable essences that can be transmitted through contact.

As Xigalas argues (2022), both ritual behaviors and sympathetic magic are definitely not only the stuff of "primitive" peoples. They are everywhere, all over the world. They are performed by sport teams before a game, by soldiers before an attack, by student before an exam, etc. Yet ritual behavior and thinking increase with the increase of stress.

Xigalas quotes a research by the psychologist Giora Keinan, who surveyed 174 Israelis about a variety of superstitious beliefs and behaviors:

> She compared people who lived closer to the Iraqi border, and were thus more vulnerable to missile attacks, with those living outside the range of the missiles.

She found that those who lived in the high-stress areas were over 30 per cent more likely to enact superstitions such as tearing up photos of their enemies or entering a bunker right foot first during a missile attack.

(Xygalatas, 2022, p. 64; Keinan, 2002)

What is interesting is that several other ethnographic observations like this one were followed by empirical studies. In Keinan's case, she tested two groups. One group was asked stressful questions, the other non-stressful ones. Then a test to assess stress was given to both groups. Keinan found that those in the first group, who had been exposed to the stressful questions, were more likely to knock on wood during the interview than those who were asked the more neutral ones. Overall, those who reported feeling more anxious were also more likely to knock on wood (Keinan, 2002).

The question is whether ritualization triggers intuitions about causality independently of those cultural beliefs, or whether this is a culture-bound phenomenon. To find out, Xigalas carried out a controlled empirical study at the University of Connecticut, in which it was clear that the responses of all the groups involved, no matter their inclinations and differences, showed a direct causal link between stress and ritualization (Xygalatas et al., 2021. For the anti-stress effect of reciting the rosary for Catholic students: Anastasi & Newberg, 2008. Or on the effect of reciting Psalms for women soldiers in war zones in Lebanon: Sosis, 2007; & Handwerker, 2011).

In a few words, rituals reduce stress (Lang et al., 2019, 2020). Such an anti-stress function of rituals is observed among children who, from around the age of 2, typically develop a variety of rules and routines that they follow compulsively (Evans et al., 2002). The studies about children socialization development show how they quickly learn to adhere to the norms and conventions of their social groups (Watson-Jones et al., 2015; Legare & Nielsen, 2015), how they adopt normative rules and, as we have seen quoting Tomasello, how they protest when social norms are violated (Rakoczy et al., 2008).

Equally important are the studies on children imitation or over-imitation as a way to facilitate social learning. In fact, a follow-up study found that children's tendency to over-imitate actually increased with age (McGuigan et al., 2011, in Xigalas, 2022).

Victoria Horner and Andrew Whiten (2005) devised a very telling experiment in which they compared the behavior of chimpanzees (*Pan troglodytes*) and 3–5-year-old children on a cognitive task. They showed to both sets of chimpanzees and children an opaque box. The experimenter would show how to slide two bars, so as to open the box and get a reward. To this, the experimenter added some redundant, useless actions – tapping on the box and on its top and side with a stick. Both chimpanzees and children quickly learned to imitate both sets of actions – the useful ones and the useless ones. Then the experimenter showed them a fully transparent box. Its transparency made it very clear that the tapping was useless and that it could be discarded without losing the reward. While chimpanzees did not tap the box but opened it in the most economical way, children kept on tapping it. If the explanation cannot be that 3, nor 5-years-olds are less intelligent than chimpanzees, then what is it?

The explanation follows precisely Tomasello's findings since these children, by far more intelligent than any primate, were not just involved in trying to get the reward (a candy), i.e., performing necessary actions to solve a *cognitive task*. They were also performing the same unnecessary actions as the experimenter, and this is a *social* process that has to do with maintaining a meaningful relationship with another person by being like him.

If one looks at the footage of the experiment and notices how the children behave, it is easy to see that this behavior looks very similar to a ritual, in which every action is carefully parsed and performed in a precise way and sequence *even if it seems clearly meaningless and whose goals are demoted*. My point is that its meaninglessness is just in the eye of the beholder insofar as *the meaning and the goal of such a ritual performance is to confirm and maintain a relationship, not just to solve a cognitive task*. Therefore, it seems legitimate to hypothesize that all rituals, regardless of their specific symbolic meanings, somehow like the mating ritualized dances of many animals when they look for and desire each other, serve a relational purpose and convey the fundamental *feeling of a "good-being-with"* – like the underpinning feeling of being safe and "understood", which is the homeostatic feeling that we all pursue in our relational life. They may do this by their performative, ritualized structure, which may also convey specific symbolic meanings. Seen from this perspective – the perspective that I am following in this book – the real motivations of rituals would not have a cognitive nature only but they would also essentially be triggered and guided by affects.

For Xigalas, or Boyer – who especially underscores the cognitive aspect of ritualization – rituals are a way to try to control the world around us and reinforce our "illusion" to have also our own minds under control and that the world functions in a familiar and predictable way. To this interpretation, I am adding a deeper emotional feature, for which what in some situations is "control" may now be described as a "monitoring" and "representing" a feeling of togetherness. Having said that, it is true that we all spontaneously engage in ritualized behaviors when we face stressful and uncertain situations, and we intuitively expect those ritualized actions to have an effect (for a groundbreaking, wonderful ethnography on the functions of protective rituals: Evans-Pritchard, 1937), the effect being that of restoring an underpinning sense of relatedness and safety like the one that is given by someone who "holds our hand".

It seems clear that this description of how all rituals work is fundamentally based on primary affects. The authors of these theories refer only to threats, which, in Panksepp and Biven's theory, would refer to FEAR, together with SEEKING. I wonder if rituals may also involve the other primary affects like, for instance, LUST, or PANIC, to give them mental and social shape and form. Furthermore, I wonder whether the religious – symbolic – aspect of rituals would imply the activation of the primary affect of PLAY. At any rate, it seems clear that such socially constructed behaviors, ritualized *like* instinctual patterns of behavior, are triggered by endogenous affects and teleologically aimed by them.

Ritualization of action is found not only in cultural ceremonies but also equally in children's rituals and in obsessive-compulsive disorder. Cultural rituals, like the religious ones, feel compelling because they take place in a context that elicits anxiety. Religious rituals are performed because neglecting them is felt to be dangerous, without the participants having any clear idea of what might happen if the proper rituals were left unperformed. Participants also have no clear idea of the supposed mechanism by which rituals bring about the desired result. Although a ritual may have a goal (healing a sick person, bring the rains, etc.), no one is able to explain how the constituent parts of the ritual relate to this general goal. In my opinion, this is a very parsimonious proposition, as it seems to me to describe the nature of rituals as archetypal structures. Yet we may now take a further step ahead and add to the nature of these (very common, universal) archetypal behavioral and mental organizations that we call rituals three extra universal features:

a) They manifest the fundamental structures of the mind.
b) The performative nature of ritual language.
c) Their symbolic nature and the quasi-universal feature of the rites of passage (Van Gennep, 1961).

Obviously, besides the ritualized structure of rituals, together with their stereotypical, repetitive, low-level characteristics, we should also examine their *linguistic* aspects. If their structure seems to be universal, are their meanings also so?

The issue of the meaning of rituals is obviously a fundamental and complex one. Still remaining at an anthropological level of analysis, what I must highlight in the context of this book are at least three points:

1. At their core rituals might express the fundamental structure of the mind insofar as they manifest its fundamental binary organization (Lévi-Strauss, 1967; Needham, 1980). Together with this fundamental property, the "savage thought" (whatever that means) contains properties – like homologies, oppositions, correlations, transformations, etc. – that are common to sophisticated thought; in a few words, it is universal. With all the due differences between Lévi-Strauss and Jung's theories, two aspects seem to be in common:

   a) The universal nature of the human mind and the universal structural nature of its social and cultural derivates.
   b) The form of its organization, which for the cognitive paradigm of Lévi-Strauss is *binary*, is oppositional for Jung.

2. That the nature of most words uttered during a ritual are *performative*; therefore, here, meanings stand for actions as much as, behaviorally speaking, actions stand for meaning.

The speech acts theory of J.L. Austin (1962), for which a proposition cannot only "describe" or represent a meaning that can be true or false but also realize what it expresses (i.e., "I now pronounce you husband and wife" constitutes marriage) is very relevant to the theory of religious ritual. In fact, Ray (1973) maintains that all relevant language in a religious ritual is performative. Although his claim has been relativized (Lawson & McCauley, 1990), the performative nature of most ritual language is quite evident.

A relevant observation may be that performative language is also the kind of language that makes possible a change in a psychotherapeutic process within the transferential relationship. Although indispensable in co-constructing the fabric of the patient's story, it is not referential interpretations (which indicate that something means something else) that heal the psyche. In their own way, first, Jung, then Winnicott, had understood that when we experience the analytic relationship emotionally through transference (when we understand the "patient's problem"), interpretations then begin to work at the moment that they, paradoxically, cease to be referential.

Suppose the analyst, having found the patient and recognized her within herself, tells her 99 times, "You are full of hatred for her mother because her love for her was betrayed". This proposition has no therapeutic effect if its nature is referential. It is just a purely cognitive, disembodied theory. One day, for the hundredth time, the patient is impressed, amazed. She may even go so far as to ask: "Why are you only telling me this now?"

The fact is that, at that moment, the nature of language radically changed, and the phrase became performative. Like the biblical "Fiat lux", the word, within the transference field, really became flesh; it (re)created not the absent meaning but the latent real body (in the referential language that said it). Now, in being expressed, this word presentifies and realizes its content, just as when the chairman of an assembly declares, "The assembly is dissolved".

The difference between a referential/interpretive language and a performative/creative language is clear, for example, from the comparison of the Protestant ritual and the Catholic ritual of transubstantiation. In fact, differently from the Protestant ritual, in which the bread *refers* to the Flesh, in the Catholic ritual, the bread *is made* Flesh. Equally, in analysis, the healing Logos is the word that, when uttered, *creates* its object and makes it become ontologically real and true. An analytical transformation is not just a change of viewpoint, it is also an ontological piece of creation in which the patient recognizes herself and her own world – that before were not – as real, inevitable and true. This ritual process, held by the performative nature of language, doesn't have to do with re-collecting lost parts or lifting the barrier of repression. It is a genuine creative act, a step in the process of *creatio continua* that cannot come from the Ego nor its personal unconscious but from the numinous space of those alien presences that Jung called archetypes – the possibilities for what we are not-yet to finally be.

For the analytical situation to transform itself into a ritual and, therefore, re-collect itself with the universal tradition of all healing techniques, it

is indispensable that a "numinous" transference happens, in which both con-
sciousnesses and unconsciousnesses of the patient and the analyst participate
and in which, as we have already recalled, subjective images are objectified. In
this situation, the analyst himself is reimagined as invested by a sacral role. It is
this performative aspect of words combined with their symbolic meaning that
transforms the analytic encounter into an effective transformative ritual. Then
the referential non-performative interpretations coagulate into sacred words in
which the meanings wholly precipitate into the present – the time of bodies.
They become perceptions, facts. All the meaning of the narratives and emotions
from which they come, they can now actually present.

Within the analytic relationship, in their being returned to being flesh and
blood again, they will be able to realize them in this new context. The performative word is not a word that, as all classical theories maintain referring to the
referential word, "depressively" refers to a lost object. It is a word of wholeness
that refers to the creative "instinct" Jung talked about. It is this word – the analytic word – that really heals: a performative and no longer interpretive word,
always inscribed within a "transference" field (i.e., a fourfold I-Thou relationship between conscious and unconscious), in which what is uttered by the analyst literally creates a recognition and objectification of the patient's previously
veiled reality, expressed in symptoms or elliptical forms.

Conversely, without the fundamental element of recognition, the analyst's
word, imposing an alien reality on the patient, would be traumatic.

3. The third characteristic of rituals is, for many authors, that the actions therein
   performed have a *symbolic* meaning and that this conveys, shapes and transforms affects into social structures. This confirms the primacy of affects for the
   organization of behavior and the role of cognition as a containing, transformed
   form of affects.

Victor Turner writes:

Although Lévi-Strauss devotes some attention to the role of ritual and mythical
symbols *as instigators of feeling and desire*, he does not develop this line of
thought as fully as he does his work on symbols as factors in cognition. [. . .]
The symbols and their relations as found in [the ritual] *Isoma* are not only a set
of cognitive classifications for ordering the Ndembu universe. They are also,
and perhaps as importantly, *a set of evocative devices for rousing, channeling,
and domesticating powerful emotions*, such as hate fear, affection, and grief. In
brief, the whole person, not just the Ndembu "mind" is existentially involved in
the life-or-death issues with which *Isoma* is concerned.

(Turner, 1996, p. 42)

Therefore, as I am also trying to show, here, symbols are at the service of cognition which is, in its turn, *at the service of the powerful affects that they express in
a transformed way*. Furthermore, I wish to highlight that when Turner refers to
the Ndembu's whole person and not "just" to the Ndembu person's mind, he is

expressing in his own language precisely what I tried to convey when I differentiated the cognitive interest on the "observed" child", the "clinical child" and the
interest on the "whole child" (i.e., the whole *real* person) as a synthesis of her
affects and cognitive competences.

Once again, referring to anthropology, it seems that at least the categories of mean-
ings/reasons/purposes that are expressed through rituals may be universal. One
may consider, for example, the formal structure of rites of passage as described
by Van Gennep and the further discussion on the dialectical relationship between
social and semantic structures and anti-structures by Victor Turner (1996), especially focusing on the liminal phase of rites of passage. Turner writes:

> for individuals and social groups, social life is a type of dialectical process that
> involves successive experience of high and low, communitas and structure,
> homogeneity and differentiation, equality and inequality. [Being] The passage
> from lower to higher status [. . .] through a limbo of statuslessness.
>
> (Turner, 1996, p. 97)

Turner is describing, at a social level, a universal structure and a structure which has
at its core the constraining and teleologically attracting force of psychological affects.

Turner describes the universal nature of rituals of passage as a dynamic, cycli-
cal process of integration and de-integration, quoting such diverse situations as
the Ndembu rites of Western Africa, the Tallensi (through Fortes' ethnography),
the Ashanti of Ghana, the Franciscan *community* (as initiated by the "spiritual" St.
Francis and continued/transformed by his successor Elias in an organized *structure*) and many Medieval spiritual movements. Other examples from Turner are
Tolstoy's peasant society, Gahndi *harijans*, the Hindu *sahajiyas* and the hippie
community of the sixties! In so doing, Turner is extending to a (quasi) universal
character the process he is describing.

Such a character of universality is based on the so-called *implicational*, or *conditional, universals* that I will discuss in the next pages, which indicate that the
character of universality would emerge when some conditions arise. Namely, in
Turner's cases, when a condition of inferiority, poverty, poorly organized social
life, etc. emerge, they will cyclically produce an opposite movement towards an
organized, eventually rigid psycho-social organization.

Not only does the symbolic interpretation of rituals confirm the ritualistic nature
of analysis in which the symbolic discourse is the central feature but the psychic character of the ritual social process, which revolves around liminality, also
becomes apparent if we look at the liminal nature of transference in which it is not
at all clear *who is who*. In fact, through transference, the stable structures and identities of patient and analyst, their Persona, become fluid, imaginal and plural, and
the relationship is subjected to the transference's anti-structuring force.

On the other side, following Turner's observations, such an anti-structured predicament is very well described by M-L. von Franz's analytical interpretation of
the role of the inferior hero (Von Franz, 1996) who must go through a liminal

condition (in Turner's words, an anti-structure) to create a new order (in Turner's words, a new "structure").

Another interesting example is Maurice Bloch's analysis of rituals of passage, as he discussed in his *Prey into Hunter* (Bloch, 2008). For Bloch, many rituals are based on a principle of *rebounding violence*, whereby native vitality (i.e., primary affects) is replaced by a conquered, external, consumed vitality (i.e., socially structured/ structuring emotions). This refers to the transformation of the material processes of life into the irreducible structures of religious phenomena and is so called because the transformation of "life" into "religious structures" is marked by (a) a rebounding dialectical process and (b) of some kind of violence.

Bloch sees this construct underlying religious rituals as varied as initiation, sacrifice, cosmogony and the state, marriage, millenarianism and mythmaking, with the latter seen as holding possibilities for intellectual analysis, critique and rejection/reconstruction of ritual.

The ethnographic examples that Bloch describes so magnificently, ranging from African social groups to the relationship between Buddhism and Shintoism in Japan, definitely have a universal function and meaning related to the possibly universal theme of *Homo sapiens* interpreted as *Homo necans*, as developed by Walter Burkert from a biological-evolutionary perspective (Burkert, 1983, 1996). In fact, ethnographic accounts seem to group the functions and symbolic meaning of rituals around a few salient categories, such as pollution and purification, danger and protection, intrusion or creation and preservation of order.

As Boyer and Liénard write, religious and magical rituals relate to the following:

a) Purification (e.g., baptism, libations).
b) Protection (so-called crisis rites, like rainmaking).
c) Creation of social order (rites of passage, such as initiations) (Boyer & Liénard, 2006; Liénard & Boyer, 2006).

If in general terms the rituals' goal is to control potentially numinous anxiety (Martin et al., 2020), now we may be more specific and say that rituals create order and guarantee the stability and coherence of the fundamental psychological, religious and social – hence, cultural – components. They guarantee and renew the integrity of the psycho-social fabric and the relationship between the living and the dead, between humans and gods and between the cosmological elements that organize the world in a predictable and meaningful cosmos.

This fundamental order-creation need, which rituals organize, begins with the first most basic ordering structure – *symmetry*, meaning the leap from the One to the Two (hence, no surprise that specularity, simmetry and asimmetry are fundamental organizational laws of Lotman's semiosphere [Lotman, 2022]). I think this aspect might help us to understand not only why obsessive-compulsive patients cannot stop at any odd number but must get to the even one – because of symmetry – but also why a musical phrase must be symmetrical; it cannot remain "hanging" in its mid sonic air.

Let's now summarize what I have been discussing:

1. Ritual structure is everywhere the same.
2. Rituals are homologues to unconscious complexes, "redescripted" (or transcended) to an interpersonal, social level. They are structured and act in a similar manner.
3. When a ritual remains private, it misses its fundamental social function and *may* represent a psychopathological ritualism.
4. Rituals are very common. They are triggered under acute condition of stress or to contain or prevent stressful situations (such as unpredictable or enigmatic emotionally charged predicaments).
5. This stressor may have to do with unpredictable and enigmatic situations, typical of the religious domain, or just with an everyday situation.
6. Rituals tend to relate to group phenomena, imitation and cohesion. They assure a sense of psychological, cosmological and social continuity, integrity and predictability, which involves this world and the world of spirits and ancestors. *Under a psychological perspective, they assure, especially on a social cultural level, what Winnicott called "illusion", i.e., the indispensable feeling and irrational certainty that experience (my own body, my experience of the world) is predictable, understandable and will respond to my actions.*
7. The minds of the participants in a ritual are intensely emotionally involved, and their autobiographical episodic memory overwhelms their semantic memory.

All these seven features seem to me describing a condition of an *abaissement du niveau mental* (Janet and Jung) in which:

1. The subject becomes more unconscious.
2. This regression implies an un-differentiation of the Ego from the group (hence, cohesion, imitation).
3. The Ego's identity is fused with the ancestors and tradition (i.e., becomes less individualized).
4. The subjects are exposed to psychic contagion.
5. The unconscious patterns now activated show the typical *automatisme psicologique* of unconscious complexes and unconscious thinking.

This last feature derives from the formal, patterned structures of rituals: rigidity, repetition and redundancy.

All these features describe what in the biological world we would call a constrained, automatic pattern of behavior. If this hypothesis is true, then we may say that, under stress, the psyche works *religiously* and is compelled by the feeling of numinosum to perform in a patterned way that derives from the precocial functions of the archaic parts of the brain.

What I wish to highlight is that, in the case of an activation in which the Ego cannot properly function (most of the time because it has not yet *learned* the nature of the threat) or, more generally, because it faces an affectively overly charged stimulus at both ends of the psycho-social/cultural spectrum (in psychopathology and religion), human behavior transculturally organizes itself like an instinctual pattern of behavior.

At this point, I ask the reader's attention, as what I am about to write is quite important.

When I say that under stress, "human behavior transculturally organizes itself like an instinctual pattern of behavior", *I am not referring to the biological patterns of behavior described by Tinbergen that I criticized in the first volume.*

My hypotheses are the following:

a) Some stressful situations may be felt as numinous because they are associated with the risk of losing the fundamental psychological Winnicottian illusion of predictability, rationality and control.
b) This means that in these cases, stress represents an unconscious feeling related to an apocalyptic fantasy – in psychological terms, the collapse of the Ego; in cultural terms, the breakdown of the cosmological, ontological and social world's integrity.
c) This emotional condition triggers a regression, which activates the typical compelling mode of functioning of the unconscious – a heavily feeling-toned compulsive, automatic (patterned) response. This feeling will constellate the ritual behavioral pattern and express itself by a performative language mode.
d) This feeling will constellate the ritual behavioral pattern and express itself by a performative language mode.
e) Both these behavioral and linguistic modalities are homologues to the way dream works. In fact, performative words *create their objects;* they collapse the distinction between word-representations and thing-representation.
f) As for the ritual behavioral patterns, they resemble a dreamlike context because the subject of these acts – the persons that participate to perform the ritual – fits into Jung's idea that if in waking life I am the subject of all objects, in the dream, I am the object of all subjects (Jung, 1959). In the ritual, the subject that performs it is actually performed *by* the ritual.

In a way, the ritual represents a situation in which the *numinosum* triggers a condition in which personal contents reveal their transpersonal nature in a social and cultural form.

If we were describing a lower animal, perhaps we would stop here (yet lower animals also adapt their behavior to the environmental circumstance), but I am not describing lower animals. I am describing humans, whose most typical feature, and therefore, the most necessary for survival, is *social cooperation* (see my discussion on Tomasello's work in volume 1). Therefore, what we are witnessing here is the activation of precocial functions *at the service of social and cultural needs, in which the subject is absorbed by the group's (the collective's) requests.* Hence, rituals seem to be direct, emergent phenomena from the collective unconscious.

Their contents may vary (but as we will see, many are quasi-universal) but not their formal structure, which is typically rigid, repetitive and redundant.

These features are now social and cultural constraints derived from the biological ones that are needed to ensure that the human social environment will not break down. Here, as I anticipated, Sahlins' distinction between causal logic and ritual logic within his theory on "the structure of conjunctures" is very relevant, as it shows us that while the causal logic belongs to the historical time where the Ego has to constantly face and interpret *events*, the ritual logic organizes experiences within recurrent social structures through which the Ego construct its interpretations of the events. Hence, the structural features of these social phenomena – the rituals – are a bottom-up, direct, transformed expression of the universal unity of the human psyche when it must face universal (collective) problems, such as the risk of a psychological and social breakdown. It will work everywhere in the same archaic (i.e., automatic and compulsive) and typical (collective) way.

As I wish to be as cautious and epistemologically parsimonious as possible, I am not claiming nor implying that ritual patterns *are* instinctual patterns. I just wish to highlight this interesting homology between instinctual patterns of behaviors and the ritualized behaviors that appear when Ego-consciousness is not (yet) able to make full sense of the situation. In this case, we may refer to behaviors that are direct expressions of the unconscious *structural* patterning that mobilizes the sensory-motor apparatus triggered and directed by our affects.

Notes

1 For an important study of religious culture and cultural universals with the study of underlying "behavioral predispositions", see: Lopreato, J. (1984). *Human Nature and Biocultural Evolution*. Boston, MA: Allen & Unwin.
2 The emic approach investigates how local people think, how they perceive and categorize the world, their rules for behavior, what has meaning for them and how they imagine and explain things. "The etic (scientist-oriented) approach shifts the focus from local observations, categories, explanations, and interpretations to those of the anthropologist. The etic approach realizes that members of a culture often are too involved in what they are doing . . . to interpret their cultures impartially. When using the etic approach, the ethnographer emphasizes what he or she considers important" (Kottak, 2006, p. 47).
3 Tulving (1972) proposed several differences between episodic memory and semantic memory. The distinguishing features of the two systems concern the type of information processed, the operations of the systems and the possible applications. First, in the episodic system, a sensation, even a nonspecific one, is a sufficient source of information, whereas it is difficult for it to be recorded in the semantic one because the content of an event must be understood, that is, related to knowledge, to be recorded in the semantic system.

The prototypical information element in the episodic system is an event, while the prototypical elements in semantic memory, in general, are facts, ideas and concepts.

The organization of information in the episodic system is temporal: an event precedes, is contemporaneous with or follows another event. The organization of information in semantic memory is governed by relations.

In episodic memory, events are related solely to the person remembering. In semantic memory, information is shared by all members of a given culture. The judgment of truthfulness is based on personal belief in episodic memory, while it requires social agreement in semantic memory.

Episodic memory stores specific events that occurred at a specific time, while this temporal component is not necessarily present in semantic memory. Episodic information is context-dependent in the sense that it is influenced by other elements present at the same time the information is processed; consequently, episodic memory is vulnerable to interference from other memories, while semantic memory is much less so. However, information stored in episodic memory is more vulnerable than that stored in semantic memory. This greater vulnerability of episodic memory stems from at least two factors.

Episodic memory, according to Tulving, is the last memory system to develop in both phylogeny and ontogeny. Recall, for example, childhood amnesia, which is not a pathological condition but simply the inability of all of us to remember episodes dating back to early life. The other factor that makes episodic memory more vulnerable is that information in semantic memory is learned, thus repeated many times over time, while episodes in episodic memory are not necessarily repeated often.

4 In my opinion, this is an evident emotional-cognitive activity. It surprising that these authors do not emphasize the obvious role of affects.

5 This double perspective refers to a concept that I think to be very valuable – divergence or convergence of patterning processes in nature (Bateson, 2002, § 2).

6 All Bion's work from his discovery of O relates to this transcendental, compelling, enigmatic nature of reality, the "absolute". The same is true for Jung's idea of the archetype, from a religious and clinical point of view (in schizophrenia).

References

Anastasi, M.W., Newberg, A.B. (2008). A preliminary study of the acute effects of religious ritual on anxiety, *Journal of Alternative and Complementary Medicine*, 14(2), 163–165.

Austin, J.L. (1962). *How to Do Things with Words*. The William James lectures delivered at Harvard University in 1955 (eds J.O. Urmson, Marina Sbisà). Oxford: Clarendon Press.

Bateson, G. (2002). *Mind and Nature: A Necessary Unity*. New York, NY: Hamton Press.

Bion, W.R. (1968). *Experiences in Groups*. London: Routledge.

Blankenburg, W. (1971/1991). *La Perte de l'Evidence naturelle: Une Contribution à la Psychopathologie des Schizophrénies Pauci-symptomatiques*. Paris: PUF.

Bloch, M. (2008). *Prey into Hunter: The Politics of Religious Experience*. Cambridge: Cambridge University Press.

Boyer, P. (2001). *Religion Explained: the Evolutionary Origins of Religious Thought*. New York, NY: Basic Books.

Boyer, P., Bergstrom, B. (2008). Evolutionary perspectives on religion. *Annual Review of Anthropology*, 37.

Boyer, P., Liénard, P. (2006). Why ritualized behavior? Precaution systems and action parsing in developmental, pathological and cultural rituals. *Behavioral and Brain Sciences*, 29, 595–650.

Burkert, W. (1983). *Homo Necans: The Anthropology of Ancient Greek Sacrificial Ritual and Myth* (trans Peter Bing). Berkeley: University of California.

Burkert, W. (1996). *Creation of the Sacred: Tracks of Biology in Early* Religions. Cambridge, MA: Harvard University.

Derrida, J. (2008). *The Animal That Therefore I Am*. New York: Fordham University Press.

Evans, D.W., Milanak, M.E., Medeiros, B., Ross, J.L. (2002). Magical beliefs and rituals in young children. *Child Psychiatry and Human Development*, 33(1), 43–58.

Evans-Pritchard, E.E. (1937/1976). *Witchcraft, Oracles and Magic Among the Azande*. Oxford: Oxford University Press.

Filoramo, G. (2004). *Che cos'è la religione*. Torino: Einaudi.

Frazer, J.G. (1890). *The Golden Bough: A Study in Comparative Religion.* London: Macmillan.

Gehlen, A. (1988). *Man: His Nature and Place in the World* (trans C. McMillan, K. Pillemer). Introduction by K.-S. Rehberg. New York, NY: Columbia University Press.

Guardascione, A. (2023, July 7). Selfhood and alterity: Schizophrenic experience between Blankenburg and Tatossian. *Frontiers in Psychology*, 14, 1214474.

Haule, J.R. (2011). *Jung in the 21st Century.* London, New York: Routledge.

Hayden, B. (2003). *Shamans, Sorcerers, and Saints: A Prehistory of Religion.* Washington, DC: Smithsonian Books.

Herrmann, P.A., Legare, C.H., Harris, P.L., Whitehouse, H. (2013). Stick to the script: The effect of witnessing multiple actors on children's imitation. *Cognition*, 129(3), 536–543.

Horner, V., Whiten, A. (2005, July). Causal knowledge and imitation/emulation switching in chimpanzees (*Pan Troglodytes*) and children (*Homo sapiens*). *Animal Cognition*, 8(3), 164–181.

Jung, C.G. (1911/1956). Symbols of Transformation. In: *The Collected Works of C.G. Jung*, vol. 5. London: Routledge.

Jung, C.G. (1959/1969). Aion. Researches on the Phenomenology of the Self. In: *The Collected Works of C.G. Jung*, vol. 9i. London: Routledge.

Kapitány, R., Nielsen, M. (2015). Adopting the ritual stance: The role of opacity and context in ritual and everyday actions. *Cognition*, 145, 13–29.

Keinan, G. (2002). The effects of stress and desire for control on superstitious behavior. *Personality and Social Psychology Bulletin*, 28(1), 102–108.

Kottak, C. (2006). *Mirror for Humanity.* New York, NY: McGraw-Hill.

Lang, M., Krátký, J., Shaver, J.H., Jerotijević, D., Xygalatas, D. (2019). Is ritual behavior a response to anxiety? In: Slone, J., McCorkle, W. (eds) *The Cognitive Science of Religion: A Methodological Introduction to Key Empirical Studies.* London: Bloomsbury Academic, pp. 181–192.

Lang, M., Krátký, J., Xygalatas, D. (2020). The role of ritual behaviour in anxiety reduction: An investigation of Marathi religious practices in Mauritius. *Philosophical Transactions of the Royal Society B* (Biological Sciences), 375, 20190431.

Lawson, E.T., McCauley, R.N. (1990). *Rethinking Religion: Connecting Cognition and Culture.* Cambridge: Cambridge University Press.

Legare, C.H., Nielsen, M. (2015). Imitation and innovation: The dual engines of cultural learning. *Trends in Cognitive Sciences*, 19(11), 688–699.

Lévi-Strauss, C. (1967). *The Savage Mind.* Chicago, IL: Chicago University Press.

Liénard, P., Boyer, P. (2006). Why cultural rituals? A cultural selection model of ritualized behaviour. *American Anthropologist*, 108(4), 814–827.

Lopreato, J. (1984). *Human Nature and Biocultural Evolution.* Boston, MA: Allen & Unwin.

Lotman, Y. (2022). *La Semiosfera. L'Asimmetria e il Dialogo nelle strutture Pensanti.* Milano: La Nave di Teseo.

Malinowski, B. (1922). *Argonauts of the Western Pacific.* London: Routledge, p. 70.

Martin, L., Krátky, J., Xygalatas, D. (2020). The role of ritual behaviour in anxiety reduction: An investigation of marathi religious practices in Mauritius. *Philosophical Transactions of The Royal Society of Biological Sciences*, 375.

McGuigan, N., Makinson, J., Whiten, A. (2011). From over-imitation to super-copying: Adults imitate causally irrelevant aspects of tool use with higher fidelity than young children. *British Journal of Psychology*, 102(1), 1–18.

Needham, R. (1980). *Reconnaissances.* Toronto: University of Toronto Press.

Nielbo, K.L., Sørensen, J. (2011). Spontaneous processing of functional and non-functional action sequences. *Religion, Brain & Behavior*, 1(1), 18–30.

Paden, W.E. (2001). Universals revisited: Human behaviors and cultural variations. *Numen.* 48(3), 276–289.

Plessner, H. (1970). *Laughing and Crying: A Study of the Limits of Human Behavior.* Evanston, IL: Northwestern University Press.

Plessner, H. (1980–1985). *Gesammelte Schriften* (eds G. Dux, O. Marquard, E. Ströker), 10 vols. Frankfurt am Main, Germany: Suhrkamp.

Pyysiäinen, I. (2012). *Cognitive Science of Religion: State-of-the-Art.* Sheffield: Equinox Publishing Ltd.

Rakoczy, H., Warneken, F., Tomasello, M. (2008). The sources of normativity: Young children's awareness of the normative structure of games. *Developmental Psychology*, 44(3), 875–881.

Ray, B. (1973). 'Performative utterances' in African rituals. *History of Religions*, 13, 16–35.

Schank, R., Abelson, R. (1977). *Scripts, Plans, Goals, and Understanding: An Inquiry into Human Knowledge Structures.* London: Taylor & Francis Inc.

Scheler, M. (2009). *The Human Place in the Cosmos.* Evanston, IL: Northwestern University Press.

Sosis, R. (2007). Psalms for safety. *Current Anthropology*, 48(6), 903–911.

Sosis, R., Handwerker, P. (2011). Psalms and Coping with Uncertainty. *American Anthropologist* 113(1), 40–55.

Stern, D.N. (1985). *The Interpersonal World of the Infant: A View from Psychoanalysis and Developmental Psychology* (Kindle ed.). London: Karnac Books. Kindle edition.

Tatossian, A. (1979/2002). *La Phénoménologie des Psychoses.* Paris: Le Cercle Herméneutique.

Tulving, E. (1972). Episodic and Semantic Memory. In: Tulving, E., Donaldson, W. (eds) *Organization of Memory.* New York; Academic Press, pp. 382–402.

Tulving, E. (1983). *Elements of Episodic Memory.* Oxford: Clarendon Press.

Turner, V. (1996). *The Ritual Orocess. Structure and Anti-structure.* New Brunswick, London: Aldine.

Van Gennep, A. (1961). *The Rites of Passage.* Chicago: University of Chicago Press.

Von Franz, M.L. (1996). *The Interpretation of Fairy Tales.* Boulder: Shambala.

Watson-Jones, R., Whitehouse, H., Legare, C. (2015). In-group ostracism increases high-fidelity imitation in early childhood. *Psychological Science*, 27(1), 34–42.

Wulf, C. (2013). *Antropologia dell'Uomo Globale.* Torino: Borighieri.

Wulf, Ch., Suzuki, S., Zirfas, J., Inoue, Y., Kellermann, I., Ono, F., Takenaka, N. (2011). *Das Glück der Familie: Ethnographische Studien in Deutschland und Japan.* Wiesbaden, Germany: VS-Verlag.

Xygalatas, D. (2022). *Ritual. How Seeming Senseless Acts Make Life Worth Living.* London: Profile Books.

Xygalatas, D., Maňo, P., Baranowski Pinto, G. (2021). Ritualization increases the perceived efficacy of instrumental actions. *Cognition*, 215.

Chapter 8

What is universal? A redefinition

The general and the specific are one; the specific is the general arising under changing conditions.

W.G. Goethe

Jung's attitude towards the issue of the universal features of archetypal images was essentially a comparative one, hence, based on an empirical method and not necessarily on the basis of further explanatory hypotheses inferred from other perspectives, like, for instance neuro-evolutionary ones. Such an experiential/empirical method does not necessarily guarantee impartiality or truth. In fact, one must always choose which features or relationships to compare and which ones to exclude. Red objects may be compared by their redness if the category is color or as writing objects if categorized by their function of writing. Nevertheless, it is always possible to find a blue pencil, which will fall just into one category and not into the other. Taking into consideration that the possible categories to which any object may be referred are, if not indefinite, surely much more than two, it is apparent that experiential comparison is far from a neutral operation. Nevertheless, this method cannot be at all underestimated. The same discourse may be referred to the finding of analogies. Bion argues:

> It has to be understood that the importance of the analogy lies not in the two objects which are compared (for example, a breast with a penis), but with the link made between the two. Speaking psychoanalytically, what we are concerned with is the relationship, not the things related.
>
> (Bion, 1990, p. 84)

An obvious, perhaps obsolete, issue in this field is the relationship between similarities (all the way up to universality) and differences, especially regarding the symbolic domain of "cultural diversities". Throughout this book, I have referred many times to the theme of the constrained nature of human psychology (not to speak of that of lower animals). Now I am dealing precisely with the domain of cultural symbolization, in which this relationship must always be kept in mind.

DOI: 10.4324/9781003586463-8

Paden writes:

Comparison per se is of course a tool of any conceptual endeavour, and a kind is not necessarily linked with the enterprise recurrences. For example, by a kind of inversion model, comparative analysis is also possible starting with particulars. That is, one could begin with what appears to be a set of common actions and then show ways that those actions (or symbols, etc.) take on different purposes and meanings in different cultures. Thus, one could set up comparison in either direction: similar functions, different acts; *or* similar acts, different functions.

(Paden, 2001, p. 288)

Within this discussion, Paden argues that Benson Saler (1999) made an apt response analogy between human and animal "escape" behaviors (Paden, 2001, pp. 288–289). The reference was Burkert's comparison of the sacrificial mutilations, like the mutilation of a finger with behaviors of a trapped fox that gnaws off its paw to escape. Paden reports that Saler observed that the act of cutting off a finger can also have different meanings according to cultural contexts. One example of this may be that of an institutionalized way of expressing grief at the death of a close relative, or the amputation of a finger as a token of fealty to a leader. Rightly, Saler argued that none of these could be called "escape behaviors".

In 1953, the anthropologist Clyde Kluckhohn had summed a view of comparativism that has the merit of making the distinction between the human and the cultural clear. Interestingly for us, between the invariants, Kluckhohn points also to the "psychological givens":

Valid cross-cultural comparison could best proceed from the invariant points of reference supplied by the biological, psychological and socio-situational "givens" of human life. These and their interrelations determine the likenesses in the broad categories and general assumptions that pervade all cultures because the "givens" provide foci around which and within which the patterns of every culture crystallize.

(Kluckhohn, 1953, p. 521)

Throughout this book, I referred to the integrating role of the core of the representational complex – the affects. Now, we may take a brief look at the issue of the relativity or universality of its images when the complex is a numinous experience.
    The first question we should ask ourselves about the local vs. universal nature of some images has to do with the definition of "universal".

In some respect and at some levels – of beliefs, of formal institutions – cultures are dazzlingly different from one another. [. . .] But are societies and cultures really so different at the level of forms and processes? Aren't they in some ways depressingly the same? Don't anthropologists, time after time in society after society, come up against the same processes carried out under a variety of

symbolic disguises? I think they do, and if they can get past the culture or ethnographic dazzle, they can see that this is so.

(Fox, 1973, p. 248)

one finds that, whatever the overt cultural male group behavior at the level of
symbolism, actual practises, beliefs, and even emotions, one thing stands out:
men form themselves into associations from which they exclude women. They
express purposes, but in many of their processes they are remarkably uniform.
Once this is grasped, seemingly bewildering variety of male behavior can be
reduced to a few principles.

Similarly, I have tried to show that the apparently endless kinds of kinship
and marriage arrangements known to man are in fact variations on a few simple
themes. The same can be said of political arrangements, which, despite their cultural variety, are reducible to a few structural forms. Once one gets behind the
surface manifestations, the uniformity of human behavior and of human social
arrangements is remarkable.

(Fox, 1973, p. 249)

These last passages by Fox are particularly important, as they hint at the "few
simple themes" as somehow biologically constrained and upon which an apparently endless number of local variations have been realized. This involves – as
I discussed in vol. I, § 6.1 – the cultural transcendence of the Darwinian biological
kinship based on consanguinity and the reference to the top-down causation of
more complex systems on their formative constraints. In our case, while we have
biological constraints, like the genetic ones, these produce complex organisms (for
example, cells) that will accumulate a higher degree of freedom and causally interact, top-down with the DNA, "harnessing" its random mutations. Exactly the same
happens at higher levels of complexity, like the psychological or the social levels.
In the latter case, the cultural-symbolic domain, thanks to its own complexity and
its emergence through generalization and metaphorization, has acquired such a
degree of freedom that it will be able to use its own lower constraints to produce
new symbolic forms. For this reason, I wrote that symbolic kinship binds persons
that do not necessarily belong to the same genetic pool through a huge variety
of customs and ways; kinship uses top-down sexual and bottom-up constraining
drives to produce extremely variated forms of kinship and social organization.

Excluding other aspects, some of which I have already discussed, among which
the issue about the *way* we compare objects and the way we find similarities and differences, one element of the quarrel on the universality of archetypal images has to do
with the fact that not all the images that Jung reports have been comparatively recorded
everywhere. It is a wise move to accept this criticism and proceed as if *no* image has
ever been found everywhere without being distributed by communication of any sort
(in fact, Coca-Cola's brand is a universal image, but it is not an archetypal one). Yet
even in the case of cultural diffusion we should still explain why those contents were
selected and sticked in the people's minds and habits. Here, once again, the issue
of susceptibility may be a valid explanation, which resolves the opposition between
innate representations and those that have been shared through cultural diffusion.

The first observation we should do is that for a content to be universal, it does not require it to be present always and everywhere. One should not confuse the actual coming into existence of a potentiality with its actualization. The best-known example in Jungian literature about this is the aforementioned description of the emerging crystal lattice from a supersaturated solution. It takes the intervention of a singularity (like a speck of dust, or the "right decision" made in the right moment, as the I Ching divine) to constellate a singularity (an individual). This process reveals that something universal had always been there potentially, as the patter of the crystal will be precisely the same always and everywhere, embedded into what the Gnostics called *Pleroma*. Universality may be totally legitimized also in the many cases of *quasi-universality* because the real issue is whether, in specific conditions (may they be also related to the ontogenetic developmental moment in a child's life), a content will emerge.

To tackle the issue of the legitimacy of the universality of images, I must once again refer to the concept of co-evolutionary environment and take into consideration what are called "implicational" or "conditional" universals, which differ from "unrestricted" or "non-conditional" universals (Greenberg, 1966, 1975, pp. 77–78), which are the ones we are used to thinking about.

In this context, *an implicational universal is a trait or complex that always appears when certain conditions are present. It takes the form "if A then B", in which A is not an individual, society, culture or language and is not itself a universal*. It is a rule that is universally applicable. This formula seems to refer to a virtual co-environment that emerges when A establishes a relation to B.

An example is that "all societies possessing paved highways possess centralized government" (Brown, 1991). Rules of this sort are common in anthropology and are often convincingly demonstrated. Implicitly, they are even more widely used, as Hempel (1942) has shown for historical explanations in general.

An example of an implicational universal refers to:

> Meyer Fortes' (1969) concept of "complementary filiation". This term was coined to refer to a phenomenon found repeatedly in societies that ideologically reckon kinship either matrilineally or patrilineally. In either case, in spite of the prevailing ideology of descent, an individual typically has strong sentimental ties to those (usually close) genetic kin who are not ideologically reckoned as kin, i.e., some close genetic relatives through the mother in a patrilineal society, through the father in a matrilineal society. By virtue of this phenomenon, the sentimental ties between kin are always to some degree effectively bilateral.
>
> (Brown, 1991, pp. 2268–2275)

This conception of universals presents a sort of optical illusion in that it illustrates relativity when looked at in one way and universality when viewed from another angle. As Brown writes, some peoples have paved highways, but some don't; some have centralized government, but some don't (relative statements); yet all that have one have the other (universalistic statements). This is in accordance, for example, with Sahlin's structure of conjuncture that I mentioned in § 1.

When one examines the causes of universals, it is apparent that the relativistic image that results from implicational universals is a surface appearance. Fundamentally, there is little difference between unrestricted and implicational universals.

Implicational and statistical universals in combination are particularly common. That is, statements of the sort "if A then a tendency to B", in which A is not an individual, society, culture or language, probably constitute the single most common form of cross-cultural generalization.

Conceptually, the archetype as the in-between dynamic organizer may be thought as the conditional constraining part of the elements that it constellates; therefore, what we are calling "conditional universals" is the description of what exactly archetypes "do".

When we consider salient images and representations imbued with an intense feeling-tone, we may often notice that such stabilized (therefore, cultural) representations (but also behaviors) differ at a superficial level but seem universal when looked from other perspectives, for instance, from the perspective of what they try:

a) To accomplish (a functionalist approach).
b) To explain (an intellectualist approach).
c) To structure and shape as categories of the mind (a structuralist approach).
d) To creatively signify (a symbolic approach).

They are, therefore, "conditionally universal".

From this perspective, we may imagine the possibility of the existence of archetypal images originally rooted in the biological sensory-motor body and imbued and fueled by affectivity which carry out all these functions. The last function – the symbolic function – is particularly important for any Jungian analyst, as it refers to the polysemic nature of the symbol and to its creative, productive nature. From this point of view, I might say that the symbolic perspective may be the context in which the three other functions take place. In fact, it is within the symbolic perspective that any specific individual contribution becomes miraculously fundamental, integrating what will be accomplished and explained within an organic context. It is thanks to the transformative, creative possibility realized by the symbol that my brief, frail existence may be rescued precisely by the meanings that the symbolic perspective produces.

It is thanks to the emotionally charged creative action of the symbol that one's life may be spared from Macbeth's destiny and lead towards Jung's numinous transferential goal:

Tomorrow, and tomorrow, and tomorrow,
Creeps in this petty pace from day to day,
To the last syllable of recorded time;
And all our yesterdays have lighted fools
The way to dusty death. Out, out, brief candle!
Life's but a walking shadow, a poor player,
That struts and frets his hour upon the stage,

And then is heard no more. It is a tale
Told by an idiot, full of sound and fury,
Signifying nothing.
      (Shakespeare, W. *Macbeth*, 5.5.16–27)

These kinds of symbolic universal images – better to say patterns – would be related to the possibility that I have already mentioned, for which the archetype is located *between* the subject and his objects, connected by an emotional bond. The archetype, seen this way, *is* what makes an environment-for-an-organism and, at the same time, an organism-for-an-environment, including the person's cultural world.. It is the archetype that, with one foot in the organism – who actively selects its environment – and the other in its environmental conditions the organism contributes to realize, creates and realizes the connection between the organism and its environment, i.e., the very conditions for life and individuation.

Now that we have established the existence of these quasi-universals and of conditional universals, I would like to discuss the validity of the hypothesis of the universality of the images' contents.

Meaningful images (i.e., not merely factual images) are always the condensed emotional representations of metaphors, and metaphors are themselves a creative product of condensed relationships (originally between observed objects in purposeful motion – as in Jean Mandler). *"Caesar is a lion"* produces a transcendent image from the condensed relationship ("is") between two incompatible images, which refer to utterly different domains: Caesar and the lion.

This is what I try to do in analysis: I participate in the production of novel, emotional, metaphorical images that transcend the original ones. I look and contribute to create new contexts for those texts which are waiting for them. I do not try to cure the symptom; I look for its lost context, the lost co-evolutionary environment in which it makes sense again.

The work of cognitive anthropologists, such as Dan Sperber, gravitate around the post-Vygotskyan paradigm, shared also by Michael Tomasello, for which development is part and parcel of the intersubjective, interpersonal, social and cultural life – in other terms, the human co-evolutionary milieu. Development and education may, therefore, be described at a level intermediary between individual emotional and cognitive development and cultural transmission (Bruner, 1996).

Now I will once again refer to the relationship between inheritance and development. This is necessary because, as I am maintaining a bottom-up perspective, I need to refer to the bottom initial part and get to the point where we are: the social anthropological domain.

Referring to the debate between domain specificity (hence, some form of encapsulated modularity, which would be inherited) and rigidity, as analytical psychology may maintain, a genetically determined disposition may express itself in different ways or not express itself at all depending both on the organism's maturational moment and on the environmental conditions. The image of the snake is a classic example of the role this disposition takes in Jungian literature.

Even in a case such as fear of snakes (and other predators), a convincing argument may be made for the existence of evolved mechanisms that trigger an appropriate self-protection response when the danger cues and the fear are not necessarily directly linked. Sperber describes such a case in which fear does not emerge "instinctively" but only after a specific sort of learning experience. Rhesus monkeys are born without fear of snakes. Enduring fear develops after a few observations of another rhesus monkey taking fright at a snake, as if *that* specific fear is *easily* elicited, vs. other potentially fearful experiences which do not trigger such a fearful response.

I argue that the "choice" of specific objects, while being expressed in variable, new forms, in phobias may also be connected to ancestral predispositions. An example may be the irrational fact that, normally, people are not afraid of riding a motorcycle but may feel anxious when jumping in the water from a spot a few meters high. In fact, the first situation is always quite dangerous, and *should* elicit fear, whereas the second is totally harmless. My hypothesis is that humans are not built to move very fast and are not susceptible for this kind of fear, which must be learned socially, but have experienced – perhaps phylogenetically from our ancestors and ontogenetically from being suspended into our mother's arms – the menace of falling; hence, any experience of falling is susceptible to trigger some form of anxiety, or excitation.

Speaking about the symbolic (not perceptual) image of the snake, Jung says that, first, it indicates something like the sign: "Achtung!" (Danger!) (Jung, 1997, 2nd vol.). Bearing in mind that something dangerous is not something that we must necessarily avoid but something that we must approach with care, here, Jung seems to agree with the sociobiological interpretation of the fear of the snake (and other fears) as a residue of ancestral disposition inherited from our ancestors that had to do with real snakes. This is a reductionist explanation – not necessarily wrong, but partial, and wrong as a unilateral perspective may be wrong.

In fact, Jung's position is much more complex; it is an anti-reductionist perspective. For Jung, the fundamental "Achtung!" meaning of this image is just a general psychological statement on an image – the snake – that, as every image imbued with a feeling-tone, is a representation of specific endogenous affects and meanings.

If interpreted situationally, as the sociobiologists do, the image of the snake is the representation of the *real* snakes that were dangerous for the human of the Pleistocene. On the contrary, if interpreted within a dispositional perspective, as Jung does and as I am doing, the existence of real snakes with their natural characteristics will turn out to be a perceptual image "good to express" endogenous meanings, a perceived image good-to-represent and express a feeling. These meanings go far beyond biological fear. Hence, the "Achtung!" refers to an extremely complex aggregate of transcendent meanings *selected and borrowed* from the real perceived snake as a good image to represent them.[1]

After all, it is true that we are chordates. Our body is anatomically built *around* the spinal cord, which is like a snake, the same way as, functionally speaking, our evolved cortical brain is built on top of its own "reptilian strata".[2] These embryological, anatomical and functional connections may be related to Jung's idea that the cold-blooded, extremely archaic nature of the snake may represent the functioning of life as an objective movement that doesn't care much of the individual per se, with its subjective, warm-blooded, mammal qualities, the most important of which is empathy. The snake is just infinite life, hence – if not integrated – psychosis.

A 34 years-old woman, a patient of mine, once dreamed of a snake standing erect in front of her. She understood in the dream that its position was polarizing two possible ways, on the right or on the left. The wrong choice would have meant to be poisoned by its bite.

She had to deal with a difficult separation from a very dependent and fragile man that she cared for. The dream helped us to understand that, as anti-psychotherapeutic as this may seem, empathy had to be put aside, because she was facing a problem whose "objective" nature did not care for the warm feelings that, at an Ego-level, are a sign of being-human.

She was called to act "cold-bloodedly" as confronting herself with a problem whose solution transcended human empathetic feelings. Unfortunately, this exclusion of warm-blooded, mammalian empathy also implied the risk of a catastrophic poisoning wrong choice.

This dream helped her to realize that she was facing an issue whose responsibility transcended her, and that she was an integral part of this problem and, before the snake, she was at risk as it was her partner.

The empirical experience of the snake as an animal that sheds its skin now becomes a perceived image good to metaphorize the same theme – the autonomous, objective process changing, transforming oneself – *to which the mind is susceptible*. This is where universality lies.

This perception of an image seems to be treated by a process similar – if not identical – to the *perceptual analysis* that for Mandler extracts patterns and primitive concepts. The only difference – and it doesn't seem to be a minor difference – is that here we are not dealing with cognitive concepts but with emotional images.

The same thing may be said for the snake's venomous bite. From its empirical experience, the poison becomes a psychological image to imagine the issue of the *pharmakon*, to which the mind is susceptible. *Had we never seen snakes or venomous bites, our susceptibilities might have produced images with similar qualities.*

What I am trying to argue is that we may use the sociobiological perspective only if we avoid its reductionist perspective and modify its situational paradigm in favor of a dispositional one for which those ancestral experiences are meaningful because they are *interpreted* by the psyche (by the organism) to give a representational form to specific complex, meaningful, "spiritualized" metaphors. Therefore, if there would not exist real snakes in nature, it is possible that the mind could have created an image similar to a snake when and if it needed to "think" those complex emotional issues that the snake represents. The ancestral disposition to be afraid of snakes would not really derive from our ancestral experiences but would be motivated by the "dangerous" emotional meanings that the image conveys. *One of them is the sociobiological inherited fear.*

This relationship between specific environmental situations (where we may encounter real snakes) and psychological dispositions is very delicate. Sperber argues:

> Both dispositions and susceptibilities need appropriate environmental conditions for their ontogenetic development. Dispositions find the appropriate conditions in the environment in which they were phylogenetically developed. Susceptibilities may well reveal themselves only as a result of a change of environmental conditions. Homo sapiens, for instance, has a disposition to eat sweet food. In the natural environment in which the species developed, this was of obvious adaptive value in helping individuals to select the most appropriate nutrients. In the modern environment in which sugar is artificially produced, this brings out a susceptibility to over-consumption of sugar, with all its well-known detrimental effects.
>
> (Sperber, 1985, pp. 80–81)

I think that the infant's social referencing activity, and her pervasive intersubjective and social nature, is the context in which these processes take place. A vast literature supports something that would be quite coherent with Jung's model of the relationship between archetype-as-such and individual complexes, among which I would add cultural complexes, in which images that reside in an individual psyche are shared by a particular social group.

So far, I have tried to justify the hypothesis of universal patterning constraints that, starting from a simple biological level, give rise step-by-step to "archetypal images" from the bottom up. I have also set affects at the very base of such a constrained transformational chain, in which contents become more and more abstract – if you wish, spiritualized and diversified. Finally, I may now explicitly say that what makes a human empirically really human is not what is universal in her but what makes her empirically different, if not unique – what makes of her a *unique and non-reproducible variation of universal themes, a singularity.*

In other words, what exists is only the empirical, historical and cultural symbolic human being. Yet what makes it possible for him to exist is the process I tried to describe is his being always embedded in an ongoing co-evolutionary field, therefore, a social group into a process of constant change yet always within a constrained – universal – set of parameters.

I may try to clarify what I am trying to say using an analogy: what formally makes geometry possible is mathematics. Yet only geometry and four-dimensional geometry *exist* – i.e., massive bodies in the historical flow of time. In my reading of Jung, this is the precious fruit and product of individuation and individual consciousness or, at a cultural level, of the inestimable preciousness of the specific ways a culture expresses itself as a particular variation of those constraints.

Seen from the empirical, historical individual experience, the archetype is an abstraction. It is its specific historical individual embodiment in the potentially infinite local variations that makes it *real*. And what may make it so for the individual are the individual's feelings. He will feel it, and only then will it really exist for him in a particular, situated form.

Previously, I criticized the risk of putting the Ego at the center of analytical psychology. Now it should be made clear that the Ego *must be* at the center, *provided that it has been becoming the Self*. Therefore, Ego-formation *is* the constant preoccupation in analysis, not referring to an "Egoic-ego" but to an "Ego-Self".

Notes

1 You may notice that this is just the repetition of the same process through which the organism selects and actively builds its own co-evolutionary environment. In this case, this dispositional process is applied to the emotional images.

2 I have already recalled the interesting fact that during the REM phase, endothermic animals lose their thermoregulatory capacity, so the body is left without its usual metabolic controls – like a cold-blooded animal – while the brain instead becomes metabolically hyperactive.

   This does not necessarily imply a direct phylogenetic descent of Homo from reptiles, which does not exist. McLean has been seriously criticized for this, although the point is there is no need for such a common evolutionary path to notice that the two brains share a common embryological and functional phylogenetic development.

References

Bion, W.R. (1990). *Brazilian Lectures. The Complete Works*, vol. VII. London: Karnak Books, pp. 1973–1974.

Brown, D.E. (1991). *Human Universals*. Kindle.

Bruner, J. (1996). *The Culture of Education*. Cambridge, MA: Harvard University Press.

Fox, R. (1973). *Encounters with Anthropology*. Harmondsworth: Penguin.

Greenberg, J.H. (1966). *Language Universals: With Special Reference to Feature Hierarchies*. The Hague: Mouton.

Greenberg, J.H. (1975). Research on language universals. *Annual Review of Anthropology*, 4, 75–94.

Hempel, C.G. (1942). The function of general laws in history. *Journal of Philosophy*, 39, 35–48.

Jung, C.G. (1997). *Visions. Notes from the Seminar Given in 1936–1934*, vol. 2. Zurich: The estate of C.G. Jung.

Kluckhohn, C. (1953). Universal categories of culture. In Kroeber, A.L. et al., *Anthropology Today: An Encyclopedic Inventory*. Chicago: University of Chicago Press.

Paden, W.E. (2001). Universals revisited: Human behaviors and cultural variations. *Numen*, 48(3), 276–289.

Saler, B. (1999). "Biology and Religion: On Establishing a Problematic," in *Method and Theory in the Study of Religion*, 11, 386–394.

Sperber, D. (1985). Anthropology and psychology: Towards an epidemiology of representations. Malinowski memorial lecture 1984. *Man (New Series)*, 20(1), 73–89.

Chapter 9

From emotionally raw images to cultural images

9.1 The ego

> The ego, has a specific content of consciousness, is not a simple or elementary factor, but a complex one, which, as such, cannot be described exhaustively. Experience shows that it rests on two seemingly different bases, the somatic and the psychic. The somatic basis is inferred from the totality of endosomatic perceptions, which for their part are already of a psychic nature and are associated with the ego and are therefore conscious. They are produced by endosymbiotic stimuli, only some of which cross the threshold of consciousness. A considerable proportion of these stimuli occur unconsciously, that is, subliminally. The fact that they are subliminal does not necessarily mean that their status is merely physiological, any more than this would be true of a psychic content. Sometimes they are capable of crossing the threshold, that is, of becoming perceptions. But there is no doubt that a large proportion of this endosymbiotic stimuli are simply uncapable of consciousness and are so elementary that there is no reason to assign them a psychic nature – unless, of course, one favors the philosophical view that all life processes are psychic anyway.
>
> (Jung, 1959, pp. 3–4)

This is the description of the Ego as a *content* of consciousness. What about the structure of the Ego from Jung's point of view? This is a difficult question (at least for me), which, nevertheless, in the context of this book, requires an answer.

I am not sure whether Jung ever explicitly refers to a structural aspect of the Ego. I think that a coherent model for an answer would be that the Ego-structure refers to the activities that in the brain lead to consciousness. There are various models for this, which I cannot discuss now, for reasons of space.

Throughout this book, I referred to the affective-sensory-motor apparatus and to the constraints that derive from it, and Jung himself describes the Ego as rooted not just in the brain but also in the whole *body*. We should differentiate the role that Jung attributes to the brain and that of the body, although they are two aspects of the same global entity. As for the "body", I would first indicate the striated muscles, which can be commanded by conscious will. They are related to the fundamental role of motricity, which I have discussed in the first part of the book. But

DOI: 10.4324/9781003586463-9

what is now important to point out is the role of the sensory apparatus, which, as I repeated many times, produces specific constraints and conditions for the imaginal expression and the organization of the fundamental movers of the psyche – the affects.

When describing what the function of the brain actually could be, Jung writes:

> In light of this view the brain might be a transformer station, in which the relatively infinite tension or intensity of the psyche proper is transformed into perceptible frequencies or "extensions" . . . Psyche=highest intensity in the smallest space.
>
> (Jung, 1953. Letter of 02–25–1952)

This idea is similar to what Bion developed later in his own life, while he was dealing with the transformation of beta elements into alpha elements as the transformation of pre-conceptions into conceptions through what he aptly called *realizations*. In fact, Bion was also dealing with some transformative function that would, so to speak, *mentalize/incarnate* O – i.e., the Absolute, the Infinite, the Numinosum.

As I said, the way that such a transformation happens is through the sensory apparatus, which dispositionally creates/selects a specific *Umwelt*. The sensory apparatus – i.e., our way we perceive whatever Reality is (Bion's O) – corresponds to the constraints of the sensory motor apparatus, which works at the service of the affects: our teleological attractors.

The sensorium – *any sensorium of any biological being* – is an extraordinary transformational device that makes the realization possible, the incarnation of a specific part of Spinoza's "God" into nature. In fact, colors, smells or musical sounds do not actually exist as such; they are specific products of the transformation of electromagnetic waves or electrochemical impulses by our sensory apparatus.[1] Humans can only see some colors and not others, which are not only imperceptible but also *inconceivable* to us. Yet these percepts may be perceived by other animals, not to mention the impossibility to conceive a reality made only by sounds, temperature, ultrasounds or electrical impulses.

This quote from Barkow, Cosmides and Tooby, which refer to the visual apparatus and therefore to images, may help us connect these threads to Jung's theory:

> one could think of the eye as a tube that traverses metaphysical realms, one end of which obtrudes into the physical realm, the other into the mental. For modern monists, however, these two realms are simply alternative descriptions of the same thing, convenient for different analytic purposes. The "mental" consists of ordered relationships in physical systems that embody properties typically running under labels such as "information", "meaning", or regulation. From this point of view, there is no Cartesian tube: both ends of the visual system are physical and both are mental.
>
> (Barkow et al., 1992, p. 58)

You will recall a passage by Jung in which he connects the somatic "instinct" to the psychological image. This passage seems quite coherent with this interpretation of the sensorium (in this case with vision, which, as we know, has a direct impact on the production of imaginal schemas and, by further abstraction, on cognition):[2]

> The primordial image might suitably be described as *the instinct's perception of itself*, or as the self-portrait of the instinct, in exactly the same way as consciousness is an inward perception of the objective life process.
>
> (Jung, 1919, p. 136. Jung's italics)

Such a somatic instinct may, therefore, be connected (also) to the sensorium (in this case, vision) and, therefore, to the Ego. The sensory apparatus and the Ego would, therefore, be part of a larger[3] transformational device that will give human shape to human experiences and produce *humanized* mental contents. Therefore, we may say that the Ego emerges from such a transformational device that is the sensorium (behind which there is, of course, a brain), a sensorium which is made by constraints specific to each species.

Now what is the embryological nature and the function of the extroverted senses (like touch, vision and smell) and of the introverted senses (like enteroception)?

You will remember that my discussion on archetypes generated the hypotheses for which universal images, which give shape and convey affects, might be something-in-between – here between the organism (the subject) and its environment (other persons but also the anthropic world). I think that the nature of the transformational device of the sensorium as the extended part of our brainbody into the environment supports this idea.

This would explain Jung's description of the relationship between Self and Ego:

> The ego stands to the self as the moved to the mover, or as object to subject, because the determining factors which radiate out from the self surround the ego on all sides and are therefore superordinate to it. This Self, like the unconscious, is an apriori existent out of which the ego evolves. It is, so to speak, an unconscious prefiguration of the ego. It is not I who create myself, rather I happen to myself. This realization is of fundamental importance for the psychology of religious phenomena.
>
> (Jung, 1954, p. 259)

In this passage, the crucial line is "[the Self] is, so to speak, an unconscious prefiguration of the Ego", for which the Ego itself would represent the *condition for the archetypal – universally constrained – images to emerge within a relational environment*. In fact, these images would arise from the archetypally built sensorium to give form and representable meaning to affects, which are, as I said, our attractors (as they are for most animals). Interpreted this way, the Ego is a potential fractal of the numinous Self. Therefore, as I wrote in the last chapter of the first volume, the Self must be put back at the center of our analytical interest. In fact, *this* Ego, being the conscious realization of the Self – therefore, its partial realization – does *not* correspond to the infantile Ego of attachment theory, or of most post-Freudian traditions, nor to the cognitive Ego studied by so much infant research. This Ego is an ongoing *process* of interaction with a co-evolutionary environment in which what we all normally call *infantile narcissism* may in fact be the first trace of the *numinosum*, as the emotional experience of something infinite, objective and universal (this is obvious in "narcissistic" patients, who are extremely sensitive about any "offence" to their "grandiose" self – an Ego still fused with the Self).

Such an Ego, along with all the studies, theories and interpretations about its development, is not the goal of psychological life or the ultimate goal of a psychotherapy. Rather, it is a condition for its own infinite and perilous transformation towards the Self. Once again, as its structure is built on the "archetypal" constraints of its affects and sensory-motor apparatus, which makes it possible for the Real (whatever it is) to contingently unveil itself into our human experience, such an Ego is relational by its own nature; it is a process of an incarnating relationality and not a" thing" of any sort. In fact, the coming into life of any organism, and most of all, a child, and then of an adult (i.e., what we call "individuation"), cannot but happen within a relationship, within a co-evolutionary environment. It is precisely the relationship with the "environment", which our senses and affects *imply*, that provides the only possible context for growth and transcendence. And this environment spans from the primary mother to the political involvement in society. Therefore, such an Ego cannot be just an organ of adaptation nor a pure product of the situation (as it is the Freudian Perception-Consciousness Ego, which is formed by the limitations of the Id imposed by the impact with the environment).

To recapitulate: for Jung, the Ego is a unique, dispositional structure that emerges from and mirrors the Self. Through the selective process of transformation and interpretation of outer and inner stimuli and by polarizing its own subjectivity with its own objects, the human Ego must carry out the infinite task of reuniting itself with the infinite (or indefinite) object-word, without losing its own existence and integrity, as this would imply a catastrophic regression into non-differentiation and unconsciousness – a fall into de Martino's Nature.

The Ego's ability to adapt corresponds to the possibility to form a container – an alchemical *vas* – into which creativity, imagination, transformations and singularity may come into being, exactly as it happens in the infinitely creative and "erotic" biological world (Kauffmann, 2021).

This whole process, which I tried to describe, is moved and attracted not by cognition but by affects and feelings. While they evolve within the relational field, they are transformed into secondary emotions and, therefore, transcend their original autistic nature of primary affects into the coronation of any psychological development – the birth of a true ethical stand.

9.2 From the collective unconscious to cultural representations

In the first volume, I criticized some psychological and analytical theories because, I wrote, they just deal with Ego development and its relationship with the repressed contents that form the personal unconscious. It is now time to complete my effort in clarifying this issue.

As I wrote in the opening pages, this book is written by an analyst whose "object" is another human *subject* – in my work, it is my patient. As I consider both the explanatory and experiential paradigms necessary, I have not restrained myself into offering several explicatory principles for the ultimately ontologically real object: the subjective emotional experience. What I intended to do is to try to recuperate some core concepts of Jung's legacy: primarily, the role of affects all the way to the *numinosum*, which is tied to the fundamental feeling of infinity, of universality and of subjective objectivity, which *may well become psychopathological*, but that, as it often happens within the paradoxical nature of existence, is a factor that saves life from utter factual and bureaucratic[4] meaninglessness.

Therefore, I tried to rescue the affective trace of meaningful ("religious") images – the feeling of *numinosum* – from psychopathology. I did it in an attempt to warn against the risk of considering health just from an adaptive point of view and, therefore, losing sight of Jung's fundamental goal of any life-process, which *includes and surpasses the analytical third phase of education* into *transformation*. Such an embedded, intrinsic goal is at the heart of Jung's idea of transference, in which what we today call projective/introjective identification is the key psychological device.

In this second volume, I turned to the images that, in their infinite diversity, may convey a sense of objective universality, while representing feelings and their specific qualities. Therefore, the aim of my work had to do with emphasizing the primacy of the affects for the "process of mentalization" via the formation of *meaningful* images *through* sensory motor constraints (via Mandler's perceptual analysis) – first of all, visual and acoustic inputs. This mentalization process, moved and organized by the affects, develops as affects turn into feelings and secondary and tertiary emotions, which motivate the fundamental representations that, at this point, do not involve just the dyad but also a triad (See vol. II, § 10) and that pave the way for the development of human perspectival cognitive *and emotional* intelligence.

To do so, I took Michael Tomasello's line of research as an example. Tomasello describes such a developmental process moved by affects, feelings and emotions that give meanings to cognitive representations as nothing less than the process of becoming *human*.

We have seen that, at this developmental stage, the child becomes an ethical being, guided not by non-egocentric and purely competitive rules but by a perspectival disposition based on cooperative norms and values rooted in fairness. This is a description of a now fully social and cultural individual. At this point, this individual is moved not only by purely self-centered aims, like the other primates, but his representations are also now deeply shared in the minds of others. If, factually, these others are the closest persons to him, what the child described by Tomasello is doing is referring to a system of values whose nature is intrinsically social. Both his social, emotional and cognitive attitude and the specific values and norms that will guide his behavior will soon transcend his kin, as they are based not on belonging but on ethical normativity.

You will recall that Sperber defines a culture as a set of shared (emotionally triggered and organized) representations stabilized in the minds of the other participants to the same social group. With this model, we have a hypothesis of the psychological developmental conditions through which a culture is born. At this point, I would like to examine this issue with some attention once again because it represents the bridge between how emotionally motivated personal representations become culture.

Once again, the starting point should be the fact that it is in the individual mind – in the mind of the infant and the child – that representations ("patterns") constrained by her primary affects and her sensory-motor apparatus emerge. They are the first building blocks for the bottom-up process of further development of much more complex, abstract (spiritual), differentiated and numerous "archetypal" images.

Considering that, like archetypes, also most of cultural contents are unconscious, *what is the difference between shared values and cultural norms on one side and pure archetypal contents on the other?* This question is important because for Jung, archetypes are *not* cultural complexes, i.e., unconscious mental organizations stably shared by individuals of the same social group, which are culturally specific. They have a biological – pre-psychological, hence, pre-social – origin.

One difference lies in the nature of affects. In fact, cultural shared values, representations and norms normally are not overly emotionally charged. They tend to be emotionally relevant and contagious but not necessarily numinous, *at least in normal times*. On the contrary, archetypes always have a numinous character.

Now the question is this: Why are they numinous? Because they are manifestations of the activation of those archaic endogenous primary affective attractors which teleologically represent "a need, or a desire, for something". The numinous quality of such needs, expressed as primary non-metabolized affects, has to do with their primary phylogenetically archaic nature. They spring from the bottom of the psyche, and being still far from any formed Ego, they have a pervasive nature.

At this point, the next question is this: *How do these primary affects get metabolized?*

The answer is that they are metabolized precisely through the complex interplay of relationships psychicized within and through the mother's mind – through Bion's *rêverie*, i.e., through the tuning between the dispositional nature of the child and the mirroring "environmental mother" (Winnicott, 1965; Bollas, 2018). Throughout ontogenesis, this phase will develop into a more complex situation in which the child will mentalize the mother and father as "other" subjects before the infant's own emergent subjectivity. It is the mother's and the father's contributions that transform the numinous, raw quality of the infant's affects into primary and secondary emotions and, eventually, cultural values and norms directed towards a shared perspective, a common goal. This transformative process of psychization is constantly guided by the infant's dispositional agentive Self; through this process, the Ego emerges from the Self as a sort of a potential, developing fractal.

From the start of ontogenetic life, whatever the empathetic mother "presents" (Winnicott) to her infant – whatever object she feels he needs – becomes an embodied metaphor of the emotional meaning of the infant's own relationship with her. In fact, any object, insofar as it is the incarnation of an emotional meaning, is not just an epistemic content but it is also a gnostic one. It becomes a re-collected part of the subject's own experience – in my example, the infant's experience.

Together with the "holding" and the "object presenting", a third paradigmatic process must be recalled – "handling". It is by presenting those objects from the perceptual world that may better represent the infant's needs and wishes through her "handling" of the infant that the mother will "hold" the process through which the infant will progressively interiorize the specific intersubjective and cultural meanings of his own world. This world spans from the infant's own emotional body and perceptions, all the way up to the way he will emotionally (hence, eventually, ethically) and cognitively categorize the flow of his own experience.

This fundamental process – hence, the way infants preverbally learn – is essentially a *practical* form of learning. As I tried to describe in the second part of this book, it proceeds from primary, innate, emotionally imbued (salient) perceptual/ motor schemas shared through the mother and the child precisely by the mother's object "presenting" and "handling". By these two relational structures, perceived "things" become sensations and emotional meanings. It should be noticed that already from the start of life, these meanings are not just idiosyncratic contents shared by two persons – mother and infant – but they are also from the very start social and cultural specific modes of existence already realized by a socialized adult (the mother), shared with the infant and interpreted in their own specific way within the dyad (and very soon, within the triad of mother, father and child).

I would like to underscore an analogy between this psychological and practical form of ontogenetical learning and knowledge and what Pierre Bourdieu, referring to the social and anthropological realm, calls "habitus" (Bourdieu, 2019).[5] Throughout this practical process, first, mother, and then father, will add language to the infant's life and shape a specific, idiosyncratic direction and shared relationality to her primary numinous motivations that had activated and constellated her representations. As we saw quoting Tomasello (vol. I, 10.1), this will be conducive to the perspectival intentionality, to the emergence of fairness, to the cooperation based on values and to an ethically based sociality, which are the foundations of any "cultural" structure. These psychological processes of exchange and interiorization seem to be necessary for the formation of the "habitus" that will take place from latency (i.e., from the post-oedipal phase of life) onward. In such a process, emotional images and behaviors are exchanged from one mind to another, starting from the primary Mother-Infant relationship.

From such a preverbal, interactive field, language emerges. A point of emergence of complex semantic and cognitive formations arising from the first preverbal conceptual primitives may be the developmental moment in which the child's vocabulary explodes between 17–24 months of age (Bloom, 1973, 2000). Such amazing increase of the child's vocabulary, now made by words composed of lexical universals (Wierzbicka, 1992), seems to prepare the way for the development of the perspectival cooperation that I mentioned previously and that happens precisely on the moment in which a constrained – archetypal – competence arises *within its proper co-evolutionary field* (in fact, without the "Mother" and "Father" functions, it could not happen).

At this point in the development of language:

1. This transformation of primary affects into secondary emotions carries with itself the possibility of also sharing the child's own (cognitive) representations. It is now that I see the birth of culture as the first form of stably shared emotional representations triggered by secondary emotions between the child and her caregivers.
2. Emotions may not be numinous anymore. They become thinkable and sayable; They have a name and are shared as emotional words between a now-existing Ego and its properly humanized environment, which contributes to regulate them. These words now have the extraordinary ability to name things present and things absent, therefore, connecting senses, representations and imagination.

Now I would like to distinguish between *divergent* and *convergent* transformations (see also Bateson, 2002. For a similar discussion in an anthropological perspective, see: Descola, 2021, pp. 127–131).

1) *Divergent transformations* belong and lead to the Ego and to consciousness. As personal complexes, they represent personal, subjective interpretations – i.e., representations produced by an idiosyncratic, possibly unique, viewpoint deriving from an archetypal disposition. As archetypal emergent contents, they may be creative, innovative and sometimes revolutionary of the overall cultural/ collective mindset. They may be the initiators of the anti-structuring process described by Turner that I discussed in the previous pages.

   They may emerge in dreams, orient imagination and choices and teleologically guide one's life in a latent way. They are the quintessence of psychological evolution, as they represent the creative emergence of new images and values, *or* they may be individual *delusions*. They may organize the individual's life or spread to the relational world and to the collective.
2) On the other hand, *convergent transformations* are culturally shared, unconscious and compelling emotional contents. Therefore, they represent and/or preserve cultural continuity.

Such contents may present themselves in two ways:

a. As already metabolized emotional contents arising from each individual psyche within the co-evolutionary field in which intersubjective relationships and *rêverie* have been taking place. The Adlerian process of "education", as Jung describes it (i.e., as the process of humanization and socialization of archetypal contents), and therefore their selection and adaptation to particular social and historical conditions are part of this.

As I described earlier, within the infant/child-mother-and-father (including the peers at a later stage) "transferential" relationship, the constrained, emotionally compelling endogenous representations in the infant/child's mind are shared by the members of the child's social group – his kin (in the West, the "family").

From the moment in which this process involves language (it always involves affects and cognition) and especially around the middle of the second year, this social sharing of emotionally meaningful representations gives birth to those implicit, emotionally charged, value-laden social structures and representations that we call *cultural complexes*. They are part of the continuity and the fabric of a culture.

The real moment in which a culture is born happens when the child develops her perspectival cooperation perspective. At this point, language becomes crucial.

Culture is, therefore, passed from parents and kin to the child as a process of socialization of the child's archetypal activity. The level of emotional charge of the environment's mind (the child's kin) in relation to these contents and in general terms (the presence, for instance, of a disturbed emotional environment) will determine the level at which those archetypal contents will become socially negotiable shared contents. Examples of collective *narratives* and representations are social/religious myths. Examples of *institutions* are rituals or normative social *habitus* (Bourdieu, 2019). Examples of physical *artifacts* may be architectures, distribution and quality of inhabited spaces, etc.

Like the mimetic analogue of the hole in the ground of the Wachandi, such cultural artifacts are symbolic, "disembodied" analogues of the psychic representations of the culture's members – for instance, as memory mediators.
These contents may eventually become the following:

i) Conscious/explicit. In this case, they represent the implicit symbolic form of stable organization of a culture; or
ii) Rigid, nonnegotiable and implicit/unconscious, from which the child (and the future adult) is not allowed to differentiate without high psycho-social costs up to forcing him into psychopathology. This would be a highly charged cultural complex. The level of its activation and polarization will be determined by the level of its emotional charge.

b. Implicit, *non-metabolized* (therefore, numinous) yet now shared (via contagion) emotional contents, *which are now culturally constellated.*

These contents represent socially unconscious aims and needs that appear within the individual psyche. They are constellated in the individual through her "education" process, starting from birth and all the way up into the participation in her cultural groups. In this situation, the child's and the adult's archetypal activation is *not* metabolized by her environment's mind (the kin's mind) since the members of her group are not in the condition to be aware of the charged contents. Therefore, they are left at the level of the collective unconscious, a segment of which is active in the cultural group and particularly constellated in some individual psyches.

This would represent a more primitive layer from which the archetypal images that the child, or the future adult that she will become, will emerge. Their unconscious-collective nature still carries a cultural and social relevance but emerges through the individual as individual formations not yet mentalized by his social group.

One example is "big dreams", another are prophetic images. In another – belonging to psychopathology – they may be psychotic delusions and hallucinations.

9.3 From conceptual primitives to lexical universals

As I wrote, language is a fundamental device for such a process of metabolization from the psychosomatic – biological – level of activation of primary affects to intersubjective secondary emotions and, therefore, to cultural complexes for two reasons. The first is for its important and perhaps unique role in the stabilization and organization of the mind/psyche. The second is for language's staggering capacity to convey, through its inherent semantics, the historically stratified cultural meanings and values.[6] Following Ana Wierzbicka's perspective, each word, used in a particular cultural milieu, contains the peculiar way through which the lexical universals are organized.

In her three-decades-long empirical comparative research, Wierzbicka pursued Leibniz's idea of the existence of an innate "alphabet of human thoughts" (1903, p. 430). All complex thoughts would arise through different combinations of simple ideas, just as references and written words arise through different combinations of letters from the alphabet. A crucial point is that such ideas are so clear to us that no explanation given can make them any clearer. Complex thoughts and meanings arise just as written sentences, and written words arise through different combinations of letters from the alphabet; all complex thoughts and meanings arise through different combinations of simple ideas and meanings. For Leibniz and for Wierzbicka, semantic definitions and understanding can be really attained by decomposing complex meanings into components that are self-explanatory.

Following Clifford Geertz (1984), for Wierzbicka, these semantic prototypes have such a self-explanatory nature because they are "experience near", whereas the meanings that are composed of them and that may be explained through them are "experience distant".

An experience-near concept is, roughly, one which an individual – a patient, a subject, in our case an informant – might himself naturally and effortlessly use to define what he and his fellow see, feel, think, imagine, and so on, and which he would readily understand when similarly applied by others. An experienced-distant concept is one which various types of specialists and analysts – an experimenter, an ethnographer, even a priest or an ideologist employ to forward their scientific, philosophical, or practical aims. Love is an experience-near concept; object cathexis is an experience-distant one.

(Geertz, 1984, pp. 227–228)

According to Geertz, experience-near concepts – and, therefore, words – "entangle" the person into a limited vernacular language. Yet this is not Wierzbicka's opinion:

Fortunately, it is not the case that *all* experience-near concepts are language-specific and that their use has to "entangle us in the vernacular". For example, concepts like FEEL, WANT, and THINK are experience-near (unlike affect, volition, or cognition), and yet using them in our explanations or definitions we do not get entangled in the vernacular, because lexical exponents of those concepts can be readily found in every language.

(Wierzbicka, 1999, p. 11)

Wierzbicka calls this "breaking the hermeneutical circle". Following Leibnitz's first hypothesis and the work of Andrzej Boguslawski (1970), in 1972 Wierzbicka embarked on an empirical investigation of several semantic domains in some European languages, and in her book *Semantic Primitives* (1972), she proposed a hypothetical list of 14 elementary human concepts, which would be expressed by specific words in each natural language.

Since then, with the cooperation of anthropologists and linguists, the empirical transcultural comparison has extended to many non-Indo-European languages (like the African Tano-Congo language Ewe, the Chinese mandarin, the Australian aboriginal languages, etc.). With time, and successive publications, the list of lexical universals amounted to ten in 1992.

The following list reports the conceptual primitives and lexical universals that Wierzbicka claims to have found throughout in an even more extended linguistic comparison.

SUBSTANTIVES: I, You, Someone (Person), Something (Thing), People, Body; DETERMINERS: This, The Same Other; QUANTIFIERS: One, Two, Some, Many/Much, All; ATTRIBUTES: Good, Bad, Big, Small; MENTAL PREDICATES: Think, No, Won't, Feel, See, Hear; SPEECH: Say, Word, True; ACTIONS, EVENTS, MOVEMENTS: Do, Happen, Move; EXISTENCE AND POSSESSION: There, Is, Have; LIFE AND DEATH: Live, Die; LOGICAL CONCEPTS: Not, Maybe, Can, Because, If; TIME: When (Time), Now, After, Before, A Long Time, A Short Time, For Some Time; SPACE: Where (Space), Here, Above, Below, Far, Near; Side, Inside; INTENSIFIER AUGMENTOR: Very, More; TAXONOMY, PARTONOMY: Kind Of, Part Of; SIMILARIT:Y Like.

(Wierzbicka, 1999)

These lexical universals, which express more fundamental conceptual primitives, are expressed in words specific to each natural language. From them, complex concepts and lexicals may be formed through a process of progressive composition and complexification. These may differ from language to language and may have limited or no semantic equivalents in other languages.

> These results tend to confirm the thrust of centuries of philosophical speculations about innate ideas, (Descartes, 1931) the "alphabet of human thoughts" (Leibniz, in: Couturad, 1903), the "midpoint around which all languages revolve" (Humboldt, 1903–1936) and the psychic unity of mankind (Boas, 1966). The main conclusion is that all languages do indeed appear to share a common core, both in their lexical repertoire and in their grammar, and that this common core can be used as a basis for a non-arbitrary and non-ethnocentric metalanguage for the description of languages and for the study of human cognition and emotion.
> (Wierzbicka, 1999, p. 36)

Wierzbicka's reference for a metalanguage precisely defines her project, based on a "natural semantic metalanguage" (NSM) made of the semantic primitives, organized in lexical universals and finally expressed by particular, precisely corresponding words that must be found in all existing and past languages. The following is an example that may also be useful to clarify the differences between what a *feeling* is in English in relation to an *emotion*.

> the word emotion is not as unproblematic as it seems. [. . .] The English word emotion combines in its meaning a reference to "feeling", a reference to "thinking", and a reference to a person's body. For example, one can talk about a "feeling of hunger", or a "feeling of heartburn", but not about an "emotion of hunger" or an "emotion of heartburn", because the feelings in question are not thought-related. One can also talk about a "feeling of loneliness" or a "feeling of alienation", but not an "emotion of loneliness" or an "emotion of alienation", because while these feeling are clearly related to thoughts (such as "I am all alone", "I don't belong", etc.) they just do not suggest any associated process such as rising blood pressure, a rush of blood to the head, tears, and so on.
> (Wierzbicka, 1999, p. 2)

Therefore, *emotion* is a word denoting a complex concept formed by the organic aggregation of lexical universals, one of which is precisely *feeling*. Therefore, not all natural languages have an equivalent word for emotion, while all do have a perfectly equivalent word for feeling. I prefer not to report the many philologically detailed examples that Wierzbicka gives, as this would encumber my discussion. I prefer to directly refer the reader to her publications. I think that these findings, if confirmed, represent an important corroboration of Jung's hypothesis of the archetypes (not necessarily meaning that such a hypothesis is confirmed but that it is not at all out of the question and that it may be confirmed through further evidence), as they not only make it possible to explain the leaps from biology to psychology to culture but they also would explain the possibility of particularly complex symbolic representations that may arise out of the most susceptible (in Sperber's words) combinations.

Within language, the most important meaning-making combination of words is surely the metaphor. In the second of Jorge Luis Borges' wonderful *Norton Lectures*, held at Harvard and dedicated to the metaphor (1967–1968), Borges, here as literary critic, argued that only slightly more than ten metaphorical patterns exist in universal literature (among which he lists stars as eyes, sleep as death, woman as flower, time as river, battle as fire, etc.). From such a surprisingly limited number of patterns, an indefinite number of variations have been crafted by all poets of all cultures throughout the centuries. Each one of these metaphorical variations is essentially a means for evoking and conveying a very specific kind of feeling – in the case of real poetry, a surprisingly precise, perfectly crafted, unique feeling among the indefinite number of feelings that we may feel.

Although I have been quite struck by Borges' idea, I have a difficult time imagining another scholar better acquainted than him with universal literature. Borges' literary analysis on the nature and variety of metaphors seems forcefully convergent with Jung's archetypal hypothesis – i.e., that of an infinite variation on specific universal themes. The fact that in the world of literature, these themes are so few – i.e., right in the domain where we would imagine that human intelligence and creativity is free from any precise limit – pushes to an unexpected extent the archetypal hypothesis.

As you might recall, I always posited affects as the source of all psychic activity, immediately organized and represented by sensory images in motion (hence, by motor schemas). The primary affects and the sensory-motor schemas would provide the initial constraints upon which all future images will form. Following an anthropic principle, for which previous constants and constraints lead to the most favorable world possible (in this case, complex archetypal images), it might make sense to interpret the universality, or quasi-universality, of the archetypal images as the product of a constrained *process*, analogous to the object-presenting feature that Winnicott describes.

This discussion on language lets me connect what I have said earlier on sensory-motor constraints and refer to the groundbreaking study by Berlin and Kay on color classification (1969).

Anthropologists and linguists had long known that the way colors are classified varies from language to language. Careful studies conducted by anthropologists after World War II, such as Harold Conklin's (1955) study of Hanunóo color words, made the point very clearly. Many anthropologists, in accordance with the "prevailing doctrine" of "extreme linguistic relativity", interpreted these findings as showing that there were no semantic universals in the domain of color terms, that the lexical coding of color was arbitrary (Berlin & Kay, 1969, pp. 1–2).

(Brown, 1991, p. 286)

Many sociocultural anthropologists conceive their task as a kind of translation from other cultures to ours. The views of a linguist described as "perhaps the leading American authority on translation" (Berlin & Kay, 1969, p. 159) were quite influential:

> *The segmentation of experience by speech symbols is essentially arbitrary.* The different sets of words for color in various languages are perhaps the best ready evidence for such arbitrariness. For example, in a high percentage of African languages there are only three "color words", corresponding to our *white, black and red*, which nevertheless divide up the entire spectrum. In the Tarahumara language of Mexico, there are five basic color words, and here "blue" and "green" are subsumed under a single term. (Nida, 1959, p. 13, italics in original) This conception of the relationship between language and color was not confined to anthropologists and linguists.
>
> (Berlin & Kay, 1969, p. 160)

To test the doctrine of extreme relativism in the categorization of colors, Berlin and Kay assembled lists of color terms from informants speaking 98 different languages representing a wide selection of unrelated major linguistic stocks. Although the number of color terms in each language did vary, they found that no more than 11 colors accounted for the basic color terms found in each language. The main defining features of a basic color term are that it is monolexemic (containing a single irreducible unit of meaning, such as "red", not two or more lexemes as in "reddish" or "dark blue"), is not included in another color term, is general in application and is psychologically salient to its users. The 11 basic colors are white, black, red, green, yellow, blue, brown, purple, pink, orange and gray. Nonbasic colors, such as "pumpkin-colored", "like the tail of a peacock", "bluish", "bluish-purple" and the like were excluded from analysis.

Once the basic color terms for each language had been determined, native speakers of those languages were asked to outline the boundaries of the colors on a color chart. The chart was composed of 329 color chips arranged along one axis in order of hue (the spectrum of colors) and along the other axis in order of brightness (brighter colors at the top, dimmer at the bottom, all at maximum saturation). To the side of the main chart were nine more chips of neutral hue, grading from white through gray to black. The informants drew a line around the chips that fit each of their basic color categories and designated the chip that was its best or most typical representative (the focal point of the color term).

Although the boundaries of color terms vary – by and large, the fewer the terms, the wider their bounds – the focal point of each basic color is substantially the same from one language to another. For example, people whose languages contain only two basic color terms tend to include the darker hues with their "black" and the lighter hues with their "white". Given the broad designation of these terms, they might just as well be glossed as "dark" and "light", but their focal points are the black and white chips. When "red" is added, to make a classification with just three basic terms, the third category typically includes some oranges, yellows, browns, pinks and purples along with the red chips that are the focus of the category. As each basic term is added – moving to languages with four, five, six basic terms, and so on – less and less of the chart remains without a basic color term label, and each of the areas designated by the new terms still tends to have a common focal point from one language to another. Considerable areas of the chart remain without designations in terms of basic colors. This definitively falsified the doctrine of total arbitrariness of color classification: color classification does not arbitrarily slice a continuum. But Berlin and Kay found a further surprising result.

> The order in which basic color categories enter languages is not arbitrary either. If a language has only two colors – and all languages have at least two – they are always white and black; if a language has three colors, the one added is red; if a fourth is added, it will be either green or yellow; when a fifth is added, it will then include both green and yellow; the sixth added is blue; the seventh added is brown; and if an eighth or more terms are added, it or they will be purple, pink, orange, or gray. Considerable subsequent research on color classification has necessitated modifications in this sequence, yet basic color terms apparently evolve in a largely universal pattern (Witkowski & Brown, 1978). Berlin and Kay (1969, p. 159) dismiss "extreme linguistic-cultural relativism", at least with respect to basic color terms, as a "myth created by linguists and anthropologists".
>
> Berlin and Kay's findings have been placed "among the most remarkable discoveries of anthropological science" (Rosh, 1973, 1978; Sahlins, 1976, p. 1).[7]
>
> (Brown, 1991, p. 340)

Recent research conducted at Georgia State University shows that native language affects how people convey information from a young age and hints at the presence of a universal system of communication that belongs to nonverbal communication. In a recent study, Şeyda Özçalışkan (Özçalışkan et al., 2023. See also: Özçalışkan & Goldin-Meadow, 2005; Özçalışkan et al., 2014, 2016a, 2016b, 2018), in collaboration with Susan Goldin-Meadow at the University of Chicago and Che Lucero at Cornell University, focused on children ages 3 to 12. The children either spoke English or Turkish. They were asked to use their hands to act out specific actions, such as running into a house. English and Turkish were the primary comparisons because they differ in terms of the way you talk about events.

If one is speaking Turkish and wants to describe someone running into a house, he must chunk the sentence up. He would say, "He's running and then he enters the house". But if it's in English, one would just say, "He ran into the house", all in one compact sentence. As such, it is easier to express both running (manner of motion) and entering (path of motion) together in a single expression in English than in Turkish.

The study wanted to find out whether gesture does or does not follow these differences and how early children learn these patterns. Researchers asked the children to describe the same action first when speaking (speech and co-speech gesture) and then without speaking with only their hands (known as silent gesture). They found that when the children spoke and gestured at the same time, their gesture followed the conventions of their language, with clear differences between the gestures of the Turkish and English speakers. When the children used gestures without speaking, however, their gestures were remarkably similar. In fact, it is easier to express both running and entering in a single gesture compared to speech, particularly for Turkish speakers who must express running and entering in two separate sentences in their speech. So when you're not speaking, gesture doesn't have to follow the separation of manner and path and you can easily actually put them together.

The study also found that these patterns kick in at a very young age. Children's co-speech gesture first begins to follow the patterns of their spoken language at 3 to 4 years of age.

Özçalışkan, in collaboration with Goldin-Meadow, has also studied sighted and blind adults. Those participants were also English and Turkish speakers. Using the same methods as in her latest study, researchers were surprised to find the same differences in co-speech gesture and similarities in silent gesture. This was even though the non-sighted participants were blind from birth, meaning they had never seen anyone gesture before. So far, all the studies carried out by the research team have produced similar results. In fact, many of the gestures used by participants resemble what are known as "home sign systems", which are informal sign language systems that are created spontaneously by deaf children, who have not been exposed to a conventional sign language by their hearing parents. According to Özçalışkan, what we see, in fact, is some of these sorts of basic structures that we see in, for instance, early sign languages. Therefore, this pattern suggests that there may be a universal gesture system that enables us to communicate with each other regardless of language, hearing ability or sightedness. This seems another example of the relationship between the physical level of motor activity and further symbolic linguistic organization of expression, in which the former must inevitably constrain the many possible local variations of the latter. The connection between Özçalışkan's finding and Mandler research is quite possible.

In my brief discussion about Wierzbicka's research, I chose not to discuss Chomsky's theory, as it is so well-known. In fact, his generative transformational grammar is still under scrutiny but not necessarily for its reference to an innate universal syntaxis. Lawson and McCauley's groundbreaking book *Rethinking Religion* (1990) successfully applied Chomsky's grammar to ritual structures and, therefore, supports another aspect of the universal character of complex cultural artifacts, such as rituals (although the date of this publication is not recent and many developments have occurred in linguistics since then). Another striking observation is Bickerton's observation that I already previously recalled:

When speakers of different languages have to communicate to carry out practical tasks but do not have the opportunity to learn one another's languages, they develop a makeshift jargon called a pidgin. Pidgins are choppy strings of words borrowed [At the time of slavery (Note by SC)] from the language of the coloniser of plantation owners, highly variable in order and with little in the way of grammar. Sometimes a pidgin can become a lingua franca and gradually increase in complexity over decades, as in the "Pidgin English" of the modern South Pacific.

But the linguist Derek Bickerton has presented evidence that in many cases a pidgin can be transmuted into a full complex language in one fell swoop: all it takes is for a group of children to be exposed to the pidgin at the age when they acquire their mother tongue. That happened, Bickerton has argued, when children were isolated from their parents and were attended collectively by a worker who spoke to them in the pidgin. Not content to reproduce the fragmentary word strings, the children injected grammatical complexity where none existed before, resulting in a brand new, richly expressive language. The language that results when children make a pigeon their native tongue is called a Creole.

(Pinker, 1994, p. 33)

This allows Haule (2011) to refer to language as a "model archetype".

Daniel Everett, among others has challenged Chmosly's theory, claiming that, differently from Chomsly's opinion, challenged Chomsly's theory, claiming that it is not all languages possess a recursive structure. Everett claims that, in fact, the Pirahã syntaxis he studied (an Amazonian language) is not recursive. It must be said that this would be *the only* language studied so far without a recursive structure, and Everett is so far *the only* scholar to have studied this language in depth, together with close idioms as the Banawá and Wari languages.

Among others (Nevins et al., 2009), some of the criticisms of Everett's theory rest on the fact that he is the only one to have found the only anomaly in a language that he only studied; therefore, more evidence should be gained by other researchers, especially because other scholars, also critical of Chomsky's theory (but for other reasons), believe that recursivity *is* a fundamental feature of the human species (Corballis, 2014)). This criticism is important, especially after the unfortunate case of the anthropological myth upon which the radical cultural relativism perspective by Edward Sapir (1929) and Benjamin Whorf was built. This had to do with the idea that minds and cultures were shaped by language and that languages had no universal grounds whatsoever – they were radically culture-specific. This theory was mostly based on Benjamin Whorf's study of the Hopi language, of which at the time he was the only "expert". One proof of the radical relativity of all languages was that the Hopi language – hence, the mind of the Hopis and their whole culture – had no sense of what time was.

I find it gratuitous to assume that a Hopi who knows only the Hopi language and the cultural ideas of his own society has the same notions, often supposed to be intuitions, of time and space that we have, and that are generally assumed to be universal. In particular, he has no general notion or intuition of TIME as a smooth flowing continuum in which everything in the universe proceeds at an equal rate, out of a future, through a present, into a past.

(Carroll, 1956, p. 57)

Since the Hopi language, Whorf said, has no conceptions of time built into it – or embodies different conceptions of time – the Hopi, therefore, perceive the world in a radically different way than we do. This was an extreme conceptualization of cultural relativism. The point is that subsequent studies proved Whorf to be wrong (as they did for Margaret Mead's myth of the uniqueness of the idyllic Samoan society [Gewertz, 1981]). Malotki (1983) amply documents the richness of Hopi conceptions of time and their essential similarities to ours.

This is the opening sentence, translated from the Hopi language, of Malotki's 1983 book:

Then indeed, the following day, quite early in the morning at the hour when people pray to the sun, around that time then he woke up the girl again.

This sentence should suffice to prove Whorf's interpretation of the Hopi language (Carroll, 1956) and to apply some caution about relativistic generalizations based on one-person studies of unknown languages, as in Everett's case.

A second important point of debate is that Everett's theory is based on the notion of a "general" form of intelligence, with no endogenous constraints. Such an intelligence would be constrained by the environment, by experience. I already have indicated some serious problems with this theory – which is disregarded by most cognitive scientists (like Karmiloff-Smith, to quote a scholar to whom I referred). Furthermore, even if Everett's works are interesting and useful for some of his interpretations, I must confess that his criticism of what an endogenous constraint is seems to me quite anecdotical and naïve.

Everett writes:

With social and cultural learning so obviously dominating a child's early years and enveloping its language-learning process, it is surprising to see a growing body of literature that proposes that learning and general intelligence are not sufficient to account for human cognitive and cultural accomplishments. I refer to this body of writing as the "strong instinct movement". A plethora of instincts has been proposed in recent years: Steve Pinker's "language instinct", Denis Dutton's "art instinct", Michael McCullough's "forgiveness instinct", Marc Hauser's "moral instinct", and Nicholas Wade's "faith instinct", among others. But instincts do not work like these authors seem to think. Instincts have zero learning curves. A baby sea turtle does not learn to walk towards the beach; it just does it. A human baby does not learn to suckle or grasp; it just suckles and grasps. A duckling does not learn to imprint on its mother; it just does. Instincts do not have different levels of attainment for healthy individuals. It is not the case that healthy sea turtle babies will be divided into those who crawl part way to the beach and those who crawl all the way. Normal human babies do not divide into those who grasp and those who occasionally grasp. Learning is not necessary with true instincts.

(Everett, 2012, p. 184)

I am afraid that Everett, through such an oversimplification, is just not getting the point of what a constraint is and how it may act during phylogenetic evolution and through ontogenetic learning. On the other hand, a sound criticism of Chomsky's idea that language arose in the human species out of a sudden biological mutation must be taken into serious consideration, and the discussion is still going on (Corballis, 1991). Yet this aspect does not involve our discussion. At any rate, I must underscore that the hypothesis of a strong innate component of the structure of natural languages is still highly debatable. Its most convincing critics come from the world of artificial intelligence, in which machine-based "pseudo" natural languages are developed. The general consensus among these scientists is that Chomsky's theory is wrong because it does not take into account the main issue of language: its use to produce meanings and not the property of its syntactic structure, especially recursive logical scaffolding. The issue of the semantic nature of language vs. its syntaxis is the same upon which Everett bases its theory.

What I would like to point out here is that Everett's point needs to be substantiated for what involves the Piranha language's syntax (we need more evidence). As for the innate structure of natural languages, there are two points that I would like to make.

First, "innate" does not mean that something is ready from birth but that what is innate is its formative *process*. This applies to any theory of innateness, for which an innate feature might be highly constrained (it will surely appear) or just probable (it has a high chance to appear).

I am connecting language, classification, sensory constraints (Berlin & Kay, 1969), ritual structure (Lawson & McCauley, 1990) and symbols (Turner, 1967, 1996; Bloch, 2008) to provide *some* elements that may help us to justify the possibility that from primitive constraints complex symbolic formations may arise. These formations will have a universal character if looked at from one angle and a specific, relative individual side if looked from another.

The second point is brought by Sperber.

In fact, we may ask ourselves: Given its inestimable role, why did language appear in the first place?

Sperber has an interesting answer. Language did not appear for a purpose: it found its own purpose when it appeared, and it proved to be so powerful and so evolutionarily useful that it became a hereditary competence. This is an interesting hypothesis. I think it is possible that some nonlinguistic competences have been used to produce the syntactic structure of natural languages by the evolutionary process of exaptation (Gould & Vrba, 2008) (vol. I, § 6 footnote 15) and that these competences were originally motor competences, a hypothesis (Hewes, 1973) that may converge with Özçalışkan's findings. This new unexpected function seems related to Kaufman's description of the *adjacent functions* (vol. I, § 2.2).

For Corballis:

> The idea that language evolved from manual gestures rather than primate calls dates back at least to the 18th century, and was revived in modern form by the anthropologist, Gordon W. Hewes, in 1973. The main sources of current evidence are: (1) Signed languages invented by deaf communities share with speech the essential characteristics of language, including such properties as reference, generativity, grammar, and prosody; (2) Great apes in captivity are much better able to learn intentional communication systems based on manual gestures than to acquire speech; (3) The manual gestures of chimpanzees in the wild are more flexible and context-independent than their vocalizations; (4) The mirror system in the primate brain provides a natural platform for the evolution of language; it represents manual gestures and some nonvocal oral movements, but not vocalizations. Vocal gestures were probably incorporated into the mirror system late in hominin evolution, perhaps only with the emergence of our own species, Homo sapiens.
>
> (Corballis, 2009, p. 2)

Discussing the foundational role of brain lateralization, Corballis pointed out that Broca's area for language, being in the left hemisphere, is contralateral to the most often dominant hand, the right hand (in 95–99% of the cases). To support his theory of the phylogenetic origin of language not from vocalizations (affects related) but from gestures[8] (i.e., procedural and "syntactic", like pointing), Corballis underscores the fact that the left hemisphere, central for language, is commonly considered the executive center of intention and will and, therefore, of purposeful acts (Corballis, 2009).

Roger Sperry, reviewing his studies on split-brain patients, argued:

> The language-dominant hemisphere is [. . .] the more aggressive, executive, leading hemisphere in the control of the motor system. [. . .] The mute, minor hemisphere, by contrast, seems to be carried along much as a passive, silent passenger who leaves the driving of behavior mainly to the left hemisphere.
>
> (In: Corballis, 1991, p. 211)

Therefore, the phylogenetic birth of language from gestures (left hemisphere) associated with vocalizations (right hemisphere) points to the association of the essential pragmatic motor activity of utterances articulation (hence, a procedural patterning) with the affective/emotional expression of the vocalizations (like other animals have). Once again, the affective element triggers the motor system, which gives a syntactic shape to it, in this case, by articulated utterances. As we would once again expect from the co-existence of the three fundamental building blocks for the construction of the psyche to which I referred in vol. 1 – affects, motor apparatus and perception – the syntactic organization provided by the motor schema (the motor apparatus) and the emotional, numinous meaning carried by the utterances' music (the affects) were probably originally referred to the impact of the perceptual world on the primitive psyche.

Here, I follow J.L. Borges' argument:

> words began not by being abstract, but rather by being concrete, and concrete, I suppose, would be the same as poetic. [. . .] it seems obvious to me that words began, in a sense, as magic. Perhaps, there was a moment when the word "light" seemed to be flashing, and when the world "night" was a dark word.
>
> (Borges, 1967–1968)

Here, Borges is describing the origin of words as responses associated to the numinous, emotional nature of sensory experience. I must underscore that this essential numinous quality infused into perceptions instantaneously transforms the latter into *sensations* and metaphors and makes of us humans the peculiar animals that we are – animals whose life is real and true only when it is lived as a shared, unrelenting, essential imagination.

The motor features of human language, which organize in a syntactic order what in other animals are purely emotional expressions coming from their sensory experiences, were exapted from motor areas that were not used anymore – perhaps at the moment in which hand lateralization differentiated the function of the dominant right hand, controlled by the left hemisphere (for manipulation and then technology), from the nondominant hand, controlled by the right hemisphere (for holding objects or perhaps branches). Subsequently, in evolution:

> Vocal language may have freed the hands for the development of tool-making and other manufacturing techniques, and facilitated pedagogy through the simultaneous deployment of demonstration and verbal description. Indeed, the switch to vocal mode may account for the extraordinary rise of technology on a scale unique to our species.
>
> (Corballis, 2009, p. 5)

The executive, procedural structure of motor patterns governed by the Broca's area could have been used as a structure for the syntaxis of natural languages, which, like motricity, according to Chomsky, has a procedural, patterned nature.

The relevant criticisms coming from the artificial intelligence community may be based on the fact, first of all, recognized by the same artificial intelligence scientists that at the moment, artificial intelligence is still *disembodied*, i.e., unrelated from the embeddedness into the physical and organic world (not only are there no bodies but today's robots are also built of inorganic matter). This disembodiment of artificial intelligence, and hence, languages, is extremely efficient for correlations but very poor for causality. On the contrary, as I have been arguing, human natural languages seem to be a direct product of the bodily motor apparatus, i.e., seem to be fully embedded in the physical world. In this regard, it might be relevant to remember that in an ontogenetic perspective, meanings (i.e., eventually, the semantic aspect of language) derive from what Mandler calls perceptual analysis (i.e., the active analysis of *moving objects*). Daniel Stern's elegant description of the process through which a core, fundamentally somatic self produces linguistic competences shows that it is precisely the active analysis of physical procedural interactions in an emotional field that provides the ingredients for the future emergence of declarative thoughts and language (Stern, 1985).

Ontogenetically, the deep syntactic structure (i.e., procedural) of the natural language of a child is the mirror of the schematic products of his perceptual analysis (Rizzolatti & Arbib, 1998).

In primates, though, the mirror system appears to be unresponsive to vocalization – indeed, primate vocalization appears to be primarily under limbic rather than cortical control. In the monkey, at least, neurons in area do respond to orofacial movements, 29 and mirror neurons even respond to the sounds of those manual actions, such as tearing paper or cracking nuts, which have distinctive sounds, but they do not respond to conspecific vocalizations. Intentional vocalization appears to have been incorporated into the mirror system at some point in hominin evolution, eventually replacing manual movements as the primary medium for language.

The intentional control of action is not of itself sufficient for language. In primates, the mirror system responds only to transitive action, such as the grasping of objects. In humans, in contrast, the mirror system, at least as understood through brain imaging studies, appears to respond to both transitive and intransitive acts, perhaps paving the way to the understanding of acts that are symbolic rather than object-related. Human language requires the further development of complex, recursive action sequences, whether signed or spoken, and it seems likely that these have evolved through extensions of the mirror system. One possibility is that language evolved at least partly as a consequence of the emergence in humans of a capacity for mental time travel, whereby remembered past episodes provide a basis for the flexible planning of future actions.

(Rizzolatti & Arbib, 1998, p. 4)

During his ontogenetic maturation, the infant will distinguish between animated and non-animated objects through his perceptual analysis, among other competencies. Then the perceptual analysis of *intentional gestures*, associated with the acquired competence (at about 7 months) to distinguish natural sounds from human language-related sounds, will eventually produce semantic concepts, while these observed motor patterns are mirrored by mirror neurons into the infant's own inner motor structure. Therefore, on one side, we have object-perception patterns (and semantics); on the other, we have patterns of motor organization of the infant's own body's motor patterns activated by mirroring the object's movements.

The existence of mirror neurons supports the plausibility of this hypothesis that would confirm Chomsky's theory of the innate universal nature of the deep structure of natural languages, provided that the subject lives in a an embodied, emotionally meaningful co-evolutionary environment in which she can accumulate empirical experiences. Hence, the fact that natural languages – and not artificial intelligences – are embodied products might have the consequence of confirming Chomsky's hypothesis of their constrained, procedural/syntactical, deep level because in the physical world, causal chains are immediately evident, and a consequence cannot precede its cause. On the contrary, as I said, artificial intelligence is extremely good in computing statistical correlations, while it does a very bad job for causality. Once (and if) we agree that, in the physical world, the immediate organization of the sensory-motor Ego is rooted in causality and linear time, it seems a logical consequence that, in the deep structure of language (which derives from mirroring such a world), a term cannot be moved in another place within a sentence without hindering its deep structure. The syntactic order would be "deeply" constrained, as it is the causal order of the ancestral physical (embodied) world, whose experience is mirrored through natural languages.

This theory, for which language emerges from emotional gestures, has another important implication: it seems that, far from not having a recursive structure as Everett maintains or an innate component, language shares the capacity for recursion with animal behaviors in general. Not only is recursivity present in language but it also seems to be present *everywhere*, embedded in the behaviors of the animal kingdom (Corballis, 2014). This observation on recursivity, together with the relationship of language with gestures, is closely connected to the discussion of the supposedly radical differences between humans and other animals – a difference that I do not deny, but which, with the passing of time from Darwin on, it seems to become always more limited. One of the examples is precisely that of language. As Haule recalls (2011), researchers such as Cheney and Seyfarth report that the velvet monkeys from East Africa that they studied indeed have a quite developed system of signs devoted to organize and hold their social structure (2007). Yet this might not be equated to human language if with language we mean symbolic communication – i.e., the emission of signs representing an absent object.

As Griffin reports (1917), Pollio (1974) sets out three criteria required to qualify an event as a symbol: it must be 1) representative of some other event, 2) "freely created" and 3) transmitted by culture. What is quite interesting is that not only at the levels of primates – the animals apparently closest to humans – but also at the evolutionary level of bees does the difference between human language and animal language become blurred. In fact, it is recognized that the dances of domestic bees are representational, although it is also argued that they are too rigid and invariable to satisfy the second criterion and that they are genetically programmed rather than culturally transmitted. Yet under the same conditions, the bees' waggle dances vary somewhat, and their performance does not necessarily occur every time a bee returns to the hive from a food source (von Frisch, 1967). There is no direct evidence in favor of cultural transmission of bee dances, but the development of individual worker bees depends to such an extent on the care provided by other members of the colony that it is difficult to exclude the presence of cultural influences. The specific dance pattern used for a given food source is, of course, learned by the individual worker during foraging flights, and thus, genetic instructions imply the ability to learn a coded form of communicative behavior. Therefore, similar reasoning to Chomsky's regarding the probable genetic basis for human linguistic ability could be made regarding domestic bees (Griffin, 1976, § 3). These considerations may contribute to the appreciation of archetypical processes that inform not only human life but also, emerging from the mathematical and physical realms, extend far deep into biological life.

Taking into consideration the 16 distinctive features needed to classify a system of communication as a language like the human language developed by Thorpe (1974), eight of them are shared between humans and other animals, while the other eight are unevenly distributed. As A.N. Whitehead wrote (1938), this makes the leap from animals to humans a matter of quantity and not of quality. Therefore, in this perspective, language emerged almost as a serendipity via exaptation because of the evolutionary process of bipedality (Corballis, 1991; Leroi-Gouran, 2018) and brain lateralization. This means that once this possibility appeared, nature (the organism) would have had to decided how to use it.

If we put affects at the center, as I have tried to do so far, the answer to the question "Why did language appear?" cannot be "To communicate". In fact, I think that we must distinguish speech, and speech acts (Austin, 1962) as the manifestation of what de Saussure called *Langage* (i.e., the empirical, social use of language), and the *Langue* – the formal system of signs from which a *Parole* (a word) acquires its meaning. Seen from this perspective, *"Langage" stayed and became hereditary because it made it possible to organize primary affects into shareable secondary emotions.* Hence, the answer to the question on the birth of language would be this: "Because language was a very good tool to shape feelings into shareable representations within a social group".

If we remember our initial discussion on the role and the connection between affects and the sensory-motor apparatus, together with their metaphorical, creative and metonymic components, we can now connect the original function of the expression of emotions by our ancestors – the unconscious (a-noetic) hominids – and their relationship with the formation of this syntactical (metonymic) structure that we call language.

As Sperber hypothesizes, human language (like life) might be born out of chance(s). Its functional usefulness would have harnessed this chancy occurrence top-down (for this top-down teleological influence, see vol. 2, § 7). Therefore, what now becomes relevant is the nature of such a function, which would be the real protagonist of this development.

I think that in an evolutionary perspective, one of the functions of language was to integrate affects and the activity of the synthetic, "creative" right hemisphere with the analytical nature of the left hemisphere, where the centers of Broca and Wernicke are located. As Paul Kugler argues (1982), following the works of Theodore

Thass-Thienemann (1957, 1963, 1967), the original level of affects, related to the singing voice (the phylogenetic animal verses of the hominids), represents the phonetic aspect of language and its *signifiers* (de Saussure's *Parole*), while the syntactic level refers to the level of meaning, provided we understand that, while if, at the level of sounds, "meaning" is the direct expression of an emotional value[9] (what I think Jung would eventually relate to the feeling function), "meaning" at the *syntactic* level refers not to the sound per se (the word, the signifier) but to its nature of a center of relationships internal to language – de Saussure's *Langue* (what Jung might have ultimately referred to as the thinking function). A word is defined by its position within the *Langue*'s network of relationships.

As Kugler writes, through his association experiments, Jung realized that, when attention is disturbed, word associations progressively lose their predicative nature; they slide towards their acoustic phylogenetic and ontogenetic origins, while the metonymic part of language dissolves into only metaphorical expressions of single numinous signifiers connected by their "musical" acoustic nature. On one end, metaphorical language is at the core of dreams, poetry and creativity, therefore, of psychotherapy, and expresses qualitative meanings that are felt as all-comprehensive; on the other end, this kind of language is marked by the apophanic expressions (Conrad, 1958) of schizophrenic language – a language made of pure affective states, each which fill the whole mind as the irruption of an infinite and absolute truth.

An example of this is the accurate description of auditory hallucinations made by A., a schizophrenic:

> The voice. For sure, it bothered me; I wanted it to go away; I didn't understand how it came. Sometimes I would hear it while chewing, so, I would try to figure out if it was coming from the food. It was not a ubiquitous voice, nor did it make complete speeches, *some "words", which had to do with some noise of the moment relatively to the sound, for example, that of chewing*: in fact, if I stopped chewing, I no longer heard it.

I am indebted to Kugler for his highlighting the fact that the associations by sounds may not be purely meaningless but that they actually may revolve and describe archetypal complexes of qualitative, numinous meanings. Therefore, the formal regression of word association within the association experiment would allow the emergence of the precocial, evolutionary, archetypal deep structure of our original emotional language.

As Kugler writes, it may be not a chancy occurrence that *car*nation, *car*nage and rein*car*nation share a similar acoustic property. Similarly, in Freud's *Rat* man clinical case, whose associations revolved around the word 'Ra*t*ten' (mouse), the emerging images plagued him, together with the preoccupations for the payments (*Rat*en) he had to make due to his father's gambling debts (Spiel-*Ratt*e). As Kugler reminds us in his book, he never recovered from his sister *Rit*a's death nor could he resolve his feelings about marrying (hei*rat*en) at the townhall (*Rat*house) or not (Kugler, 1982, § 4).

Previously, I argued that the process of finding similarities and analogies is not always based on a precise, unique logic. In this case, we are confronted with something similar to something like an acoustic form of Wittgenstein's "family resemblances". It was Jung's genius to imagine that the apparently meaningless words associated symptomatically by their sound may actually reveal a deep layer of archetypal emotional meanings. If we look at the relative stability of, for instance, the Indo-European languages through the millennia, not just in regard to etymologies but also to sound assonances, we may imagine that this deep emotional layer of language is a direct manifestation of Jung's collective unconscious, yet it is the layer that is, *at the same time*, intrinsically both biological and cultural.

At this level of the helix that I quoted from Bion as an exergue to this book, the dispositional nature of the psyche reveals itself into language. In fact, as Wilden argues in his comment on Lacan (1968), the signifiers as intended by de Saussure – i.e., arbitrary (and differential) phonetic sounds within the complex connecting structure of the *Langue* – can be seen in a wholly different way. Referring to what is called the "triangle of reference" (Figure 9.1), in his interpretation of de Saussure, Wilden argues that the arbitrary nature of the signifier that de Saussure discusses derives from its reference *not to the language but to the real objects to which they refer*. On the other hand, if we relate the signifier to its phonetic nature, *internal to the language*, then, as Thass-Thienemann and Kugler argue, the signifier reveals its intrinsic, necessary, non-arbitrary belonging to a common, dispositional, archetypal affective meaning. This is clearly an interpretation of the *internal coherence of language based on affects* – an introverted perspective on language as an endogenous organizer of affects. It is from this endogenous area that the deep, underlying meaning emerges from the phonetic complex of associations of words, like, as I have already said, *rat-rat*ten-*rat*house-*rat*en, etc.[10] At this level – an evolutionary and ontogenetic precocial level (since it refers to a prelinguistic stage of phylogenetic evolution and ontogenetic development, when the mother's idiom is a pure erotic musical song waiting for its future logos) – language is the expression and the communication of endogenous, dispositional feeling-states, quite like many other

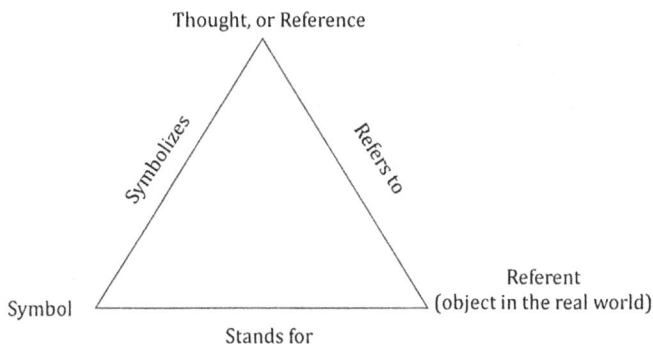

Figure 9.1 The triangle of reference.

animals. It will be the association with the syntactic organization exapted from the sensory-motor patterns that will promote the altricial development, up to a stage in which the signifiers are totally arbitrary – the intellectual language of the False Self.

My references to the phylogenetic birth of language from gestures associated with vocalizations – in which the affective element triggers the motor system, the embodied origin of syntactic recursivity, Özçalışkan's findings and the mirror neurons – all are aspects that point to Merleau-Ponty's theory of language that, he suggests, arises from and is intertwined with our perceptual experiences, underscoring the inseparable connection between language, embodiment, perception and intersubjectivity (Merleau-Ponty, 1965, 1973).

When we discussed the theme of the stabilization of representations, I introduced Sperber's notion of Cultural Causal Cognitive Chains, which are stabilized sets of representations shared by a social group. *Language is the most important and stable domain in which common representations that are psychologically susceptible are stored.* In this case, the specific area of study is that of etymologies, i.e., the fact of the incredibly resilient passage – throughout millennia – of stable associations of certain words and their meanings. This is the same temporal perspective that we deal with when I discussed Warburg's *nachleben*, in vol. 1.

I will soon summarize one example from the proto-Indo-European origin of a set of words that are still used today within the Indo-European linguistic basin (i.e., by a good portion of the world's speakers), yet I must once again point out that, also for languages, the source is always the same: the affects, which, in this case, are expressed by those *sounds* that will compose a signifier. It is in this perspective that the study of etymologies may be seen as something like an association experiment on a historical, collective scale.

If we refer to Sperber's theory of susceptibility – which is generally accepted in the field of cognitive anthropology – language would be the most surprising testimony of the stability of certain psychological representations through time in the person's mind and at the social level. Therefore, the fact that a natural language is transmitted *culturally* from the caregivers to children should not mislead us since its intrinsic etymological stability points to the fact that the representations that gave origin to those words are still highly susceptible to be thought, used and passed to the next generation and, therefore, contain a constraining force. The telling aspect of this phenomenon is that through this passage, connected through susceptibility to the psycho-biological foundation of human culture, we witness, at the same time, a universal feature, from which etymologies remain stable, and, at the same time, great cultural variations since the modern institutions, technology, habits, etc., of an Indo-European speaker is very different from that of his ancestors.

All these observations may be referred to Jung's initial studies of word associations. The following example will show that words and their associations into a *Langage* do not exist just as isolated expressions for isolated representations but also refer to those nuclear psycho-social situations, or constellations, which Jung called "archetypes". We should remember that isolated words, devoid of their metonymic organization within the *Langue*, are felt by the speaker as numinous absolutes and form the essence of the prophetic revelation or of the revelation of a schizophrenic. Thus, words *metaphorically refer to representations and, at the same time, metonymically connect within the language other representations to metaphorically represent complex nuclear narrative themes*. One easy example is the following: What may be associated with, for instance, the concept and word "King"? The semantic cloud that may constellate around this word is organized and organizes the representation of "King" in a coherent way. The cloud would be very different if the word would have been, for instance, "Hammer".[11] Furthermore, we must keep in mind that no semantic word has ever been uttered in the void. From its evolutionary origin, language vocally expressed emotions (and, obviously, bodily changes) through its sounds, within a specific situation or, we might say, within a specific existential script. In fact, what is necessary to realize is that *the metonymic narrative organization – the plot – always precedes the word (the logos)*, as the relational field precedes the emotion that will trigger what will eventually become a word. Hence, a word will always be a contextualized product of a specific interactive semantic cloud, which, on its turn, will recursively constellate it.

This semantic cloud refers to the probable components of a "theme" – a specific situation, a narrative, an institution, etc. – and at its core (considering its staggering historical etymological stability in the minds of billions of Indo-European speakers), it resembles a miteme with an archetypal nature.

In his groundbreaking book *How to Kill a Dragon: Aspects of Indo-European Poetics* (1995), devoted to the comparative study of poetical features, Calvert Watkins seems to point in the same direction as mine. Watkins refers to what he thinks are the central features of ancient poetry, the "formulas". They are the following:

> set phrases which are the vehicles of "themes", which in turn make up the culture of the given society.
>
> (Watkins, 1995, p. 9)

In fact, Watkins' goal is this:

> to emphasize the longevity and specificity of verbal tradition and the persistence of specific verbal traditions, whether in the structures of the lexicon, or syntax, or of style.
>
> (Watkins, 1995, p. 10)

In his work, Watkins focuses on the formulas related to "dragon slaying" in the various Indo-European languages and ultimately proves, by way of reconstruction, that the formula was present in the poetic repertory of the Proto-Indo-European language, and its development may be followed through most of the branches of the language family.

Watkins identifies the root of the formula of the "dragon slaying" instance as being "HERO SLAYS SERPENT". In its core, he identifies the Proto-Indo-European root *gwhen* – from which he reconstructs the historical transformation of this root in the Indo-European languages throughout the millennia. The stability of this linguistic root (which historically changes because of its varying ways of pronunciation throughout oral transmission) may be equated with the stability of the formula, which, on its part, may refer to a miteme to which the mind was, has been and still is particularly susceptible – in other words, with an archetypal image.

For Watkins, the formula "HERO KILLS SERPENT" is a quasi-universal. Yet the *image* that this formula represents may also be surely generalized to non-Indo-European cultures.

Besides its immemorial stability (at least 6000 BC) the particularly interesting feature of this proto-Indo-European poetic formula is that it may be interpreted as a psychological statement. In fact, in all the stories that refer to this formula, the hero must kill a serpent which seems to constantly refer to something like a chaotic state of "nature". Hence, slaying, or sacrificing, the serpent might refer to the psychological process of mental organization – in a way to the process through which the brainmind and its world are paired and form a coherent whole. If we refer to the unconscious as formed by an indefinite plurality of complexes, the emerging feeling of such plurality by an individual mind may cause an immediate sense of chaos, unless subjectivity immediately emerges to *perceive this in(de)finite plurality in a unitary perspective*.

One specific variation of the formula "HERO KILLS SERPENT", in which the hero is Hercules that has to kill the nine-headed Hydra, or Apollo with Python, or Perseus, who has to kill the Gorgon, may confirm this essential feature. In fact, both chaotic monsters convey the image of a chaotic, multiheaded mind, or of an equally plural, chaotic mental process under the forms of serpents coming from a head.

Even more striking is what Pindar recounts (Pythian Ode, XII): that the reflection of such a chaotic state of mind onto Athena's aegis made it possible to transform the chaotic plurality into a song (once again, music is the organizing, mentalizing, regulating function of affects), which Athena herself composed out of the snakes' hissings. The same image appears in the 7th-century Saxon poem Bēowulf, in which the hero has to kill a dragon-nature, or a few millennia earlier, in the myth recounted in the Rigveda, in which the God Indra (the Lord, an equivalent to other Indo-European gods, such as Zeus, Jupiter, Apollon, Odin, Perun, Perkūnas, Zalmoxis, Taranis or Thor), associated with lightning, weather, thunder, storms, rains, river flows and war, has to kill the serpent-dragon Vṛtra.

All these heroes-gods essentially have to create a cosmology if their deeds are seen from an extroverted perspective (that of perceptions), or a psychology, if we look at them through an introverted one (that of sensations). It should be clear that these two perspectives – the cosmological, object-related, extroverted one and the psychological, subject-related one – *are two complementary version of the same thing*.

Seen under this light, the miteme "HERO KILLS SERPENT" represents the phylogenetic origin of subjectivity, in which the hero is not exactly Jung's Ego yet. In fact, at this point, this emergent subjectivity does not need to be meta-noetic (self-representational); it may well still be "just" noetic. This phylogenetic hero seems to be the emergence of a new phylogenetic form of Self imbued with unique synthesizing/categorizing capabilities, and perhaps, with language. No wonder that for Greek philosophy, the main issue was the dialectic between unity and plurality.

Before such an occurrence, Lucretius, who, in his *De rerum naturae*, was dealing exactly with these issues regarding the "nature of things", could never have written these words:

Suave, mari magno turbantibus aequora ventis,
e terra magnum alterius spectare laborem;
non quia vexari quemquamst iucunda voluptas,
sed quibus ipse malis careas quia cernere suave est.

[it is] pleasant [to watch] in a great sea when the winds are buffeting the waves on the great sea, to watch from the land the great struggle of another.
(Lucretius, 2013, I-61, my trans.)

This interpretation for which the miteme of the killing of the serpent represents the phylogenetic origin of subjectivity may be confirmed by another contribution from comparative linguistics. In fact, the way the word "Father" is regularly coupled with "Sky" in the proto-Indo-European and Indo-European languages seems to point to the role of the "Father" as a cosmic (in its being the "sky") or earthly point of reference, i.e., an organizer of a totality. For instance, in the cosmological perspective, the Latin *Jupiter* (Sky-Father) would be, like Zeus, the overarching organizer, while for the earthly matters, the *Pater* (*familias*) would be the point of reference of his "clan".

This equation seems to hold for all the ancient Indo-European populations, which seemed to consider the individual subject – always male, *alas!* – as the quintessence of the organizing entity. What this means is that the idea of the birth of subjectivity, associated with the "HERO KILLS SERPENT", is compatible with the concordant traces of the meaning the coupling of the words "Father-Sky".

I am quite convinced that the comparative perspective that includes the study of language and its etymological stability may help us to understand that, as also Sahlins argues in his theory of the "structure of conjuncture", universal and local, structural and contingent are two sides of the same coin. One of these two sides is rooted in the body – *is* the body, *whatever the body may be.*[12] The lack of acknowledgment of the embodied nature of language by the artificial intelligence community is part and parcel of the widespread blindness towards the role of affects in cognitive sciences – cognitive anthropology included. This produces very interesting and heuristic, but insufficient and reductive, theories.

In closing this book, I wish to emphasize, once again, the primacy of affects to frame and understand the function and role of cognition within phylogenesis and ontogenesis. This is an indispensable perspective avoid confusing secondary epistemic knowledge (which has a purely intellectual nature) with primary gnostic knowledge (which regards the whole person – what Daniel Stern called the "clinical" child). Therefore, when a baby learns a language, she is not only learning to communicate (a social activity) nor learning to categorize (an epistemic activity) but she is also transforming her own essence into a wholly cultural being made not only of individual original and unique traits but also by a shared emotional and representational ethical world.

Essentially, this transformation expresses itself by one's ability to find/create new metaphors and stories. This makes the analytical process not a scientific quest for explanations but an essentially artistic venture that requires an artistic mind – a venture in which two (or more) persons are not precisely looking for one's own story but, more precisely, for a story of one's own. Therefore, after these pages in which I mostly referred to epistemic knowledge and science, I think it is necessary to emphasize the fundamentally creative nature of the analytical process, during which the patient (but not just him) not only will "understand" but also, above all, will *become* the story that he himself will have to recognize as his own. As individuation proceeds, this story will weave deeper into the past and the future, extending farther to include all his "objects" encompassed in such a receding and proceeding horizon.

This is what an analyst deals with: not necessarily interpretations and explanations, which may occur *between* sessions, but with the emotional *experience* that takes place within the co-evolutionary space we call transference – the alpha and omega of human experience.

Notes

1 The way the sensory apparatus works, for example, the eye, and therefore, the very nature of the Ego as a transformational apparatus, matches the way a photon behaves when it has to go through two parallel slits, as in the experiments by Davisson and Germer first and Thomson afterwards. Perception is nothing like a mere transduction of a signal. What exactly is beyond our perception is only partially graspable by technological apparatuses that "extend" the Ego's limitations. Yet, once again, this is a transformation too. The possibility to imagine, to mathematize (like science does) and to build such apparatuses (like technology does) springs from human creativity – one of the five Jungian "instincts". What our Ego cannot perceive directly, the Self may imagine in imaginal or mathematical forms.

2 Therefore, on the fact that, in the cognitive domain, every species is endowed with different inferential systems.

3 Because it would include the brain, the autonomic system, the immune and endocrine systems, the axes of the brain-heart, brain-lungs and brain-guts, probably all the way down to cellular functions.

4 I have in mind Max Weber and Walter Benjamin's *loss of enchantment*, which began with the advent of modernity. But I also have in mind Hannah Arendt's *banality of evil*, in which within a bureaucratic universe, one cannot be even evil. A beautiful text on this existential tragedy is Sartre's *The Devil and the Good God*.

5 Habitus is composed of "systems of durable, transposable dispositions, structured structures predisposed to function as structuring structures, that is, as principles which generate and organize practices and representations that can be objectively adapted to their outcomes without presupposing a conscious aiming at ends or an express mastery of the operations necessary in order to attain them" (Bourdieu, 1977, p. 72).

Although this is a sociological construct, primarily used to describe implicit social relationship based on power, in my opinion, its origin may be found within the primary interactive field between the mother, as a fully socialized person, and the infant/child, as a human being in her way to be socialized. Insofar as the process of socialization and interiorization of cultural structures, like language, behaviors or values, is a "natural" process, Jung would probably say that, through it, the archetype of the Persona is activated in relation to the process of the Ego's emergence from the Self.

6   A striking proof of this may be Émile Benveniste's study on the Indo-European social and cultural institutions analyzed, interpreted and understood through his analysis of words' etymologies (Benveniste, 1969).

7   The psychological saliency of basic color terms has been explored cross-culturally in a variety of ways (Bolton, 1978; Heider, 1972), attempts have been made to explain why humans perceive colors uniformly (e.g., Ratliff, 1976; Boynton & Olson, 1987), studies of the classification of botanical and zoological life forms have revealed evolutionary sequences similar to those that Berlin and Kay found in the classification of basic colors (Brown, 1977, 1979; Witkowski & Brown, 1977), and the discovery of cross-culturally stable focal points for color (and other) categories gave rise to new conceptions of how humans categorize and reason (Rosch, 1975, 1983).

8   This does not mean that vocalizations, together with the phylogenetic development of the larynx, of its function and its position are not important.

9   This is connected to what I wrote in vol. 1 – that the affective core of the complex is organized by acoustics, while its gravitating representations are organized by vision.

10 This does *not* imply that the unconscious is structured like a language, as Lacan maintained. It means that in its deepest layer, it is structured by sounds as primary carriers of affects and emotions (Carta, 2009). They are then represented by images, from whose abstractions language emerges.

11 There is a statistical probability to that "Royalty", "Aristocracy", "Leadership", "Power", "Authority", "Crown", "Throne", "Dynasty" and "Scepter" will be closely related to the concept of "King", whereas concepts like "Construction", "Handle", "Head", "Nail", "Forge", "Mallet", "Pounding" and "Blacksmith" may be closely related to the concept of "Hammer".

12 Since there is no discourse on any body without a mind that imagines it. Once again, we are facing a recursive helix.

References

Austin, J.L. (1962). *How to Do Things with Words*. The William James lectures delivered at Harvard University in 1955 (eds J.O. Urmson, Marina Sbisà). Oxford: Clarendon Press.

Barkow, J., Cosmides, L., Tooby, J. (eds) (1992). *The Adapted Mind: Evolutionary Psychology and the Generation of Culture*. Oxford, New York, Toronto: Oxford University Press.

Bateson, G. (2002). *Mind and Nature: A Necessary Unity*. New York: Hampton Press.

Benveniste, E. (1969). *Vocabulaire des Institutions Indo-Europeennes*, 2 vols. Paris: Les Editions De Minuit.

Berlin, B., Kay, P. (1969). *Basic Color Terms: Their Universality and Evolution*. Berkeley, Los Angeles: University of California Press.

Bloch, M. (2008). *Prey into Hunter: The Politics of Religious Experience*. Cambridge: Cambridge University Press.

Bloom, L. (1973). *One Word at a Time: The Use of Single Word Utterances Before Syntax*. Mouton: The Hague.

Boas, F. (1966). *Introduction to Handbook of American Indian Languages*. Lincoln: University of Nebraska Press.

Boguslawski, A. (1970). On Semantic Primitives and Meaningfulness. In: Greimas, A.J. (ed) *Sign, Language, Culture*. The Hague: Mouton, pp. 143–152.

Bollas, C. (2018). *The Shadow of the Object. Psychoanalysis of the Unthought Known.* London: Routledge.

Bolton, R. (1978). Black, white, and red all over: The riddle of color term salience. *Ethnology,* 17, 287–311.

Borges, J.L. (1967–1968). *The Norton Lectures. The Craft of Verse.* www.youtube.com/watch?v=YSLV7t9DvN8&t=5568s.

Bourdieu, P. (1977). *Outline of a Theory of Practice.* Cambridge: Cambridge University Press.

Bourdieu, P. (2019). *Habitus and Field: General Sociology, vol. 2 (1982–1983).* Cambridge, Oxford, UK and Boston, New York, USA: Polity Press.

Boynton, R.M., Olson, C.X. (1987). Locating basic colors in OSA space. *Color Research and Application,* 12, 94–105.

Brown, C.H. (1977). Lexical Universals and the Human Language Faculty. In: Saville-Troike, M. (ed) *Linguistics and Anthropology.* Washington, DC: Georgetown University Press, pp. 75–91.

Brown, C.H. (1979). Folk Zoological Life-Forms: Their Universality and Growth. *American Anthropologist* 81:791–817.

Brown, D.E. (1991). *Human Universals.* Kindle.

Carroll, J. (ed) (1956). *Language, Thought, and Reality: Selected Writings of Benjamin Lee Whorf.* Boston, MA: Technology Press of MIT.

Carta, S. (2009). Music in dreams and the emergence of the self. *Journal of Analytical Psychology,* 54, 1.

Corballis, M.C. (1991). The *Lopsided Ape: Evolution of the Generative Mind.* Oxford: Oxford University Press.

Corballis, M.C. (2009). *The Gestural Origins of Language. Homo Sapiens.* John Wiley & Sons, Ltd. (Wires Cogn Sci. 2010. 1, 2–7).

Corballis, M.C. (2014). *The Recursive Mind: The Origins of Human Language, Thought, and Civilization.* Princeton: Princeton University Press.

Couturat, J. (ed.) (1903). *Opuscules et Fragments Inédits de Leibniz.* Paris: PUF.

Conrad, K. (1958). *Die Beginnende Schizophrenie.* Thieme: Stuttgart.

Descartes, R. (1931). The Search after Truth by the Light of Natura. In: *The Philosophical Works of Descartes* (Vol. I). Cambridge: Cambridge University Press.

Descola, P. (2021). *Oltre Natura e Cultura.* Milano: Cortina.

Everett, D. (2012). *Language: The Cultural Tool* (English ed.). Kindle.

Geertz, C. (1984). From the Native Point of View: On the Nature on Anthropological Understanding. In: Shweden, R., Levine, R. (eds) *Culture Theory: Essays on Mind, Self and Emotion.* Cambridge: Cambridge University Press.

Gewertz, D. (1981). A historical reconsideration of female dominance among the chambri of papua New Guinea. *American Ethnologist,* 8, 94–106.

Gould, S.J., Vrba, E. (2008). *Exaptation, il Bricolage dell'evoluzione.* Torino: Boringhieri.

Griffin, D.R. (1976). *The Question of Animal Awareness. Evolutionary Continuity of Mental Experience.* New York, NY: Rockfeller University Press.

Haule, J.R. (2011). *Jung in the 21st Century.* London, New York: Routledge.

Heider, E. R. (1972). Universals in Color Naming and Memory. *Journal of Experimental Psychology.* 93:10–20.

Hewes, G.W. (1973). Primate communication and the gestural origins of language. *Current Anthropology,* 14, 5–24.

Humboldt, C.W. von (1903–1936). *Wilehelms von Humboldts Werke,* 17 vols. Berlin: B. Behr.

Jung, C.G. (1919). The Instinct and the Unconscious. In: *The Collected Works of C.G. Jung,* vol. 8. London: Routledge.

Jung, C.G. (1953). *Letters.* Selected and Edited by Gerhard Adler in collaboration with Aniela Jaffé, 2 vols. Princeton: Princeton University Press.

Jung, C.G. (1954/1966). General Problems of Psychotherapy. In: *The Collected Works of C.G. Jung,* vol. 16. London: Routledge.

Jung, C.G. (1959). Archetypes of the Collective Unconscious. In: *The Collected Works of C.G. Jung,* vol. 9ii. London, New York, NY: Routledge

Kauffmann, S.A. (2021). *Ontogenesis Beyond* Complexity. London: Routledge.

Konrad, K. (1958). *Die Beginnende Schizophrenie.* Thieme: Stuttgart.

Kugler, P. (1982). *The Alchemie of Discourse. An Archetypal Approach to Language.* New York: Associated Press, Inc.

Lacan, J. (1968). *The Language of the Self. The Function of Language in Psychoanalysis* (trans A. Wilden). Baltimore: John Hopkins University Press.

Lawson, E.T., Mccauley, R.N. (1990). *Rethinking Religion: Connecting Cognition and Culture.* Cambridge: Cambridge University Press.

Lucretius, T.C. (2013). *De Rerum Natura.* Torino: UTET.

Leroi-Gouran, A. (2018). *Gestures and Speech.* Cambridge, MA: The MIT Press.

Malotki, E. (1983). *Hopi Time: A Linguistic Analysis of the Temporal Concepts in the Hopi Language.* Berlin: Mouton.

Merleau-Ponty, M. (1965). *The Structure of Behavior* (trans Alden Fisher). London: Methuen.

Merleau-Ponty, M. (1973). *Consciousness and the Acquisition of Language* (trans Hugh J. Silverman). Evanston: Northwestern University Press.

Nevins, A., Pesetsky, D., Rodrigues, C. (2009). Evidence and argumentation: A reply to Everett. *Language,* 85(3).

Nida, E.A. (1959). Principles of Translation as Exemplified by Bible Translating. In: Brower R.A. (ed) *On Translation.* Cambridge: Harvard University Press, pp. 11–31.

Özçalışkan, Ş., Gentner, D., Goldin-Meadow, S. (2014). Do iconic gestures pave the way for children's early verbs? *Applied Psycholinguistics,* 35, 1143–1162.

Özçalışkan, Ş., Goldin-Meadow, S. (2005). Gesture is at the cutting edge of early language development. *Cognition,* 96(3).

Özçalışkan, Ş., Lucero, C., Goldin-Meadow, S. (2016a). Is seeing gesture necessary to gesture like a native speaker? *Psychological Science,* 27(5), 737–747.

Özçalışkan, Ş., Lucero, C., Goldin-Meadow, S. (2016b). Does language shape silent gesture? *Cognition,* 148, 10–18.

Özçalışkan, Ş., Lucero, C., Goldin-Meadow, S. (2018). Blind speakers show language-specific patterns in co-speech gesture but not silent gesture. *Cognitive Science,* 42(3), 1001–1014.

Özçalışkan, S. et al. (2023). What the development of gesture with and without speech can tell us about the effect of language on thought. *Language and Cognition,* Volume 16, Issue 1, March 2024, pp. 220–241.

Pinker, S. (1994). *The Language Instinct.* London: Penguin Books.

Pollio, H.R. (1974). *The Psychology of Symbolic Activity.* Reading, MA: Addison-Wesley.

Ratliff, F. (1976). On the psychophysiological bases of universal color names. *Proceedings of the American Philosophical Society,* 120, 311–330.

Rizzolatti, G., Arbib, M.A. (1998). Language within our grasp. *Trends in Cognitive Sciences,* 21, 188–194.

Rosch, E. (1973). Natural categories. *Cognitive Psychology,* 4(3), 328–350.

Rosch, E. (1975). *Universals and Cultural Specifics in Human Categorization. In Cross-Cultural Perspectives on Learning,* edited by Richard W. Brislin, Stephen Bochner, and Walter J. Lonner, pp. 177–206. New York: Wiley.

Rosch, E. (1978). Principles of Categorization. In: Rosch, E., Lloyd, B.B. (eds) *Cognition and Categorization.* Hillsdale: Lawrence Erlbaum.

Rosch, H.E. (1972). Universals in color naming and memory. *Journal of Experimental Psychology,* 93, 10–20.

(Rosh, E. (1983). *Prototype Classification and Logical Classification: The Two Systems. In New Trends in Conceptual Representation: Challenges to Piaget's Theory*. edited by Ellin Kofsky Scholnick, pp. 73–86. Hillsdale, New Jersey: Lawrence Erlbaum Associates.

Sahlins, M. (1976). Colors and culture. *Semiotica*, 16, 1–22.

Sapir, E. (1929). The status of linguistics as a science. *Language*, 5, 207–214.

Stern, D.N. (1985). *The Interpersonal World of the Infant: A View From Psychoanalysis and Developmental Psychology*. Kindle.

Thass-Thienemann, T. (1957). Left-handed writing. A study in psychoanalysis of language. *Psychoanalytic Quarterly*, 26, 140.

Thass-Thienemann, T. (1963). Psychotherapy and psycholinguistics. *Topical Problems of Psychotherapy*, 4, 37–45.

Thass-Thienemann, T. (1967). *The Subconscious Language*. New York: Washington Square Press.

Thorpe, W.H. (1974). *Animal Nature and Human Nature*. Garden City, NY: Doubleday.

Turner, V. (1996). *The ritual process. Structure and anti-structure*. New Brunswick, London: Aldine.

Turner, V. (1967). *The Forest of Symbols*. Ithaca, New York: Cornell University Press.

Von Frisch, K. (1967). *The Dance Language and Orientation of Bees*. Cambridge: Harvard University Press.

Watkins, C. (1995). *How to Kill a Dragon. Aspects of Indo-European Poetics*. Oxford: Oxford University Press.

Wierzbicka, A. (1972). *Semantic Primitives*. Frankfurt: Athenäum.

Wierzbicka, A. (1992). *Semantics, Culture and Cognition. Universal Human Concepts in Culture-Specific Configurations*. New York, Oxford: Oxford University Press.

Wierzbicka, A. (1999). *Emotions Across Languages and Cultures. Diversity and Universals*. Cambridge: Cambridge University Press.

Winnicott, D.W. (1965). The Theory of the Parent-Infant Relationship. In *The Maturational Processes and the Facilitating Environment*. New York, NY: International Universities Press.

Witkowski, S.R., Brown, C.H. (1977). An explanation of color nomenclature universals. *American Anthropologist*, 79, 50–57.

Witkowski, S.R., Brown, C.H. (1978). Lexical universals, *Annual Review of Anthropology*, 7, 427–451.

Chapter 10

Conclusions by amplification

α' Μελέτη τὸ πᾶν.
["Take good care of everything" (that there is)]
Periander (c. 628–588)

I would like to close this book, and both volumes, through an amplification of an image that Jung considered to be archetypal – the Trinity. In fact, this image can somehow include and condense the main topics that I have discussed so far. Yet the closing of these volumes cannot happen but at the point at which one whole turn of the helix, from which I have begun this whole discussion, is complete – when one finds himself almost exactly where he had started his spiral-ambulation.

Our point of departure were these words by Jung:

> The spirit of our time spoke to me and said: "What dire urgency could be forcing you to speak all this? This was an awful temptation. I wanted to ponder what inner or outer bind could force me into this, and because I found nothing that I could grasp, I was near to making one up. But with this the spirit of our time had almost brought it about, that instead of speaking, I was thinking again about reasons and explanations. But the spirit of the depths spoke to me and said: "To understand a thing is a bridge and possibility of returning to the path. But to explain a matter is arbitrary and sometimes even murder. Have you counted the murderous among the scholars?"
>
> (Jung, 2009, p. 230)

Jung's words point straight to the core – the meaning of understanding as "a bridge and possibility of returning to the path". In fact, now close to the end, I first of all wish to point out something that may seem paradoxical and that has to do with questions like these: What can we actually do with "archetypal images"? How can we deal with them? How can we manage them?

My answer is that the only way that such images may acquire meaning is through their being embedded in a specific co-evolutionary environment – in this case, in a

DOI: 10.4324/9781003586463-10

specific historical moment of a specific social group in which a specific individual, who experiences the emergence of such images in his mind, belongs.

After so many pages dedicated to understanding universal images, my paradoxical answer to those questions is that we cannot say anything of these images if not by and within such specific empirical conditions. The only thing we can do is to say something *from* them but not *about* them. The claim to say something of an image that we think is archetypal corresponds to an interpretation and not to an amplification and is always an illegitimate projection of the interpreter's personal perspective, i.e., of his own biases. In fact, if an archetypal image represents an archetype-in-itself, then it represents the unconscious formal possibility of having any phenomenological, conscious experience. Therefore, as Jung pointed out referring to the fact that we can have direct experience of the collective unconscious only through consciousness (see vol. I, § 5), an image that we consider to be archetypal can also be understood only through the Ego, i.e., through the subject's empirical, cultural and historical specific predicament.

The empirical validity of our understanding of an archetypal image will be confirmed only if, by gravitating around it, the historical, culturally determined, empirical, phenomenological experience of the particular person reaches its psychological, meaningful, creative form. This is valid also for "psychotic" patients, for whom an image that may seem archetypal may trigger and organize specific meanings that belong to their own specific historical predicament.

Taking into account these cautions, we may now deal with an archetypal image – the Trinity.

Following Sperber's theory of susceptibility, the image of the Trinity is surely an image to which the mind *is* susceptible. Perhaps it is not a universal image but given its success in the last millennia – starting at least with the Egyptian *Ka-mutef* up to today – the fact that it has not been imagined all over the world would not be sufficient to exclude its potential universal, easy-to-imagine nature, which would produce it "in case of need". Therefore, it would fall into the category of "quasi-universal" images.

I would approach the image of the Trinity by noticing its numerical, Platonic ternary structure,[1] in which the quality of the Three (Von Franz, 1986) seems to organize in a peculiar way how we humans perceive and organize conscious experience.

The quality of ternary consciousness is meta-noetic (Panksepp), theoretical (epistemic, not fully gnostic) and reflective. Following Jung's "reflective instinct", it describes the conditions for both the "gnostic", transformational transcendent function as well as for Karmiloff-Smith's intellectual and representational redescription process.

As Jung emphasizes in discussing the relationship between the Three and the Fourth (Jung, 1948, § 195), because of its triadic structure, the Trinity's reflective, transcending process has a purely spiritual (hence, also epistemic) nature. But ternary consciousness is not the only one. There can be a conscious experience structured by the Two and, as I will show following Jung, a consciousness of the Four.

The consciousness of the Two is a noetic, *representational* form of consciousness available also to non-human animals up to primates. As I wrote, such representations of whatever the Real is is different for each species and determines a specific ecological niche within the co-evolutionary field. In this case, as with many others, the axiom of Maria Prophetissa is like a compass, as it describes the most abstract – mathematical – structure of emerging, creative, new levels of reality out of the One.

> Out of the One comes the Two, out of the Two comes the Three, and from the Third comes the One as the Fourth

You may remember Tomasello's refined description of the ontogenetic maturational moment in which, as he writes, the child *becomes human* – i.e., ethical. This is the moment in which, out of the relational twoness, the perspectival three emerges; and with this, emerges the world of higher values beyond the mere satisfaction of competitive, egocentric needs – at which the development of our closer phylogenetical relatives, the chimpanzees, stops.

Figure 10.1 represents the ontogenetic triadic relational field studied by Tomasello.

If we use this image in the context of this discussion, it would be a representation of the ontogenetic transcending relationship of the twoness into a threeness, which, for Tomasello, is psycho-biologically common to the whole human species.

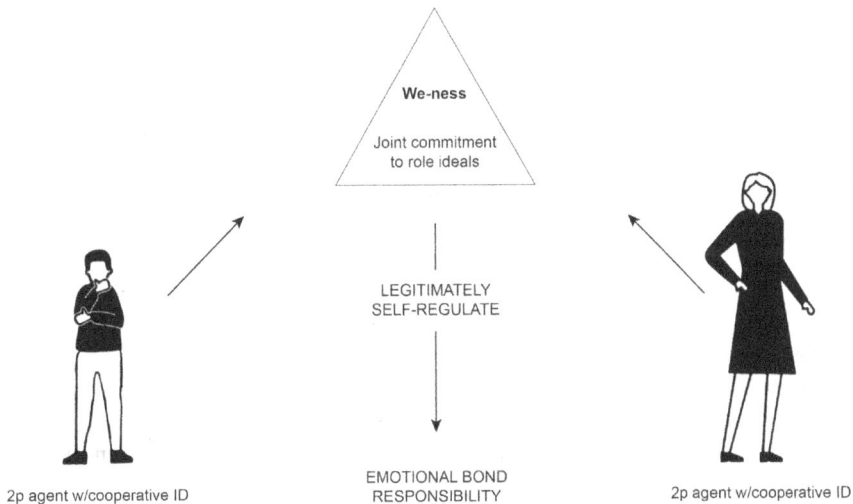

We-ness
Joint commitment
to role ideals

LEGITIMATELY
SELF-REGULATE

EMOTIONAL BOND
RESPONSIBILITY

2p agent w/cooperative ID

2p agent w/cooperative ID

THE TERNARY STRUCTURE OF THE PERSPECTIVAL NORMATIVE RELATEDNESS

Figure 10.1 Normative cooperation.

THE TRINITY
AN EXAMPLE OF AN IMPLICATIONAL UNIVERSAL METAPHOR
FROM AN ORIGINAL CO-EVOLUTIONARY *SOCIAL* ENVIRONMENT

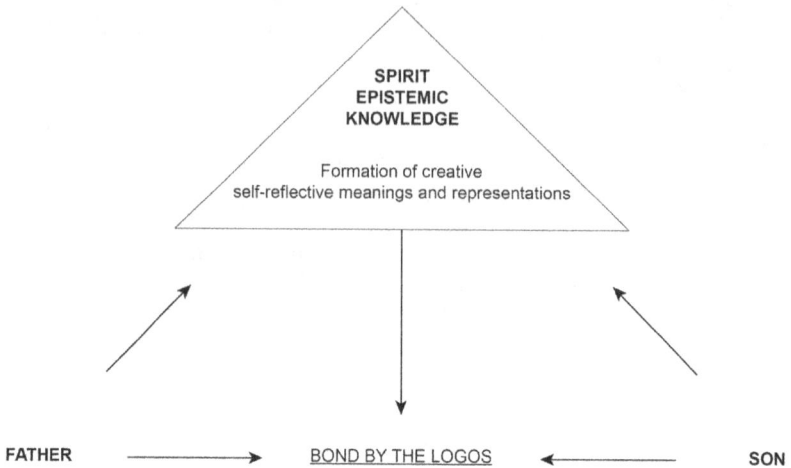

Figure 10.2 The metaphorization of the normative triad in the Trinity.

Seen from Tomasello's perspective, such a situation looks very much like a universal, like a real archetype.

The Figure 10.2 represents *a metaphorization* of the previous image; hence, it is an image that not only reflects but also transcends a ternary relationship into a Trinity. If we use this second image in the context of this discussion (since being treated as a symbol, it represents an indefinite number of other possible interpretations), it would represent a transformation of the previous image which takes the form of the Trinity. Hence, within this context, the perspectival normative relatedness triadic field would be homologue to the Trinity, as this represents a union in the spirit – a union not for immediate egocentric instinctual pleasure but for the fulfillment of a higher value, a truly ethical (i.e., transcending, spiritual) one. This is an objective that represents the union of the two into the "spirit of the ethical law".

Now, one could say this: The maturational moment in which the transcending threeness appears *produces* the image of the Trinity. Seen this way, the Trinity would just be a referential *sign* for the perspectival normative relatedness triadic field that *caused* it. This would be a reductionist, causal point of view. On the contrary, from Jung's perspective, there is a latent triadic organizing principle *that constellates and is common to both situations at different creative levels of abstraction.*

I wholeheartedly agree with Jung. In fact, I do not wish to derive the Trinity from Tomasello's momentous evolutionary step that transforms the human animal into a symbolic animal, the step in which "perspectival normative relatedness" appears. The latter seems to me close to an implicational universal, whose emotional constraints guide the production of a whole transcending central metaphor which develops through cultural historical time and ontogenetic life.

Therefore, with this metaphorization, I do not intend to derive, nor interpret, the image of the Trinity from the triadic relational co-evolutionary field that is constellated at around 3 years of age. I am not at all trying to interpret this image. I only wish to propose a way to consider the emergence of an image that seems homologous to a conditional universal situation in which "if A, then B" and that seems to develop through ontogenetic and historical time.

IF
there is a good-enough relational environment in the co-evolutionary field and the child has matured at the right point in his ontogenetic path (A)
THEN
a peculiar ternary structure is formed as an "image" – an emotional/cognitive pattern. We will call this perspectival normative relatedness (B).

In the ontogenetic period in which perspectival normative relatedness is born, the conditional universal formula may be translated as such:

This conditional formula may apply also to social and cultural situations, in which this spiritual bond rooted in perspectival relatedness and ethics may appear as a shared cultural value – in fact, as the very possibility of any culture to exist.

I would like to point out that *at this ultimate level*, the image has not yet been historically accomplished, as I do not see any real sign of ethical spiritualization in our culture(s). Deep down, we are still blocked at a chimpanzee-like level, or at the scapegoating structural violence described by Reneé Girard (1977, 1987). I believe this happens for the correlation between large social numbers and unconsciousness. If, in fact, in a small group, humans manage to safeguard their ethical, and therefore, "human", nature, when social networks expand the dimensions of the group, this process towards massification automatically entails a psychological regression and a reverting to a phylo-ontogenetic evolutionary stage in which the human animal returns to being a primate. The problem is that such a primate now has the wrong neurobiological apparatus, as it is partly de-specialized. This is the essence of human tragedy.

If we interpret this ternary emotional emergence as a dynamic potentiality that incarnates itself in various successive forms, one of which is perspectival normative relatedness, this would imply that we may interpret all subsequent images, from the ontogenetic development of the child to the loftiest symbols inherent in the image of the Trinity, as *means* for a goal that constantly transcends its own ends towards an infinite creative process of metaphorization and symbolization and a further expansion of Ego consciousness.

In volume 1 (§ 7), I wrote these words:

> [Already starting at the level of molecular developmental biology] It is much more efficient to intervene top-down at the highest possible level of organization than at the lowest one, as it is the higher level that informs and organizes the lower one. If this is valid for biology, it is even more valid for psychology, where the non-reductive top-down action at the highest possible level, that of meaning [. . .] may be the most efficient one, as it would inherently involve all the other lower levels, out of which it has emerged.

This means that at the lower level we find constraints that provide the minimal information necessary for the emergence of a next, higher level (for instance, from the genomic level to the cellular level, to the tissue and organ level, to the organism level, to the social level, etc.). Along such a bottom-up formative process, a top-down process also takes place, a process of crucial importance through which the higher levels interact top-down, as an attractor, on the lower ones, using the latter's constraints for *their own purposes*, for instance, for the preservation of a specific morphology or function in unexpected circumstances. Thus, what now is always more and more clear is that the best locus of control of the whole developmental ladder is always not the causal, lower one but the higher one (Along with Michael Levin, as a punch, I may say, "Not drugs, but mindfulness").

The progressive bottom-up unfolding of patterns, from atoms to language – my metaphor of the infinite ladder – is beautifully theorized and quite impressively researched by Manolis Kellis, a computational biologist of MIT and Harvard University in Boston. Kellis is known for his work in genomics and his contributions for the understanding the relationships between genes, biological function and evolution. Kellis' "theory" is not a singular framework but rather a set of approaches and insights that integrate evolutionary biology, computational methods and experimental genomics to understand life's complexities. His overarching perspective emphasizes the systemic level in which the interaction of genes, regulatory networks and epigenetic states take place, all shaped by evolutionary forces, as central to decoding the genome's nature. Within his overarching perspective, Kellis is on his way to explaining how we can find some common, repeating, recurrent patterns developing bottom-up through specific sets of precise, recurrent design principles (archetypes?) from the world of microphysics to that of cognition. In fact, according to Kellis, these design principles are not unlike some of the design principles that we humans have come up with in the social and cultural domain, which evolved from the same tinkering of the four fundamental basis of the ACGT (the four chemical bases that make up DNA, Adenine, Guanine. Cytosine, Thymine). According to Kellis, the DNA, which has its own language and code, evolved a construct that has its own language and code. *This is a learning construct* that can adapt to learn almost any language and code. From this fundamental biological level, yet related to the underlying physical and chemical ones, patterns of patterns develop towards more encompassing and complex layers.

Kellis' research (for an overview: Kellis, 2016) is individuating patterns and rules of translation of these different languages, initially from atoms and quarks to molecules, to the abstraction layer of ACGT to the next abstraction layer of the 20 amino acids and, from this, to the abstraction layer of folds and proteins and, eventually, to the abstraction layer in which a learning system emerges by evolving neurons that are able to perceive the outer world in which they are entangled and so store perceptions as memories. From this cognitive level, differences in patterns of thinking emerge. As we have already seen (quoting Damasio on bacteria), from the layer in which perceptions are stored and processed, sensations develop. In fact, once again, from the level of intero- and exteroception, a next level is about to arise – the level of consciousness and language.

Hence, the attractor of all lower-level constraints, the supreme, irreducible level of the ontological ladder is subjective experiential consciousness. Now, the overarching primacy of consciousness (i.e., of the psyche) as the teleological destination of nature's unfolding (at least from our human point of view) is the essence of Jung's life's effort. In fact, as Jung reminds us, we may appreciate not just the functions but also the very existence of the material world only by and through consciousness, not the other way around.

As David Chalmers maintains (1995), subjective experiential consciousness may be one of the fundamental constants of nature, such as mass, space-time or electrical charge. As a matter of fact, while the correlates of the subjective experiential consciousness can be explained causally bottom-up (Chalmers, 2010, pp. 4–5) (yet always through and by conscious subjective experience), phenomenal consciousness itself will be never constitutively explained by any lower-level structures, functions or processes, such as (quantum?) physics, biochemistry or neurosciences (Chalmers, 1995; also: Witkowski et al., 2022). In fact, it is consciousness that may constitutively explain the material, physical world out of which it seems to emerge and bring it into meaningful ontological existence, not the other way around. Hence, subjective experiential consciousness is, for us humans, the ultimate, teleological, encompassing apex of the evolutionary ladder that I have tried to describe so far.

Let's imagine that the font of the words that you are reading, or their being a "signifier" for a "signified" (the sound of the word "dog", for instance), belong to a specific ontological layer, while their *meaning* (the category of dogs or a specific dog belonging to this category) belongs to a higher layer, which is the transformation of the lower one. A fundamental property of the bottom-up developmental ladder that I am describing is that, in order to understand the meaning, you may *not* pay attention to the lower-level properties of the words (their typographical font, their acoustic characteristics). Hence, for my developmental perspective, the top-levels (from the genome to the way the brain works) encompass the lower ones all the way up to consciousness, which represents the ultimate ontological leap – the transformational emergence of a latent fundamental property of nature. Therefore, from the highest layer of this evolutionary model (i.e., consciousness), the top-down perspective implies that the deepest form of understanding of the lower levels (i.e., of the "material, Newtonian" levels) through the Ego may transcend causality and ego-consciousness and, moved by affects all the way upward, ultimately refer not to causes but to *meaning* and synchronicity.

Within the analytical tradition, this top-down perspective is the paradigmatic center of Alfred Adler's individual psychology. Adler's influence on Jung cannot be underestimated – for example, his teleological perspective, the principle of compensation, the role of what Jung called "education" or the theory of psychopathological conditions as *arrangements*. One of these paradigmatic Adlerian points of view, which have become part of Jung's analytical psychology, is Adler's underscoring of the directing role of the organism for the parts that make it. According to Adler's individual psychology:

> As soon as organic causes can be ruled out [i.e., when the "causal", "material" lower ontological levels are transcended (SC)], one should ask the question: To what does memory weakness tend? What does it want to achieve? This goal will only reveal itself to us from *an intimate knowledge of the whole individual, whereby the understanding of a part arises solely from the understanding of the whole.*
>
> (Adler, 1967, p. 14. My transl. My italics)

I would now like to introduce a second analytical perspective, related to memory, for which of the creation and re-creation of meaning, this top-down influence, may resemble what Freud ingeniously pointed to when he referred to a concept of Nietzsche's that he called *Nachträglichkeit*:[2]

> an attempt to give oneself, as it were, a past *a posteriori* [after the fact], out of which we may be descended in opposition to the one from which we are descended.
>
> (Nietsche, 2010, p. 13, italics in the original)

By such "afterwardsness", the subject's present interpretation of his own past *re-creates* the past. Such an influence corresponds to the transformation of supposedly past "facts" into new symbolic forms of understanding through that particular form of creative imagination that we call memory. However, I interpret this fundamental reconstructive process in a way different from Freud's and also Lacan's, as I think that, following Jung's teleological principle, the new forms of understanding that the present produces on the past – this top-down creation of the past from its future – has a true individuative value, a value of truth, only when it recursively *matches with the original dispositional goal that was embedded in the past itself.* In Winnicott's perspective, this is the same matching required for an object to be the right object to be presented to a child. It is only thanks to this entelechy that, through *Nachträglichkeit*, the past's future may be fulfilled in the present – the real time in which time and life exist. Within our perspective, therefore, the analytical process, hinged on the creative action of the present on the past through memory, consists in a continuous teleological, entelechial transformation of biology into history, i.e., into the symbolic unfolding of the libido through and by each singular subject.

The Trinity and Jung's archetypal images seem to me one of those high-level formations that, through an ongoing psychological, self-reflective, subjectively conscious level – the highest level we know – may express and partly regulate the lower-level (biological) occurrences, deep down the ladder's steps to the genome (through epigenetic feedbacks). This top-down effect is produced by the emotional meaning of these kinds of images, which attain their evolutionary destiny when they are fully integrated into consciousness.

For ease, we may say that this process towards consciousness, towards the expression of an emotional meaning, described by the Trinity seems to embody itself *psychologically* in the empirical world at around 3,5 years of age and proceeds as a form towards a gnostic knowledge – a most complete form of subjective experiential consciousness – that progressively transforms the person's consciousness and empirical life by universalizing and spiritualizing it.

Therefore, the infantile situation would not be the cause of the process, but it would be the archetypal progressive formation of an image that keeps unfolding itself.

I now wish to amplify another aspect of this image.

The Trinity is rooted in a paradox, something impossible in the natural world: the begetting of a Son from a Father united by the Spirit. In this paradoxical feature, there is something that represents another part of the topics that I discussed in these two volumes – the transcendence into cultural symbols of the biological body – what Jung called psychization.

We have seen that, using Sperber's language and according to Jung and Maria Prophetissa, the human mind is susceptible to representing a conscious and differentiated wholeness as a *quaternio*. The triad would represent something like a cognitive step towards it as, being the representation of the difference emerging from the twoness, it opens the mental space for self-reflective consciousness.[3]

In Aion (Jung, 1959/1969), Jung discusses these issues at length and in depth, and it is far from my intention to add anything to such an astounding intellectual *tour de force*. I am referring to Aion just to emphasize the incomplete nature of the Triad. In fact, in the representation of the Trinity, something is missing, and this something is the feminine, terrestrial element – the body.[4,5]

Figure 10.3 represents a second triad made by the filiation from the Mother to the Daughter via a bond that, in this case, is not spiritual but experiential, corporeal, sensory and affective. The Mother-Daughter filiation does not necessarily imply that the Mother's offspring is a real female person, but it implies something that might be expressed as follows: "From the emotional body, another emotional body is created".

This feminine, terrestrial triad seems to me good-to-imagine some of the issues that I have discussed in these volumes (therefore, it is susceptible to being imagined).

In fact, it seems to represent the *biological* (and ontogenetically infantile) level from which my bottom-up discussion has begun. This biological level is the Darwinian level of analysis in which, for instance, organisms will tend to reproduce to pass their genetic endowment to the next generation. This order of affairs obviously implies that the only relevant channel for this to occur is through consanguinity (carrying plus or minus the same genome). Furthermore, the phylogenetic goal of this process fundamentally uses all possible egoistical strategies for survival. In fact, nobody that is dead or submitted to a stronger inhibiting competitor will be able to pursue the goal of selective inheritance. At this level – the biological level – sociality is mostly related to biological kinship, as it is for primates. But as I have tried to show through Sahlins' work, this is *not* how kinship works in the human *cultural* world, in which kin does not necessarily need to be "one of the blood family". The idea that the "family" is rooted in blood may be true for the Western world, but sadly, it represents an (another) "underdeveloped" aspect of our inflated, arrogant culture.

In fact, as Sahlins showed us, in many cultures, biological kinship (here represented by the biological-"feminine" triad) is transcended into the cultural one – the spiritual trinitarian triad – for which a kin is somebody with whom I share a belonging based on *values and cultural norms*, not on blood, and what will be passed to the next generations are not genes but stories and institutions (vol. II, § 1).

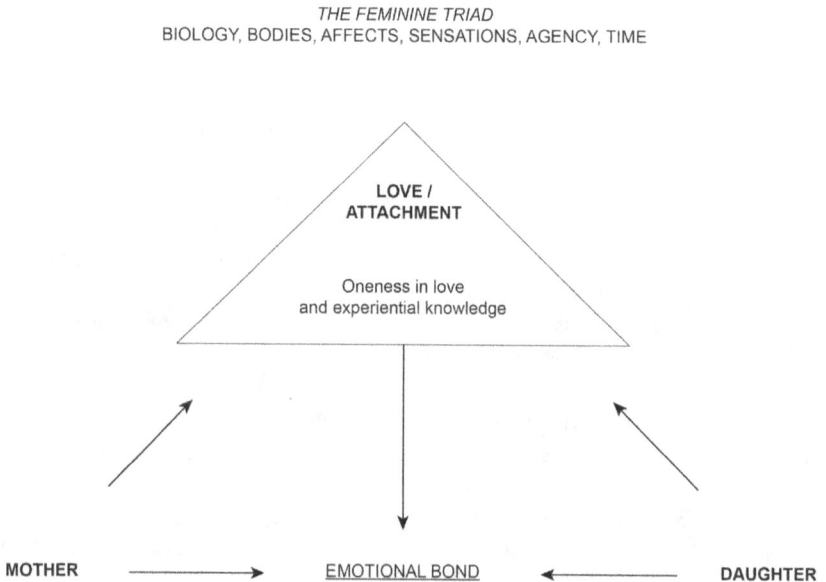

THE FEMININE TRIAD
BIOLOGY, BODIES, AFFECTS, SENSATIONS, AGENCY, TIME

LOVE /
ATTACHMENT

Oneness in love
and experiential knowledge

MOTHER   ⟶   EMOTIONAL BOND   ⟵   DAUGHTER

THE **TRINITARY** STRUCTURE AS AN "ARCHETYPAL" FURTHER METAPHORIZATION OF THE ORIGINAL
"PERSPECTIVAL NORMATIVE RELATEDNESS"

Figure 10.3 The natural triad.

From a psychological perspective, this transformation from the earthly triad to the heavenly one seems to be the representation of what Jung called psychization.

Yet the trinitarian triangle is also unilateral and incomplete, as it represents just the *theoretical* (Jung, 1948) aspect of the possibility that what the 3,5/4-year-old child has become – an ethical human (vol. I, § 10.1) – is not lost within the typical regressive, unethical, uncooperative, narcissistic, competitive, scapegoating behavior: *Alas!* the behavior typical of adults.

The transcendence and the full realization (the embodiment) of the natural, biological archetypal endowment into the spiritual one (its psychization) create the conditions in which all living creatures are finally part of the same family in which they are all kin, even if not related by blood (brothers and sisters, or better said, *friends* [Carta, 2012]). *This condition is psychologically and culturally far from being realized*, and I personally doubt that humankind will ever be able to transform itself and attain the goal of the Holy Ghost in the Pentecost, when each person will speak his language and everyone will understand each other.

Following Jung, for this to happen we must integrate both triads into a *quaternio*, which could be represented as the image in Figure 10.4, in which the two triads are connected at one point: The spirit is connected with the affect. The masculine spiritual triad and the feminine natural triad, represented as two triangles, connect on one vertex, which would represent the gnostic kind of knowledge created by the integration of the "masculine spirit" into the "feminine nature".

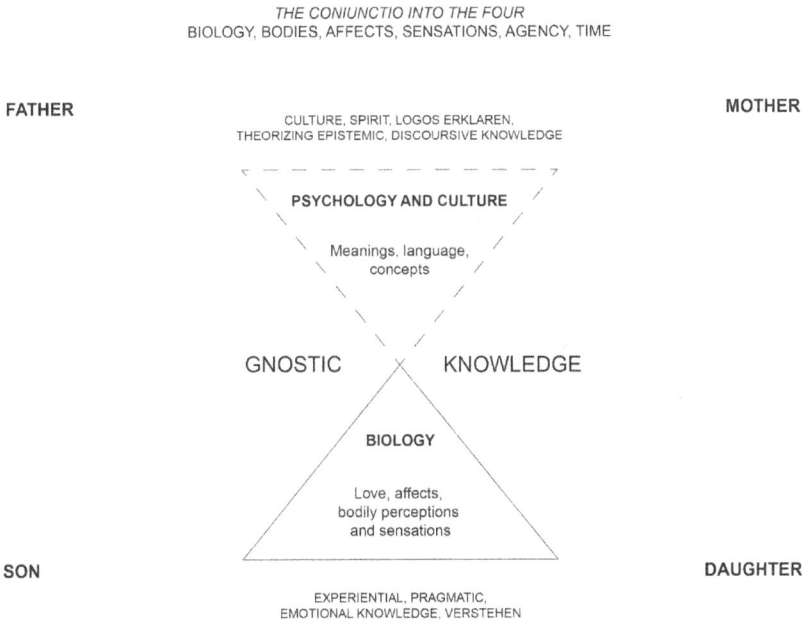

THE CONIUNCTIO INTO THE FOUR
BIOLOGY, BODIES, AFFECTS, SENSATIONS, AGENCY, TIME

FATHER   MOTHER

CULTURE, SPIRIT, LOGOS ERKLAREN,
THEORIZING EPISTEMIC, DISCOURSIVE KNOWLEDGE

PSYCHOLOGY AND CULTURE

Meanings, language,
concepts

GNOSTIC   KNOWLEDGE

BIOLOGY

Love, affects,
bodily perceptions
and sensations

SON   DAUGHTER

EXPERIENTIAL, PRAGMATIC,
EMOTIONAL KNOWLEDGE, VERSTEHEN

Figure 10.4 Two triads are connected at one point: the Spirit is connected with the affect.

This process may be described more thoroughly by the following two images. They try to describe the fact that the fourth unit of each triad is *the whole opposite triad* and that the *coniunctio* between them is the union between Eros (the Physis) and Logos (the Image and then the Word).

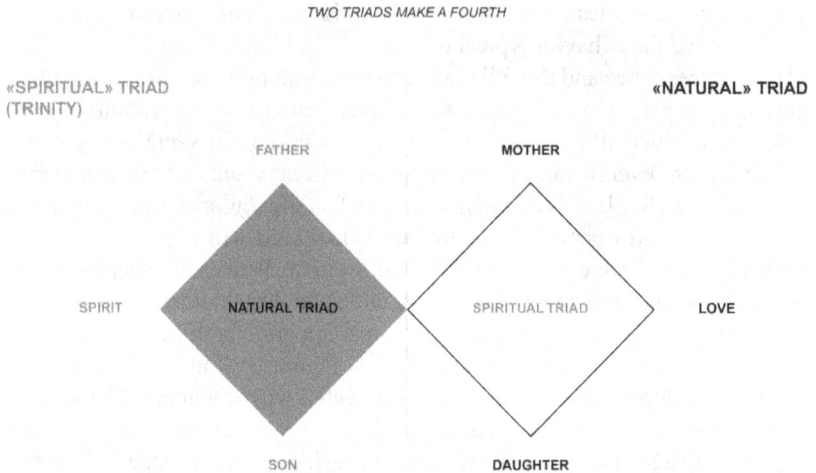

TWO TRIADS MAKE A FOURTH

«SPIRITUAL» TRIAD
(TRINITY)

«NATURAL» TRIAD

FATHER

MOTHER

SPIRIT

NATURAL TRIAD

SPIRITUAL TRIAD

LOVE

SON

DAUGHTER

Figure 10.5 The completion of each triad into the quaternio. If + does not mean "adding" but "integrating", then 3 + 3 = 4.

PHYSIS

LOGOS

Figure 10.6 The previous figure, Figure 10.5, should be "folded", imagining that the process of transcendence of each triad (the Natural and the Spiritual) is a circular process, actually an infinite, recursive *Moebius helix*. This helix may be also a representation of the circular interaction between the organism and the genome that I have recalled in vol. 1, §7.

As shown in Figure 10.6, the relationship between Physis (in our perspective, "biology") and Spirit (in our perspective, "symbolism and culture") is a recursive developing and transformative relationship. This represents the fundamental trans-formational helix that has been the inspiration for these two volumes. In fact, in this context, I don't imagine the recursive infinity of the strip as a closed circle but as an open, infinite helix – *an infinite ladder*.

Let me use a simple example: If the idea that conscious qualia emerge from the brain is commonly accepted (actually, so far, this is a true mystery), the possibility that, for example, a perception might be transformed by language into a differ-ent sensation is much less noticed. Yet this is what happens when, after sipping and smelling a glass of good wine, a sommelier tells me the flavors – the sensa-tions – that he has individuated. Suddenly, a miracle happens: like a blooming sensory flower made of taste and scents, we sensorially recognize.

spiced pear mixed with candied lemon rind, wildflowers and fresh honey all swirl in concert in the glass. Each sniff brings out a new element from the wine: fruit, mineral and flower. The palate is full in body with a texture that will make you keep coming back and rue the moment the glass is finished, capped with apricot and a salty minerality.

(This is the bouquet of the 2021 Giacomo Borgogno & Figli Derthona Timorasso Colli Tortonesi)

This top-down effect of symbolic, abstract language on bodily sensations has been aptly described by Paolo Virno (2003) as "second-degree sensism" and, in my opinion, shows the possibility that the whole physical realm and the spiritual one are conjoined in an evolving, transcending, recursive manner.

In the *quaternio*, purely cognitive thought – the logical Logos – finally fulfils its mandate and becomes an emotional thought/a thoughtful emotion. This is the point in which raw emotions and the body take an imaginative form within a complex relationship.

Here, Bion is of help: the complex nature of the relationship that makes it possi-ble to really transcend the biological, experiential, emotional triad into the spiritual one *and vice versa* is the point in which Bion's L is united with K – in which Love *is* Knowledge and Knowledge *is* Love[6] "with mutual benefit and without harm to either" (Bion, 1962, p. 27). If the spiritual, meta-noetic Logos of the trinitarian triad is what I called *epistemic* knowledge – the knowledge of explanations – and if the emotional form of knowledge of the feminine triad is an a-noetic or a noetic, purely experiential knowledge, the knowledge produced by the *coniunctio* of the two triangles is what I called *gnostic knowledge*.

This knowledge emerges from the transcending process in which the "biologi-cal", terrestrial, affective triad blooms and completes itself into the spiritual one while, at the same time, making it possible for the latter to embody itself in the relational, intersubjective world. This gnostic knowledge makes it possible not only a representation of one's experience but also the experience of a representation – what Jaspers referred to as *Verstehen*.

If the union of these two triads really represents a good image of this psychological growth, we should never forget that at its base, there is the body – its emotions, perceptions and agency. This is why I insisted on treating cognition, as well as the cognitive interpretations of religion and rituals, as a secondary form of knowledge based upon emotional and sensory experiences.

Lastly, we should remember that these exceedingly complex cultural images, like the Trinity, are representations of a process that seems to be archetypal. They seem to be patterns whose first appearance is *through* biology and infancy. They are patterns good-for-imagining a process that not only has to be historically completed by humankind but, as I said, is also still far from being completed.

The *coniunctio* of the triangles in a *quaternio* regards the problem of the "second mixing" that puzzled Plato in the *Timaeus* (Jung, 1948, § 179ff.). This (probably) had to do with the transformation of a bidimensional reality (made of pure thoughts and structurally expressed by a Two transcending into a Three) obtained by the first mixing of two pairs of opposites into a tridimensional temporalized reality (expressed as a Three transcending into a Four) for which a second mixing is necessary. It is intuitively clear that this problem involves nothing less than the "top-down" incarnation of the eternal spirit in the flesh and into time – a problem that occupied Plato five centuries before Christ. This makes very apparent that the shift from a triad to a *quaternio*, which involves the inclusion of the "Other" as the fourth element, opposes a fierce resistance. So fierce that, after two millennia, there is little sign of that transformation of humanity for which Christ sacrificed his life.

In all truth, what we have witnessed has been a resistance so very fierce that the historical end-result seems to be the enantiodromic destruction of most of the planet's native populations by colonialism, of nature itself by greed and, finally, of a possible self-destruction.

The birth of the spirit at 3,5 years of age is still a natural outcome of a biosocial process. The possibility and necessity that the child, who has now become a fully human animal, permanently incarnates himself in a truly "human" psychology and culture(s) without regressing to a behavior typical of a primate (yet a now-mad Prometheus literally *unchained* by his own neotenic nature) seems a far utopia and the second mixing too hard to attain, if not in theory.[7] So far, the nature of this *cultural* symbol, as it has not yet been accomplished, is that of an infinite, open object of reflection to promote further growth. In fact, its not-yet-accomplished "realization" would imply the possibility of a top-down transformation through which a cultural symbol may modify its lower formative bio-psychological constraints.

The mandate of analytical psychology, for which I decided to write these books, is to try to hold fast to this *coniunctio* between Love and Knowledge held by the eternal weaver that saves and re-creates human experience, transforming it into meaningful stories: memory.

Notes

1 Or at least the "Pythagoreanized" Plato, where he is interpreted as building a mathematical ontology. Obviously, this is an enormous challenging issue and a beautiful one not just for its cognitive aspect related to the thinking function of human consciousness but also especially for the possibility of connecting, if not deriving, *ethics* – which is rooted in the feeling function of consciousness – from mathematical knowledge (in a reductionist perspective, connecting Tomasello's triadic relational structure with the secondary feelings that allow the foundation of ethics on human fairness).

   Among the many, one of the ancient protagonists of this "Pythagoreanizing" interpretation is Proclus. In accordance with Plato's *Republic*, he distinguishes between a lower *dianoetic* access to empirical truth and higher *noetic* knowledge which accesses the pure (mathematical) forms.

   The dianoetic intellection of mathematics consists of two sorts of power, according to Proclus' interpretation of Plato. Its "lower" powers form the basis not only of the branches of mathematical science, as Plato distinguishes them (arithmetic or number theory, geometry and stereometry, astronomy and harmonics), but also applied mathematics. With respect to its higher powers, which lead to *noesis*, Proclus Pythagoreanizes: "The range of this thinking extends from on high all the way down to conclusions in the sense world, where it touches on nature and cooperates with natural science (physiologia) in establishing many of its propositions, just as it rises up from below and nearly joins intellectual knowledge in laying hold of the first principles of contemplation (theôria)" (In pr. Eucl. 19–20–24; trans. altered from that of Morrow in Proclus 1970, pp. 16–17).

   As White notices (2006, p. 9): "He [Proclus] adds that the 'beauty and order of mathematical discourse, and the abiding and steadfast character of this *theôria*, bring us into contact with the intelligible world itself'" (In pr. Eucl. 20.27–21.2, in Proclus 1970: 17). Thus, mathematical science, "directed upward", makes contributions of the greatest importance to philosophy and theology; in the realm of human value, it benefits political philosophy and "perfects us with respect to moral philosophy (*êthikên philosophian*) by instilling order and harmonious living into our characters" (In pr. Eucl. 21.25ff., 23.12ff, and 24.4–6, respectively).

   See also: Burnyeat, 2000, pp. 1–81.
2 With "afterwardsness", or "deferred action", Freud indicated "a memory [which] is repressed which has only become a trauma *after the event*" (Freud, 1975, p. 435).
3 The huge difference between Sperber and Jung has to do with Jung's problems of category B (synchronicity) that in this book I did not discuss, for which the archetypal image is not just a representation but is the best possible image representable by the human mind of the unknowable underlying reality.
4 These words ("feminine", "terrestrial", "body", etc.) should not be approached as clear and distinct concepts but as imaginative amplifications, whose semantic borders are and must remain blurred. In fact, their purpose is not to express a clear conceptual knowledge but to help me shape my own attempt to understand what I am trying to think. It is not impossible that this attempt might also help some reader, but this is not inevitably necessary.
5 I am not mentioning the scotomization of evil because I think that this is a local, cultural variant of the trinitary structure, in which the Father is interpreted as pure Good.
6 I realize that, since the feminine triad is a bodily/biological/emotional one, I should not speak of Love but of "attachment", but I have too many resistances to use such a

biologistic term for such a complex experience. In fact, I would propose to speak of Love also for Harlow's primates.

7 To my eyes, the materialistic, unilaterally competitive, atomizing myth of capitalism, based as it is on blind greed, is a thoroughly chimpanzee-like cultural organization. It works using an *emotional* mind younger than 3 years old. After 3, a child aims at preserving common higher values and wishes to cooperate.

In this regard, what comes back to mind is the controversy between Herbert Spencer and Thomas Henry Huxley about the possibility of an evolutionary ethics. The central idea was that human morality (moral sense and moral codes) could be explained as a function of biological adaptation. For Huxley, it is no longer a matter of dominating and possessing nature, as Descartes claimed, nor of submitting to it by restoring its laws in civilization as Spencer thought since the doctrine of evolution (in its restrictive terms) cannot provide a foundation for morality because the purported "fittest" for survival may be the worst on the ethical level (Huxley, 2009).

I side with Thomas Huxley, not to refute our animal nature but on the basis of the more comprehensive Darwinian vision that Kropotkin defended.

References

Adler, A. (1967). *Teoria e Prassi della Psicologia Individuale.* Rome: Astrolabio.

Bion, W.R. (1962). *Learning from Experience.* London: Karnak Books.

Burnyeat, M.F. (2000). Plato on Why Mathematics is Good for the Soul. In: Smiley, T. (ed) *Mathematics and Necessity: Essays in the History of Philosophy.* Oxford: Oxford University Press.

Carta, S. (2012). Narcissism, solitude, friendship. Notes on the therapeutic alliance in the context of the Freud-Jung relationship. *Journal of Analytical Psychology,* 57(4), 483–499.

Chalmers, D. (1995). Facing up to the problem of consciousness. *Journal of Consciousness Studies,* 2.

Chalmers, D. (2010). *The Character of Consciousness.* Oxford, UK: Oxford University Press.

Freud, S. (1975/1895). Project for a Scientific Psychology. In: Strachey, J. (ed & trans) *Standard Edition of the Complete Psychological Works of Sigmund Freud,* vol. I. London, UK: The Hogarth Press, pp. 283–397.

Girard, R. (1977). *Violence and the Sacred* (trans Patrick Gregory). Baltimore: Johns Hopkins University Press.

Girard, R. (1987). *Things Hidden Since the Foundation of the World,* Research undertaken in collaboration with Jean-Michel Oughourlian and G. Lefort. Stanford: Stanford University Press.

Huxley, T.A. (2009). *Evolution and Ethics.* Princeton: Princeton University Press.

Jung, C.G. (1948). The Psychological Approach to the Trinity. In: *The Collected Works of C.G. Jung,* vol. 11. London: Routledge.

Jung, C.G. (1959/1969). Aion. Researches on the Phenomenology of the Self. In: *The Collected Works of C.G. Jung,* vol. 9i. London: Routledge.

Jung, C.G. (2009). *The Red Book* (eds S. Shamdasani). New York: Norton.

Kellis, M. (2016). *Computational Biology: Genomes, Networks, Evolution.* MITcourse 6.047/6.878. https://ocw.mit.edu/ans7870/6/6.047/f15/MIT6_047F15_Compiled.pdf

Nietsche, F. (1874/2010). *Untimely Meditations. On the Use and Abuse of History for Life.* Luverne, MN: EZreads Publications.

Proclus. (1970). *A Commentary on the First Book of Euclid's Elements* (English trans G.R. Morrow). Princeton, NJ: Princeton University Press.

Virno, P. (2003). *Quando il verbo si fa carne. Linguaggio e natura umana.* Torino: Bollati Boringhieri.

Von Franz, M.L. (1986). *Number and Time: Reflections Leading Toward a Unification of Depth Psychology and Physics.* Evanston: Northwestern University Press.

White, M.J. (2006). Plato and Mathematics. In: Benson, H.H. (ed) *A Companion to Plato.* Malden, MA: Blackwell, pp. 228–243.

Witkowski, T., Solomonova, E., Duane, B., Levin, M. (2022). Biology, buddhism, and AI: Care as the driver of intelligence. *Entropy*, 24, 710.

Jung as a contemporary scientist

*Silvano Tagliagambe**

This work by Stefano Carta is an important work because it highlights a curious as well as an obvious basic contradiction in the current situation of analytical psychology: a marked "internal" distancing from Jung by the Jungians at the very moment when many aspects of his thought are the focus of interest in various directions of today's scientific research, from physics to neuroscience.

Let us begin with the first of these aspects. In his latest work, *Metafisica Concreta* (2023), the Italian philosopher Massimo Cacciari writes:

> Of great fascination regarding the problem of simultaneity are the reflections of W. Pauli, (1949)[1] in relation to Jung and his psychological research, a relationship that began in 1932 and lasted for twenty-five years. The acausal connections discovered with regularity by Jung (1952)[2] would correspond, analogically, for Pauli, to the co-implication at a distance between two particles observed in microphysics. One has "memory" of the other and tends to preserve the behavior it had with the other even when this has disappeared. In the unconscious-conscious life we continually experience similar situations.
>
> (Cacciari, 2023, p. 268, my transl.)

Of particular interest is the fact that this reference to the Jung-Pauli principle of synchronicity from physics is being matched by a similar and increasingly pronounced interest from neuroscience, and it is instructive to understand why.

Recently, the American evolutionary psychologist Nicholas Humphrey (2006) has taken up and developed an idea proposed in 1785 by Thomas Reid (1975), who dealt with the problem of sensible perception and the conditions necessary for it to occur. In this connection, he argued that the object, either directly or by some means, must produce an impression, and therefore, an action, on the bodily organ without which the impression could not impress itself first on the nerve and then, through it, on the brain. The function of external matter is finished at this point: what remains is up to the intellect.

Therefore, while the layman knows only an object that exists in perception as something external, in memory, this object is something that has existed; in the mind, however, as a *conception*, it may be something that never existed. Thus,

DOI: 10.4324/9781003586463-11

philosophers must recognize the need to "distinguish objects into two types". In this regard, Reid proposed a significant distinction between two representational modes:

- *Perception*, which presupposes a reference to external objects and their incidence on a subject; and
- *Sensation*, which, on the contrary, does not imply this conception.

Here is how Reid presents this distinction:

> If I suffer a pinprick, is the pain I feel a sensation? Undoubtedly. [. . .] But is the pin also a sensation? I am obliged to answer that it is not a sensation and bears no resemblance to it. The pin has a determined length, thickness, figure and weight. A sensation possesses none of these qualities. [. . .] However, the pin is a sensible object; and I am sure that I perceive its shape and hardness with my senses, just as I am sure that I feel pain when I am pricked by it.
>
> (Reid, 1785/1975, p. 421, my transl.)

Therefore, we can speak of perception only at the moment when there is an "objectification", that is, when our experience takes on the sense of an experience of a world independent from the mind. Of this process of objectification, Reid provides a tripartite analysis; for him for there to be perception, three conditions must be met:

- First, an external object must be present to the percipient's mind;
- Second, the percipient must believe that the object in question actually exists; and
- Finally, this belief must be non-inferential.

Generally, both the fact that the percipient finds himself having the object in his mind and the related belief have as their proximate cause the fact that a certain sensation, or a certain set of sensations, has been produced in the percipient's mind, which, nevertheless, are not the objects of perception. The relation that sensations entertain with external objects is an external relation. No similarity is at stake. It is rather a matter of causality, that is, of the action and incidence of the external object on the surface of our body, on its bio-border. Thus, there is a process that is triggered by the action of the external object on the body's bio-border (perception) and that produces as a reaction within the body – a counterpart (a sensation) that is the effect of this action. Therefore, what occurs may be presented as the coincidence, on the skin boundary, of the aforementioned action, together with the reaction that it caused within the body structure.

Sensations, as we know, have a hedonic character: they may be pleasant, unpleasant or indifferent and give us a conception and a "natural", irresistible belief in the existence of external objects. Perception has always an external object; the object of my perception, in our case, is given by the shape and hardness of the pin, which I perceive when I am pricked and which causes the painful (and, therefore, unpleasant) sensation in me. As I said, and as is appropriate to repeat it, this sensation has no relationship based on any resemblance to the object that produced it: it is the result of an internal process based on an intuition that out there, beyond my body, there is something external affecting it and causing it to respond.

Reconnecting with this 1785 Thomas Reid's idea, Nicholas Humphrey points out that the stimulus that lands on our body's bio-border has a dual function:

- It produces a local body reaction in the form of a homeostatic change in body states, giving rise to a sensation; and
- It can be the distinctive sign of something that is external to the boundaries of one's body and not simply upon it and that presents itself in the form of a perception.

Giorgio Vallortigara writes:

The scent of the rose that we can smell for itself, without reference to the object-rose, constitutes the sensation. It exists as long as someone can smell it. As Bishop Berkeley would say, its "existing" consists in being perceived (*esse est percepi*). But the smell of the rose also arouses in us the recognition of the external object; that is, the smell acts as a signal of one of the qualities of the external object. The correlation with the object can be easily verified, because if I move that specific rose – that specific object – away from me, its fragrance will become fainter and fainter, until it disappears.

(Vallortigara, 2021, p. 98)

The two representational modalities, as Humphrey himself was among the first to demonstrate, run in parallel and not one after the other, but they can also proceed disconnected, resulting in a perception that is not accompanied by a sensation, as in the case of the in blind sight; or the reverse situation may occur – to which also Stefano Carta refers – in which the presence of a sensation without any perception, as in agnosia, a kind of mental blindness that produces, on the part of patients, even in the absence of disturbances of memory or the sense organ involved, an inability to recognize objects, people, sounds and shapes that are already known.

Despite the possible disconnection experienced between the perception (as a stimulation caused by an external stimulus arriving at the surface of the organism) and the sensation (as a stimulation caused by the active movement of the organism itself, whose surface has encountered an external stimulus), it is clear that, based on the correlation with the object of which Vallortigara is referring in the passage just quoted, the intensity and quality of one influences that of the other. As we move away from the rose of the previous example, its fragrance becomes more and more faint until it fades away. Therefore, the characteristics, requirements and the level of the sensations present in our inner universe depend on those of the external objects of the physical world in which we live, in particular, on their incidence on the surface that delimits our body.

As Carta also writes, as a result of further research, the original idea of the cancellation and substitution of the externally perceived stimulus (the incoming sensory signal) by the so-called "efference copy" – created to compare the movement that the brainmind expects with the actual one, which creates a feedback system capable of stabilizing the organism – has been substituted by the reference to an *anticipatory* control mechanism capable of monitoring and evaluating motor commands *before* the effector (the muscle that controls the movement to be made) goes into action. The fact to be noted, however, is that what underlies the distinction between self and non-self, and thus, the explanation of the process by which our experiences come into being, is not the idea of the *ex-afference* of objects existing out there, and thus, of our perceptions, but that of the *re-efference* of what is produced by the subject's own action, and thus, of our sensations.

Regarding the previous point, it is important to remember that vision should be associated with movement since "seeing", as it is evident from the research conducted to explain this process, does not have to do with generating representations and images in the brain, but instead, it is an exploratory activity mediated by our knowledge of sensorimotor contingencies. Therefore, what would be at play is a continuous active process of interrogation and control in which the role of the efference copy is, once again, crucial. We see movement because of the following:

> along with the command to move the eye muscles, an efference copy is sent to the comparator, which then receives a signal that we interpret as movement of the object.
>
> (Vallortigara, 2021, p. 121, my transl.)

In this perspective, the reference to time thus becomes crucial, because, as Vallortigara again highlights:

> What we call feeling would be nothing more than the sensory signal, *held in time*, awaiting a revelation, that is, a comparison between the sensory/body signal and the efference copy of a motor action that may or may not have already occurred. So, yes, it is a memory, but of a special kind, because it is in fact the memory of a bodily reaction which carries with itself the sense of having been accomplished (hence the sense of the belonging and authorship of the sensation) together with its hedonic value.
>
> (Vallortigara, 2021, p. 98, my transl.)

This is a very significant step, indeed, because it highlights the importance of the role of synchronization of which Jung spoke of at the time. In order to make the comparison, the comparator must receive both signals together, for example, by delaying the one that arrives first. The corollary motor signal must then be delayed and held in memory while waiting for the signal produced by the sensory stimulation to arrive. It is crucial that our brain does this, and it is to Jung's unquestionable credit that he first emphasized the importance of this process.

The founder of analytical psychology also places great emphasis on a concept – that of energy – which, as Carta appropriately points out, Jung formulates explicitly by referring to the physical laws of thermodynamics and the conservation/transformation of motion and energy. This aspect is rightly pointed out and emphasized in this book because it is consistent with contemporary psycho-biological models, some of which are cited and used and have several significant implications.

The first of these models concerns the concept of *"movement relations"* in reference to the development of the psyche. In this regard, Carta points out that there is a broad consensus among contemporary cognitive scientists, neuroscientists and developmental psychologists precisely on the role of these relations. Essential in this regard is what Vallortigara again writes, pointing out that the distinction between what happens on the body surface and what is out there is related to movement:

> the only way to determine whether a part of our body is ours is to move it. [. . .] This is because as the organism moves actively, it becomes essential to distinguish the sensory signals that come from the world out there from those that are instead the consequence of the organism's own movements in the world.
>
> (Vallortigara, 2021, p. 121, my transl.)

This is a reversal of perspective of paramount importance, as Vallortigara again effectively points out, in that it shifts the role of motor action from perception to sensation. In short:

> the first organisms endowed with active movement found it necessary to produce a splitting in an otherwise unitary sensory signal: does something touch you because it came upon you or because by moving you went upon it? The mechanism that can enable this splitting is the phenomenon of *efference copying*, or *corollary discharge*, which we have known in detail since the early part of the last century thanks to the work of Erich von Hoilst and Roger Sperry (but which had been intuited by many other scholars well before that).
>
> Whenever the organism enacts an active movement, a copy of the command related to the movement is generated and compared with the incoming sensory signal, so that the latter is cancelled out. As many authors have noted, what is put in place by the afferent copy mechanism constitutes in effect a primitive distinction between self and non-self, the crucial step in the emergence of consciousness (aka experience, in the sense of the term we use here.
>
> (Vallortigara, 2021, p. 121, my transl.)

Here, we have another instance where Jung's theory reveals its astonishing scientific validity, confirmed by a great deal of research and findings. From this, Jung drew deep and pervasive cognitive implications for his theory of the unconscious, which is far from being based on a purely drive-and-discharge principle, as is the Freudian Id. To underscore this distinction, Carta, not surprisingly, devotes much of his book to the relationship between cognition, affects, feelings and emotions and to the primacy of affects over cognition within Jung's psychology, which is confirmed, as we have seen, by the hedonic character of the stimuli arriving on the boundaries of the organism, which determine the appropriate automatic behavioral responses of reactions to them and the subsequent development, on this initiating basis, of cognitive processes. At the end of the author's convincing analysis devoted to images, their formation and their role in shaping affects and producing new forms of meaning, the role of what we call "cognition" in preconscious and unconscious processes also becomes quite clear.

Another indisputable merit of this book is to point out that for Jung, archetypes constitute collective preconscious complexes of biological and evolutionary origin. This gives rise to the idea, already credited by Kant in the *Critique of Pure Reason*, that space and time do not stand on the same plane, for while it is true that we inhabit space, the same cannot be said of time, which we do not inhabit at all, for *we constitutively are time*.

Consequently, it is of the utmost importance to note that there is a distinction, and an ineliminable tension, between a "spatial" and a "temporal" consideration of the Self, by virtue of which "the latter perpetually *disquiets* the former", as Cacciari points out in his already cited work, where he stresses:

> to the knowing ourselves, to the introspective exercise so much praised by "popular philosophy", should be granted no privilege. No object can be given to us except through the form of an internal sense, and yet this form – time – holds no absolute reality. It is relative to our representation of the thing. Thus, its relativity is affirmed and, at the same time, the insuperability of its being relative. Here lays the aporia.
>
> (Cacciari, 2023, p. 121, my transl.)

What results from this is the character of the person's meta-stability to define which we have to resort to notions, such as that of "potential energy of a system", "order" and "the increase of entropy", and which must be considered the result of the following fact:

> below the continuous and discontinuous, there subsists the quantum and the complementary meta-stable (the more-than-unity) which consists of the truly pre-individual.
>
> (Simondon, 2020)

To understand what this "pre-individual" concretely consists of, it is appropriate to refer to Giorgio Vallortigara's latest essay, *Il pulcino di Kant* (2023), which addresses crucial questions for biology, epistemology and psychology. The underlying problem is to try to understand how organisms form and develop their capacity to "take hold" of the physical and social world in which they live, constructing a cognitive process that enables them to orient themselves and to move and act in accordance with its structure. Through a series of rigorously conducted experiments to explore the contents of the mind in the nascent state of small vertebrates, especially chicks, and also referring to the phenomenon of imprinting, Vallortigara asks whether the answers that may come out of empiricism can be considered sufficient to adequately account for the origin of information – the wisdom that living beings possess as their basic equipment. In particular, what he sets out to determine is whether the latter's availability can be explained by referring only to gradually *acquired* sensory data and to the reactions to them.

The answer is no:

> Ultimately, – it is observed – the problem with empiricism is that, quite simply, there are far too many possible associations available in the world, and without some kind of instructional mechanism an organism would find itself utterly lost in the infinite web of potential causal connections.
>
> (Simondon, 2020, p. 132)

The mechanisms to be called in to duly address the question of the "innate guidelines for learning" can be traced back to a deep biological memory, which has the long timescale of natural history and not the short timescale of individual development. Hence, they are a priori for the individual and a posteriori for the species to which the individual belongs. They are the results of experience acquired along the timescale of phylogenetic history.

Experiments carried out and illustrated with exemplary clarity tell us what the nature of these mechanisms is made of. It is made of the predispositions from birth to perceive objects as cohesive and continuous entities extending in space and persisting in time; the ability to distinguish possible and impossible objects; the principle that sensory objects occupy space exclusively; the assumption that the reflectance of an object does not change with illumination, an effective guide to learning the properties of visible surfaces; of the general aptitude for grasping relations of equality or difference regardless of the objects; of the sensitivity to probability, by virtue of which animals succeed in the mighty feat of spontaneously grasping the probabilistic structure of a sequence; and of an innate sense of geometry, which precedes and guides our experiences of navigation in the environment, an idea that would have appealed to Immanuel Kant and which explains the title of the essay.

These mechanisms underlie the formation of two categories of abstract concepts: "*sortals*" and "*modes*". The sortals are types of objects, both natural and artifacts, and identify the "type" of entity with which one is dealing – that is, they provide the criteria for identifying and counting objects. The modes, on the other hand, are the properties enjoyed by the objects thus identified. The process by which an organism comes to have these concepts requires on its part the ability to evaluate a novel stimulus based on performing two different types of analysis with mutually incompatible logical demands. It is important to understand in what sense and why.

> First, on the basis of previous experience, [the organism] must estimate the degree of novelty of the stimulus and, to do so, it must recall stored memories

and then process them for future use. Second, it must use some properties of the stimulus, despite variations in many other properties, to try to assign it to a category, and then decide what kind of rapid response, if any, should be provided.

(Vallortigara, 2023, p. 39)

So, in order to classify events or stimuli, the organism must recognize the invariance of features of an experience, while ignoring or discarding those variations between episodes that are instead crucial in order to detect novelty and construct a detailed record of episodic experiences. In the former case, it must provide rapid responses based on all-or-nothing categorization; in the latter, it must know how to make the necessary discrimination within categories by making use of variable properties of stimuli instead.

These two types of processing, which are clearly incompatible, must be performed simultaneously for an animal to be able to both classify objects and events and notice novelty. To be managed together, these two activities require functionally separate systems. According to Vallortigara, this is one of the main reasons for the differentiation of functions between the two sides of the brain.

Ceruti's complexity studies are another excellent application of the concept of metastability and of the further confirmation of its validity. One example among many that could be proposed is related to the idea that, while the person undoubtedly lives in the present, he:

protects within himself a laboratory where experimentation are in his daily agenda, through which the variety necessary for the future can originate and develop without immediately interfering with the processes necessary for the present. We could say that the human genome has turned out to be the paradigmatic model of a dual organization, in which the purposes of the short term and the purposes of the long term are integrated in a very complex mechanism that is not only very efficient but also very effective. I like to recall the way Stephen J. Gould summarized the issue: In nature, redundant material is almost never *garbage*, that is, waste that is thrown away, but almost always junk, or scrap ready to be reinterpreted and reused. Reuse is not a marginal strategy, but a high road of biological evolution.

(Ceruti, 2018, p. 108, my transl.)

It must then be concluded that, for living systems:

there is precisely a need to be dual, with one foot in the present and one foot in the future: one must be able to do routine work well, consolidating current trends and generating adaptations to these trends. But one must also preserve the awareness that these trends are getting closer and closer to the breaking point and that other equilibria and other technologies characterized by very different logics and rules, in any case not reducible to those of the present moment, will soon emerge.

(Ceruti, 2018, p. 150, my transl.)

This orientation towards the future must be complemented with the reference, always at the center of Ceruti's interests and reflections, to the crucial importance of narrative, time and on the incidence of the past – all inescapable constituent parts of any complex system, and therefore, also of the person – since in any universe of discourse, the set of evolutionary possibilities is not fixed a priori and once and for all. Any set of possibilities recurrently regenerates itself discontinuously and unpredictably from the initial conditions. Every story is a narrative in which new universes of possibility are produced coinciding with major turning points, major discontinuities and major thresholds of evolutionary processes. In its course, certain possibilities become fixed and transformed into constraints that eliminate some alternatives but produce others. So constraints and possibilities – as Carta argues, too – are not to be set against each other, according to the logic of mutually exclusive oppositional pairs, but are to be thought of together, as they co-evolve. The result is a dance, a game that is characterized by the co-existence of rigid rules and factors of unpredictability, in which each constraint describes a *limes*, the Latin word for a boundary, an end point, the conclusion of a story, but simultaneously represents a *limen*, a threshold, the beginning of a new story, as reflected in the dual meaning of boundary that I tried to explore in a text of mine several years ago (Tagliagambe, 1997). Consequently, the constraints of history are to be interpreted not only as limits of the possible but also as conditions of new possibilities. This is confirmed for us by the dynamics of scientific theories themselves – a constraint like Heisenberg's uncertainty principle, according to which it is impossible to simultaneously measure incompatible observables, such as position and momentum, which gives a quantum particle a very wide spectrum of possible behaviors, far more than before it was introduced.

The co-existence, interaction, hybridization and fusion of the three temporal dimensions in the person as a metastable complex system means the following:

> on the level of the individual being, the being is necessarily already *polyphasic*, for the pre individual past survives parallel to the existence of the individual being and remains a seed for new amplifying operations; individuation intervenes in the being as the *correlative birth of the distinct phase* based on that which did not include them, insofar as what did not include them is pure omnipresent potential. The individual, which is the result but also the *milieu* or *milieu of individuation*, must not be considered as singular: it is singular only with respect to other individuals, according to a very superficial here and now.
>
> (Simondon, 2020, pp. 360–361)

Metastability thus presents itself as that precise condition of equilibrium in which a system finds itself when *unexpressed potentials* are detected within it and that, even in the presence of the constraints that condition both its internal structure and its relation to the environment, constantly take the system on the verge of going out of phase itself and opening to opportunities compatible with the presence of the aforementioned constraints. By virtue of the *apeiron* it carries, being is not just an individuated being but it is also a pair formed by an individuated being and nature. Through this remnant of nature, it communicates with the world and with other individuated beings, discovering meanings of which it doesn't know not whether they are a priori or a posteriori. The discovery of these meanings is a posteriori since an operation of individuation is needed for them to appear; the individuated being cannot accomplish this alone. In fact, copresence with some other being is necessary for individuation – as this is the origin and the environment by which meaning manifests itself. But such manifestation of meaning also presupposes a real a priori: the inherence to the subject of that power of nature, a remnant of the original, pre-individual phase of being. The individualized being carries with it an absolute origin.

The term "individualization", initially used in relation to biological life in the sense of a "perpetual genesis", must then be extended to technology and its objects since they, like the living being, presuppose for their functioning an "associated milieu". Hence, they must be thought of and viewed in close and inseparable relation to their environment, with which they form an indissoluble pair. In this way, Simondon, a philosopher of technology and an expert about techniques and their history, believes on the substantial convergence of biology and technology and, after extending to the latter the aspects that characterize the living organism in its relation to the environment, takes Wiener's cybernetics as an interpretive key. Referring to Wiener's perspective, for Simondon, it is not only suitable but also necessary to understand that the metastable system that is the person is the result of continuous processes of complete positive feedback not only between the remote and near past, the present and the future but also between perception and imagination, between constraints and opportunities, between sense of reality and sense of possibility. In fact, Simondon understands and defines metastability as a supersaturated state rich in potential that he, too, like Wiener, borrows from thermodynamics to lead us to the idea of a "pre-individual" as the primordial condition of reality, of which, as he sees it, only the quantum wave-corpuscle duality provides the index since it refers back to the "more than one" – to the condition of possibility that precedes all effectual individuation.

This pre-individual state is always characterized by a constitutive disequilibrium, by a series of "disparate" potentials tending towards the resolution of their conflict in a new dimension. Thus, Simondon regards the process of individuation as a true act of creation, i.e., the invention of a dimension suitable for resolving a previous state of tension.

In short, any theory of form must be integrated through considerations of polarity, movement, co-existence and tension between opposites that gives rise to that process of continuous interaction and positive feedback between the constraints of effectuality and the broad spectrum of opportunities that they nonetheless make available. By virtue of this, perception, like any process of individuation, cannot consist in a mere emergence of the formal principle but in a true invention of it. Perception, from this point of view, means inventing a system of stability capable of holding together the incompatible potentials of a system in a metastable state. The example that recurs most often in Simondon is that of binocular vision:

> there is desperation when two twin ansembles that are not completely super-posable, such as the left retinal image and the right retinal image, are grasped together as a system, allowing for the formation of a single assemble at the higher degree that integrates all their elements due to a new dimension f(or example, in the case of vision, the layering of depth of field).
>
> (Simondon, 2005, p. 44, my transl.)

This is a true individuation, that is, an invention of forms which constitutes a new field (or three-dimensional image, in the case of binocular vision) from a previous state of potential tension. The example of stereoscopic vision particularly clearly shows how the perceptual mechanism is a mobile and creative process capable of bringing into existence a new (present) dimension from a (pre-individual) field that is constituted as a condition of possibility for its own genesis.

By virtue of this fundamental characteristic:

> The living being resolves problems, not just by adapting, i.e., by modifying its relation to the milieu (like a machine is capable of doing), but by modify-ing itself, by inventing new internal structures, and by completely introducing itself into the axiomatic of vital problems. The living individual is a system of individuation, an individuating system, and the system that is in the midst of undergoing the process of individuating; internal resonance and the translation of self-relation into information take place in this system of the living being.
>
> (Simondon, 2005, p. 7, my transl.)

This is something that is emphasized in particular on the previously cited pages by Stefano Carta in this twofold direction:

- First, regarding the inner universe of the person and the developmental pro-cesses by which it is characterized.
- Secondly, in terms of the relationship between the individual and the environment.

Regarding the first question, it is pointed out that Jung's ingenious approach is not the interpretive one but one based on amplifications, which can only be multi-ple. This is demonstrated by the fact that for him, the Ego is a means and not an end for a process in which becoming myself is the necessary path to becoming another. This explains the significance of Jung's idea of the two moments of the analytic process – a "first" part devoted to the Ego and a "second" part in which the Ego is called upon to step back – or of the existence of interpretation and amplification.

In the first part of an analysis (but this *should not* be interpreted diachronically since the second part is always embedded in the first), the protagonists are, in fact, the Ego itself, the Persona and the Shadow. At this preliminary stage, the analysis of Ego-related contents would aim at the coalescence of an Ego to allow the Ego to transform and progressively integrate the non-Ego (the unrepressed unconscious).

In the second part of the analytic process, the Ego (assuming it ever formed) must withdraw. This is an aspect of the psychotherapeutic process completely neglected by all psychotherapies, with their pseudo-medical idea of psychotherapy as something that is supposed to cure someone of his or her "defects". Centered exclusively on the Ego and its personal unconscious, all alternatives to analytical psychology seem to look at the present only in reference to a causal past and not at the past and present as movements towards a creative future.

In relation to the second of the two aspects referred to, Carta rightly points out that while for the animal, the environment is a natural place, for the individual, it becomes a *world*, a cultural milieu. In this case, therefore, the motivation inherent in the individual soul, the *individual's subjective experience*, must also include the world in which we humans are involved.

The author reminds us, in this regard, that the situation in contemporary biology is not exactly that of Darwin's time, and there is a correction to be made to evolutionary theory. Introducing the first and most general principle of this correction is Lewontin, according to whom:

> just as there can be no organism without an environment, so there can be no environment without an organism. There is confusion between the correct statement that there is a physical world outside an organism that would continue to exist in the absence of the species and the incorrect statement that environments exist without species.
>
> (Simondon, 2020, p. 48, my transl.)

As Carta reminds us, von Uexküll (1962) also argues that the organism chooses within the general environment the stimuli that are specific to itself and turns its relations to certain characters of the things around it, understanding them in a network that leads to its existence. Its stated goal is explicit: to definitively challenge an anthropocentric prejudice, the idea that the various animal species, jellyfish and cats, earthworms and hedgehogs, live in a sense-motor space identical to our own, as if our modes of meaning and action constitute the reference point for the life of any organism. Through a continuous work of investigation and popularization, Uexküll describes how each life form carves out its environment according to the perceptual structures and conformation that distinguish it: for the dog, space has first and foremost an olfactory organization that structures its environment into territories in which to leave odorous traces; the places flown over by the fly are affected by the particular morphology of the eyes composed of thousands of elements, each with its own lens. A stimulus to be such must not only produce itself but must also be felt, that is, it presupposes the interest of the living person; thus, it does not come from the object but from the living person's demand. Of all the richness of which a given environment is made up, as a bestower of potentially unlimited perturbations, the animal considers only a few signals. What we call "environment" thus represents a selection of part of the entire geographical sphere that only humans can perceive. What the environment offers to the living is a function of the demand itself.

In this systemic framework, to summarize:

1. The organism determines which parts of the environment will be put together to create its specific environment.
2. The organism actively *constructs* its own world, its own environment.
3. This represents a constant and active process of altering the world to sustain the process of life. The simplest example is that every living organism consumes and produces.
4. The organism can constantly modulate and adjust the statistical properties of the environment over time. This property shows the inherent intelligence of life.
5. Each organism selects and interprets in a peculiar way the physical signals it perceives. It is the arrangement of the organism that determines the existence of one specific world and not another. This property means that not only we humans but all biological life also has a dispositional nature and that every species on the planet inhabits a partially or totally different world (Lewontin, 2022, cited in Yong, 2022).

Every human co-evolutionary niche is also a *cultural* niche, so this is not just a biological description but what Laland et al. (2000) call an "eco-cognitive perspective".

For these reasons, Carta rightly argues that both a nonspecific form of environmental plasticity and a rigid genetic predetermination are abstractions. Looking from a complementary perspective, both the specific, "unique" individual and the environment are inherited (predetermined by, or rather, *through* evolutionary laws), unique and specific. That is why he believes it might be fruitful to imagine the function of archetypes *as being something in-between the individual and his or her environment.*

This is an extremely important point on which we need to dwell in order to emphasize, once again, two different but closely related aspects with significant mutual implications. The first concerns the relationship between humans and their environment as proposed by models of the brain based on quantum field theory; the second relates to the reliability of oppositional pairs, such as those of internal/external and inside/outside.

Regarding the first question, according to the model of the brain inspired by quantum field theory, the relationship between our brain processes and our world is a constant dynamic process of doubling, in which the action observed and the action performed are structurally equivalent so that everything that seems static and "substantial" (the dissipative brain, its objects as "things") actually emerges as an effect of equivalences from this dynamic process of mutual and co-evolutionary mirroring. It is, therefore, important to summarize its fundamental aspects.

It was Ricciardi and Umezawa who formulated, in 1967, a quantum model of the brain in which the external stimulus, perceived by the brain, is assumed to be responsible for spontaneous symmetry breaking. This is a process of second-order phase transition that, upon the change of a critical internal parameter, following an input from outside, causes the whole system to move from one state to another extremely quickly, with a radical energetic reorganization that allows the appearance of a completely new order, endowed with less symmetry and, therefore, more organization. What occurs as a result of this process is a transition from one less structured and homogeneous phase to another more structured and less homogeneous phase, with the system compensating for the constraints of the new energetic ordering in the form of internal correlations and the system compensating for the constraints of the new energetic ordering in the form of long-range correlations related to some extent to its new internal organization. It is called spontaneous because any dynamic regime that is compatible with the internal state of the brain is allowed, and the choice among possible states is made on the basis of a myriad of conditions.

For this to occur, as Goldstone's theorem demonstrates, the existence of a particle is necessary, which is given the name Nambu-Goldstone quantum (NG), associated with the wavelike nature of the fields, whose role is that of a messenger, or carrier, responsible for propagating the ordering information between the elementary components. This NG correlation quantum is a real particle, observed by the same techniques by which other particles are also observed (division techniques or "scattering", in which a "probe" particle, or projectile, is collided with the particle to be observed, called the target, from whose properties the effects produced by the collision are traced).

When we say that in the state of the system (we usually refer to the lowest-energy state, called the fundamental or vacuum state), NG quanta are condensed, we mean that ordered structures are observed in that state. The phenomenon of condensation of NG quanta thus involves the formation of configurations in which the elementary components are correlated over large distances. The phenomenon of condensation involves a change in scale, in that, as we have seen, we move from the microscopic dimensions of the interactions between the elementary components to the mesoscopic and/or macroscopic dimensions of the ordered domains. Thus, ordered systems are macroscopic quantum systems (Anderson, 1984; Umezawa, 1993; Vitiello, 2001) and, as such, manifest classical behavior. The "classical" properties they possess and manifest by virtue of their own organization are not derivable except by recourse to quantum dynamics, which makes it possible the mechanism of symmetry breaking.

Ricciardi and Umezawa's model fits within the quantum field theory (QFT) scenario. The external stimulus to which the brain is subjected induces a spontaneous breaking of symmetry. The endogenous dynamics of the brain, then, generates the long-range NG correlation quanta predicted by Goldstone's theorem; what follows is the correlation quanta condensation in the fundamental states. According to Ricciardi and Umezawa's model, this is the mechanism that presides over memory.

For simplicity's sake, their model did not consider the fact that the brain is a system in continuous, ineradicable interaction with the environment. This "approximation" is a severe limit since the brain is an inherently *open* system to the world around it, and to close it off means to eliminate all functionality, as medicine, neuroscience and epigenetics observe and affirm. This is why, from 1995 (Vitiello, 1995, 1997, pp. 171–198; Pessa & Vitiello, 1999, p. 339; Alfinito & Vitiello, 2000, pp. 853–868; Pessa & Vitiello, 2004, pp. 841–858) perfected the model by extending it to dissipative dynamics in the context of quantum field theory. Vitiello refers to the results of observations obtained in the laboratory by the American biologist and neuroscientist Walter Jackson Freeman (Freeman, 2004a, 2004b, 2005a, 2005b, 2006), which highlight the property of the brain to accumulate experience and build knowledge, that is, to learn to have "maximum grip" on the world. To this end, copying – i.e., pure mirroring – is not enough, as a creative and productive operation is needed, involving the possible, and not just what simply happens.

This model, the result of a collaboration that began in 2005 between Freeman and Vitiello (Freeman & Vitiello, 2005; pp. 1–9; 2006, pp. 93–118; 2008, pp. 1–17; 2016), fits within the scenario of quantum many-body field theory, in which neurons and other cells, unlike other quantum models of the brain, are not considered as quantum components. It predicts that the external stimulus to which the brain is subjected induces spontaneous symmetry breaking, yet the orderly structure that goes into formation depends on the *internal* dynamics of the brain. It is precisely the prevalence of an inner field for "decoding" signals that entails the possibility that a certain memory will be evoked by stimuli completely different from those that induced its storage and under conditions that are partly or entirely different from those in which the person was when the memory was stored.

The aspect of this model that interests us for the purposes of the *vexata quaestio* of the relationship between external and internal is that, as already I pointed out, it sees the brain as an inherently open system, permanently coupled with the external environment and leading to the image of a mind that experiences a continuous series of phase transitions and, thus, new emergent levels. Such coupling is considered "inescapable" since the mathematics at our disposal dictates that in the study of an open system, defined as system A, one must proceed to the "closure" of the system itself by necessarily taking into consideration the environment in which it is immersed. In fact, only in this way the balance of the flows of matter, energy, etc., between system A and the environment, which we can now refer to as system B, is consistently obtained. For the purpose of the energy balance (and the balance of fluxes of any other exchangeable quantities between A and B), system B behaves like the double of system A, in the sense that it behaves exactly like system A as far as fluxes are concerned, provided that its direction is reversed: in fact, what for A is inward, for B is outward and in the opposite direction. Clearly, reversing the direction of flows is equivalent to exchanging A for B, and vice versa. Since, technically, the direction of flow is reversed by changing the sign of the time variable, we can say that B behaves as the copy of A for which the direction of time has been reversed (the copy of A reversed in time). In summary, B is the system that describes the environment with regard to the equilibrium of A's energy flow, and it is also the image of A in the mirror of time (the temporal mirror image of A). In other words, B is the double of A.

To understand this reference to the environment as dual to the brain one must, as Barkow, Cosmides and Tooby (1992) point out, distinguish 'the environment' in the sense of the actual total state of the entire universe – *which, of course, is not caused by an individual's genes or developmental mechanisms* – from 'the environment' in the sense of those particular aspects of the world that are made mentally developmentally relevant by the evolved design of an organism's developmental adaptations. It is this developmentally relevant environment – the environment with which the organism interacts – that, in a significant sense, can be said to be the product of evolution, evolving hand in hand with the organism's organized response to it. The confusion of these two quite distinct meanings of "environment" has obscured the fact that the recurrent organization of the environment contributes to a biological inheritance parallel to that of the genes, acting in parity with them to evolve.

That is why it can be said that A and B, the brain and "its" environment, are intertwined, as entangled particles are in quantum mechanics, inextricably linked, that is, by that sort of "long-distance embrace", as a result of which what happens to one determines what happens to the other, and the former can also transfer its state to the latter, becoming, in fact, identical to it, its twin. Entanglement plays a central role in the dissipative model. It indicates that the relationship, the "dialogue" between the self (the brain) and its double (the environment) cannot be disrupted (disentangled). This entanglement is that between brain activity and mental activity, with no possibility that they can be separated. There are not two entities, not any double level of existence, but one indivisible entity, within which the dialogue between A and B, between the brain and its environment, continually reshapes, with each new perceptual input, the landscape of attractors constructed in previous experiences. The external input is thus transformed into an internal meaning whose reliability is verified on the basis of the appropriateness of the resulting action, which is the premise and content of the concept of "pragmatic information" (Atmanspacher & Scheingraber, 1990, pp. 728–737; Atmanspacher, 2018, pp. 39–44).

Memory is not memory of information; it is memory of meanings.

With regard to the second of the two aspects mentioned earlier, the one concerning the possibility of still referring, on the basis of all that has been considered, to oppositional pairs, such as those of internal/external and inside/outside, it is appropriate to consider the European Landscape Convention, signed in Florence on October 20, 2000, which describes its object as follows: "a certain part of the territory, as perceived by the people, whose character derives from the action of natural and/or human factors and their interrelationships".

We, therefore, speak of territory, hence, of something that exists out there, as perceived by people, thus, as living inside people, in their inner universe. It is then inevitable to ask to what extent this definition is compatible with the sharp distinction between external and internal, between outside and inside, that we are used to.

A convincing answer in this regard is given to us by Fabio Merlini (2022), who acutely investigates and analyzes the complexity of the operation of matching the borders of two contrasting worlds, such as the external reality and our inner universe. He delves into the broad spectrum of possibilities with which this relationship must be interpreted and experienced – with the two extremes made by their mutual estrangement, on the one hand, and by an interaction in virtue of which they instead not only adhere to but also, on the other hand, mutually support and regenerate each other with the whole range of the varied modalities intermediate between them. Thus, a valuable reconstruction of the processes of mediation and incorporation that reinvent the outside through its internalization is concretely offered, giving a sense of how one can go beyond the oppositional outside-inside pair, thus constituting that balance between the outside of perception and the inside of sensation of which landscape is precisely the expression. The ideal point of arrival of this path, the "perfect coincidence between the inner and outer worlds" (Merlini, 2022, p. 59, my transl.), is the result of an action, like the poetic one, that begins not only from the awareness of the presence of these two dimensions but also reach the awareness of the "painful friction" between them – of the incidence of a gap that must be recomposed, something which can be done only by interrupting the apparent and fallacious *continuum* of an experience burdened and conditioned by a suffocating complex of automatisms and routines:

> At the moment when the *continuum* of the everyday is interrupted, when the conditions are given so that a reality untethered from the time of custom or urgency can arise, it is precisely there that interiority and exteriority become the welcoming place of one another. It is an interruption that corresponds to a *feeling otherwise* than the current dissent, to the flow of images, representations, thoughts, projects and purposes that render routine or disrupt our everyday life. A rupture thus creeps into the perception of the world, and a new desire can assert itself through this unseen temporality that opens things up in the direction of another configuration of meaning.
>
> (Merlini, 2022, p. 59, my transl.)

Merlini identifies the linearity of the fracture and its recomposition through the process of adherence, along with all the motivations and actions it presupposes and entails, as the emergence of a "time horizon by virtue of which another sense of the self can surprisingly take shape", as truly remarkable. And it is certainly no coincidence, then, that in describing and analyzing this process and the conditions of its enrichment, that Merlini uses the adjective "hospitable":

> Externality, so exciting and exhilarating, requires a continuous work of internalization. If the richness of outer space is not constantly modulated by a hospitable

inner space, appearance remains mere exteriority, sense incapable of becoming meaning. *Erlebnis* without *Erfahrung*, an experience that does not rise to the understanding of experience.

(Merlini, 2022, p. 67, my transl.)

On the contrary, when this dissymmetry between external reality and the inner universe is overcome and their correspondence realized, the spirit:

gains a vigor that keeps existence in balance, assuring it a gravity that never borders on dryness: a life, at once, posed and joyful.

(Merlini, 2022, my transl.)

The adherence between perception and sensation, between exteriority and interiority through the recomposition and coincidence of their respective edges achieves a "return to self and an enriched self", which is the exact opposite of the "corrosive curiosity" that goes in constant search of an inconclusive "'beyond' that turns on and off the distracted and unfulfilled attention, always in search of new stimuli to feel alive" (Merlini, 2022, p. 9, my transl.). This operation of recomposition, if carried out in the proper way, produces an outcome, by virtue of which:

one becomes greater than oneself. To become greater than oneself is to go beyond the limit established by self-perception as it is delineated through everyday experience. It is a going beyond one's self-image.

(Merlini, 2022, p. 126, my transl.)

To achieve this requires gaining the awareness of the following:

One can "become greater than oneself" when in relationship with the external world the feeling of interiority makes the soul the horizon of a potentially infinite integrative reception. A limitless receptive space – unlike physical space – by virtue of which experiences and knowledge are preserved unlike in collecting and, in general, in those forms of property accumulation where objects are added to one another. The principle here is not the same. It reflects a desire not so much for possession of the world, but for self-appropriation, in the sense of a never-ending work of redefining one's apprehension of the spectacle of the world, which playfully pushes ever further the capacity to retain with oneself what one has witnessed.

(Merlini, 2022, p. 126, my transl.)

How then do we anchor subjectivity to the reality beyond itself? The inner world to the outer world, the inside to the outside? With what perceptual and cognitive tools can one make them fit together and interact? And where to begin to realize this process? These are the questions that cannot be avoided by those who intend to conceive themselves and then conceive.

Clearly, no satisfactory answer to questions of this kind can be found if we remain prisoners of the oppositional pair "inside"/"outside", to which we owe both the problematic nature of the coincidence of the edges between exteriority and interiority, so as to produce the process of incorporation and assimilation of reality that Merlini speaks of and the difficulty of really understanding, for example, the definition of landscape proposed by the 2000 European Convention, which considers it an intermediate space between the material physicality of the territory and the internal universe of symbols.

One way out is offered to us by Lacan, who, in the third seminar, addresses the relationship between linguistic formulations and sensations, questioning, in particular, the relationship that exists between the feeling of relaxation experienced at the end of a day of storm and fatigue and the linguistic formulation in which this sensation is embodied, namely, "the peace of the evening", an internal discourse (or *endophasia*) that nevertheless seems to come from outside. "The peace of the evening" is described by Lacan as an expression that, in the act of signaling the distinction between outside and inside, on the basis of an idea of the border as a sharp demarcation line, blurs its frontier, bringing out rather the idea of the border as a *trait d'union* because it oscillates on the threshold, so much so that we cannot tell whether it comes "from outside or inside" (Merlini, 2022, p. 164, my transl.).

The topological ambiguity of these voices is, according to Lacan, fundamental to making a comparison between mental health and madness since in psychosis, it often happens that their liminal-metaphorical nature is not recognized and that the subject, interpreting them literally, consequently attributes them to a totally external source. The ability to stand on the threshold without crossing it, fully recognizing the function of the boundary on which to stand, would thus be the discriminating factor in distinguishing health from illness.

It is precisely from these reflections that Lacan elaborates the concept of *estimity* to explore some of the most complex and controversial aspects of subjectivity, the unconscious and analytic practice itself. The term *estimity* translates the French *extimité*, a Lacanian neologism that merges the prefix "ex" of *exterieur* with the adjective "intime" to create the oxymoron of an "intimate exteriority" (Lacan, 2008, p. 165, my transl.). While this concept is used in the seventh seminar to denote the "generative phase" of subjectivity that logically precedes the opposition between inside and outside, in the tenth seminar (Lacan, 2007), the analysis of subjectivity is approached by explicitly referring to non-orientable surfaces, such as the Moebius strip.

To understand what happens when we are confronted with surfaces of this kind, it is useful to refer to the three-color woodcut on head wood that Escher dedicated to the Moebius strip in 1963:

> the insect that travels across the surface [. . .] can believe at any moment that there is a face that it has not yet explored, the one that is the reverse of the face it is traveling across. The insect may believe this reverse, although in fact there is

not. [. . .] Without knowing it, it explores the only face there is, and yet, in every moment, there is also a reverse.

Lacan (2007, p. 148, my transl.)

Man, too, according to Lacan, is subject to the same illusion when he does not realize that the self (*moi*) is nothing but the result of a successive series of identifications, a line of fiction, a mirage, which is the basis of the famous Lacanian dictum "I think where I am not, therefore I am where I do not think" (Lacan, 1974, p. 512, my transl.), which highlights the irretrievable gulf that opens up within the Cartesian *cogito* that preached the coincidence of being (*sum*) and thought (*cogito*): if the subject sees itself where it is not and as it is not, the being of the subject, in the act of thinking itself, escapes itself by producing a series of illusory images.

To stem this divide and heal it, it is necessary to overcome the dualism between body and mind, matter and psyche by starting from the reference to affective consciousness that Panksepp and Solms are particularly concerned with and to which that this book also refers. We have seen how, underlying the relationship between the external stimulus and the internal sensation, there is a reaction of a hedonic nature, based on the fundamental role of affectivity, which today is gaining ground in neurobiological research, which considers it the initiation and subsequent developmental stage of cognitive processes as well. This is an important, even decisive, aspect, but it should not make us forget that affects are not only the result of a response to the environment and its inputs, i.e., of a generating process that starts from what is out there, outside, to produce its effects *within ourselves*, in our *inner universe*.

In addition to this function, there is another one, which emerged clearly during the proceedings of the 12th International Neuropsychoanalysis Congress, held in Berlin in June 2011 on the theme of "Dealing with the Body", where Bud Craig, Antonio Damasio, Jaak Panksepp, Vittorio Gallese and Manos Tsakiris, among others, summarized the current state of knowledge regarding how human mental functioning is embodied. In his closing remarks at the conference, Mark Solms pointed out that the speakers had referred to two different aspects of the body, without always distinguishing them with the necessary clarity. In his view, this can give rise to confusion that prevents due consideration of the internal articulation of the body, its splitting between the *external body and the internal body*.

There is, in fact, a first level of the body that hinges on the somatotopic maps of the cortical surface that originate from the sensory receptors on the surface of the body itself. This aspect of body representation corresponds directly to the cortical homunculus. The body representation, however, does not coincide only with the somatosensory cortex; it also includes the projection zones of the other sensory modalities, which consist of topological maps of the different sense organs. It includes the modality-specific subcortical thalamic structures and those of the cranial nerves: these structures connect these terminal sense organs with the cortex. The "body image" originates not only from these modality-specific cortical maps.

This aspect of body representation, corresponding to what we perceive when we look at ourselves externally, for example, in the mirror and think, "This thing is me", "It is my body", is called the "external body" by Solms and Panksepp, who emphasize that it must be supplemented by the various perceptual streams that originate from the projection zones and converge in the associative cortex. The resulting representation is the work of the same brain mechanisms that also represent external objects. *The external body is, therefore, an object that we treat in the same way as all other objects in the reality that surrounds us and in which we are immersed.*

Motor maps also contribute to this external body image since the sensation of possessing a three-dimensional body is determined not only by exteromodal sensory convergence but also, as mentioned, by movement, which produces kinesthetic sensations and may have intrinsic brain emotions on its own. The close relationship between movement and muscle and joint sensations is reflected in the anatomical proximity of the respective cortical areas: the somatosensory and motor projective areas form an integrated functional unit.

There is, however, a fundamental difference between this specific external object, which is represented more deeply and at a lower level in the brain by structures that have their basis not only in the hypothalamus but also in the circumventricular organs, the parabrachial nucleus, the area postrema, the solitary nucleus and the like. These enteroceptive structures not only monitor the state of the body but also actively contribute to ensuring the balance between the internal and external environments, which Cannon explained by introducing that specific biological function he called *homeostasis* (Cannon, 1929).

What is particularly noticeable and to be emphasized is that the brain mechanisms of the internal body function largely automatically, but they also stimulate the external body to meet vital needs in the external world. This complex process is presented by Solms and Panksepp in the following terms:

> It is important to note that an interdependent, hierarchical relationship therefore exists between the two aspects of the body. Considering the evolutionarily ancient roots of visceration, situated as they are more caudally and medially in the brain, there are reasons to believe that cerebral visceration (and hence emotionality) provided a bodily-coherence generating substrate for future brain developments, including the more cognitive domains. However, as some forward-looking scholars have long emphasized, from David Hume to Antonio Damasio, the emotional components are still critically important for the way the cognitive overlay operates.
>
> Furthermore, it is becoming ever more evident that the internal body generates a very different type of consciousness from the consciousness associated with exteroceptive cortex. The interoceptive brainstem, along with diverse emotional networks, generates internal "states" rather than external "objects" of consciousness. [. . .] In other words, the internal body is not represented as an object of perception. Rather it gives rise to a background state of "being"; this

aspect of the body is the *subject* of perception. We may picture this type of consciousness as the neurodynamic page upon which, or from which, exteroceptive experiences are written in higher brain regions.

(Solms & Panksepp, 2012, p. 147)

Panksepp and Solms point out that these "states" of the body-as-subject involve not only varying levels of consciousness but also varying qualities of consciousness, in which affects, rather than representing discrete external events, are experienced as positively and negatively valenced states. Therefore, they are the crucial functions to establish homeostasis within a metastable process through the regulation determined by the continuum delight-distress, or pain-pleasure. As Carta constantly reminds us, this pre-imagistic level, in which affects are the protagonists, is the original level in which consciousness and subjectivity appear. For Panksepp and Solms, whereas the classical sensory modalities represent discrete external (knowledge-generating and objective) *noetic* happenings, affective consciousness represents diffuse internal (automatically evaluative and subjective) *a-noetic* reactions to those happenings. Affectivity is, in this respect, not only a unique experiential modality but it is also an intrinsic property of the brain which is expressed in the emotions.

Therefore, along with Carta's work, we speak of affective consciousness, considered the primary conscious state not only of man but also of mammals in general, as an intrinsic function of the lower regions of the brain, as a dynamic process consisting of a drive of the organism that has its source in a somatic arousal and whose goal is to suppress this state of tension in or through the object. In this process, what Freud called "drives" are to be differentiated from instincts, in that while the latter constitute a preformed and hereditarily transmitted behavior that is relatively fixed and characteristic of the species, drive stimuli take their start from a biological function with an unambiguous and relatively stable purpose, in that they are an expression of the specific historical vicissitudes of the human subject, with the relationships he has woven in his life. Since drives are, as we have seen, a boundary concept and an intermediate space between the psychic and the somatic, they represent the measure and outcome of the activity required of the psyche by its inescapable and problematic connection with the body. The two authors in question refer, in particular, to the essay *Triebe und Triebschicksale* (*Instincts and Their Vicissitudes*), in which Freud speaks of the "drive" as something specific and different from the other physiological stimuli acting on the psyche and outlines its fundamental characters as follows:

We have now obtained the material necessary for distinguishing between essential stimuli and other physiological stimuli that operate on the mind. In the first place, an instinctual stimulus does not arise from the external world but from within the Organism itself. For this reason it operates differently upon the mind and different actions are necessary in order to remove it.

(Freud, 1915, p. 118)

By virtue of the fact that the drive:

since it impinges not from without but from within the organism, no flight can avail against it. A better term for an instinctual stimulus is a "need". What does away with a need is "satisfaction". This can be attained only by an appropriate ("adequate") alteration of the internal source of stimulation.

(Freud, p. 118)

In Freud's opinion:

these stimuli are the signs of an internal world, the evidence of instinctual needs. The perceptual substance of the living organism will thus have found in the efficacy of its muscular activity a basis for distinguishing between an "outside" and an "inside".

(Freud, p. 119)

If we now:

apply ourselves to considering mental life from a *biological* point of view, an instinct appears to us as the concept on the frontier between the mental and somatic, as the psychical representative of the stimuli originating from within the organism and reaching the mind, as a measure of the demand made upon the mind for work in consequences of its connection with the body.

(Freud, pp. 121–122, Freud's italics)

Thus, overcoming the dualism between them.

Solms and Panksepp frame the Freudian contribution within the framework of Endel Tulving's division of consciousness into three forms (Tulving, 2002):

- A-noetic (forms of unreflective experience, which can be affectively intense without being "known" and which might be the inherent characteristic of all mammals).
- Noetic (thought-mediated forms of consciousness related to perception and exteroceptive cognition).
- Autonoetic (abstract forms of perceptions and cognitions, enabling conscious "awareness" and reflection on experience in the "mind's eye" through episodic memories and fantasies).

Solms and Panksepp note that this kind of a scheme can be readily overlaid on some major evolutionary passages of the brain, which roughly correspond to the evolution of (a) upper brainstem (up to the septal area), which permits *a-noetic* phenomenal experiences, (b) lower subcortical ganglia and upper limbic structures, which permit learning and *noetic* consciousness, and (c) higher neocortical functions (including all association cortices). These anatomical and functional systems provide the fundamental substrates for the *autonoetic*, reflexive experiential blends that yield the stream of everyday awareness (Solms & Panksepp, 2012).

This tripartition of consciousness is applied by them to a correct interpretation of Libet's well-known experiments, which record a delay of up to 400 ms between the physiological onset of premotor activation and the voluntary decision to move, a result that is typically interpreted to mean that free will is an illusion; Solms and Panksepp, on the other hand, derive an opposite belief, based on the idea that it shows only that reflexive re-representation of self-initiating a movement occurs somewhat later than the core-self actually initiating it. Solms and Panksepp's opinion is that this confusion is avoided if we use different terms to refer to the different levels of self-experience.

We might, for example, call the re-represented (prefrontal) self of everyday cognition the "declarative" noetic self, and the primary affective (brainstem) state of being might be called the "core" anoetic affective self. The intermediate (posterior cortical) somatosensory-motor self might then be called the "bodily" self. With autonoetic consciousness we can have vast varieties of idiographic selves.

[49]

thus: the core self, synonymous with Freud's "id", is the font of all consciousness; the declarative self, synonymous with Freud's "ego", is unconscious in itself. However, because the ego stabilizes the core consciousness generated by the id, by transforming affects into object representations, and more particularly verbal object re-representations, we ordinarily think of ourselves as being conscious in the latter sense. This obscures the fact that our conscious thinking (and exteroceptive perceiving, which thinking re-represents) is constantly accompanied by low level affects (some kind of residual "free energy" from which cognitive consciousness was constructed during developmental psychogenesis). However, the underlying primary, affective form of consciousness is literally invisible, so we have to translate it into perceptual-verbal imagery before we can "declare" its existence.

The dumb id, in short, knows more than it can admit. Small wonder, therefore, that it is so regularly overlooked in contemporary cognitive science. But the id, unlike the ego, is only dumb in the glossopharyngeal sense. It constitutes the primary stuff from which minds are made; and cognitive science ignores it at its peril. We may safely say, without fear of contradiction, that were it not for the constant presence of affective feeling, conscious perceiving and thinking would either not exist or would gradually decay. This is just as well, because a mind unmotivated (and unguided) by feelings would be a hapless zombie, incapable of managing the basic tasks of life.

(Solms & Panksepp, 2012, p. 168)

The consequences of this aspect, explicitly enunciated by the two authors in the conclusion of their work, are of extraordinary importance for the purposes of both the understanding and the very definition of what we can appropriately call a "polychronic perspective" as an inescapable horizon and indispensable component of the awareness of what we humans are and of the meaning to be attributed today to the cultural heritage left to us by Freud:

> Our goal here was to re-establish a primary-process affective foundation of mind to the higher mental apparatus that is receiving the lion's share of attention in cognitive science and cognitive neuroscience, as well as consciousness and psychoanalytic studies. We chose to frame our argument in classical Freudian psychoanalytic theory, since during the 20th century, perhaps he came closest to the vision we have shared. Although he, in the modern vein, situated consciousness on top of the brain, the weight of evidence now indicates that raw affects arise from the "basement" of the brain. Our argument has been largely restricted to the basement, and we recognize that when it is interfaced with unconscious secondary learning-memory and the resulting affectively energized cognitive thought processes, there will be vast additional complexities to be faced, along with the possibility of many mereological fallacies (part-whole confusions and conflations), as discussed superbly by Bennett and Hacker, in their exceptional 2003 book.[3]

> Of course, primal emotions unfold in relation to individual lives, but they are built into the brain as nomothetic endogenous behavioral and affective resources of the organisms. We have not sought to address how these ancestral powers of the mind percolate through the subsequent idiographic layers of brain-mind emergence. Freud attempted to do that, but future cognitive neuroscience and related neurophenomenological consciousness studies, will need to flesh out those processes, with a full recognition that the bottom-up developmental-epigenetic emergence of minds needs to provide a solid foundation for the vast complexities of the automatized top-down regulations and effortful conscious mental controls that a mature (fully-constructed) mental apparatus permits and promotes.

> (Solms & Panksepp, 2012, pp. 171–172)

What we have called the "polychronic perspective" thus consists of, as we have already had occasion to point out, the anchoring and reference to the remote past, which characterize the complexity of the human person. This is the result not only of the archetypes and the cultural inheritance of the generations that historically preceded us but also of the affectivity and emotions which constitute the most powerful reactive mechanism we have because they are the most ancestrally ancient, the one that roots our cognitive mechanism and our behaviors in relationships with the environment characterized by feelings of well-being or discomfort, of pleasure, tranquility, joy and euphoria or, on the contrary, of anger, fear, panic, anxiety and depression.

Figure 11.1 represents a schematic presentation, which summarizes Solms and Panksepp's view of the nested overlapping bottom-up/top-down hierarchies that regulate the brainmind activity. This is a further description of the Moebius strip that Carta discusses throughout his two books and that he summarizes in the last chapter of this second volume. Within Panksepp's motivational architecture, the primary motivational systems that ignite and regulate the whole process are his seven primary affects, those with positive valence (seeking, pleasure, caring and play) and those with the negative ones (anger, fear and panic/pain).

In this approach, the authors themselves do not fail to point out:

> the brain is not merely an information-processing device but also a sentient, intentional being. Our animal behaviors are not "just" behaviors; in their primal affective forms they embody ancient mental processes that we share, at the very least, with all other mammals.
>
> (Solms & Panksepp, 2012, p. 171)

The polychronic perspective that sees the person as the result of a metastable balance between the present and a past rooted as far back as the earliest stages of man's natural evolution could not be presented in sharper and clearer terms, presenting subcortical energies as that which provide the basis for the epigenetic construction of the higher, perceptual and non-perceptual forms of consciousness. From this perspective, perceptual experiences, as Carta also argues, were initially affective, belonging to primary processes and originating in the brainstem; they

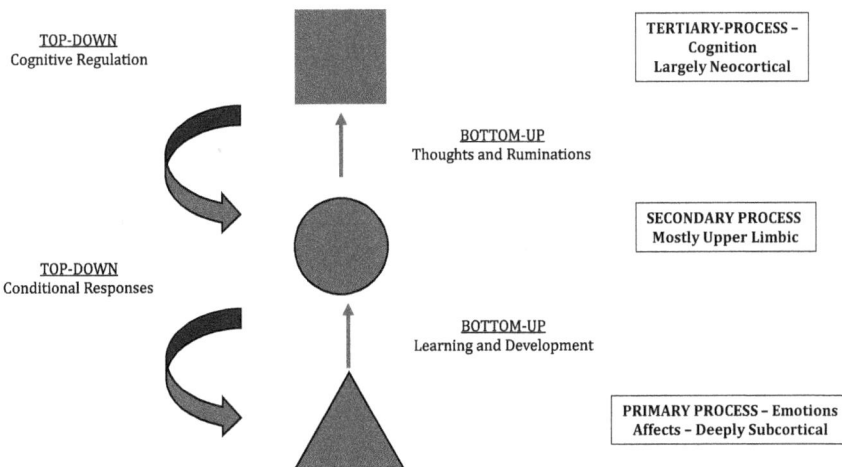

TWO-WAY CIRCULAR CAUSATION OF NESTED BRAIN-MIND HIERARCHIES

Figure 11.1 A schematic presentation of the overlapping hierarchies of brain functions.

then proved capable of being processed through secondary learning and mnemonic processes and evolving into the tertiary cognition forms of consciousness.

This recovery of the fundamental importance of non-self-reflective, representational (noetic) consciousness is in total agreement with the conclusions Jung and Pauli reached in discussing the persistent presence of archetypes and archetypal ideas and speaking of the principle of synchronicity. In their common opinion, it would be impossible to understand and explain the incidence in the present of contents from an unidentified, deeper, wholly timeless stratum by starting from the identification of consciousness with cognition and assuming the idea that consciousness is always and only cognitive and that it cannot, consequently, have anything to do with the functions of the deeper regions of the brain that generate physiological changes and emotional-instinctive behaviors since these deep substrates are non-cognitive and must, for this reason, be intimately unconscious.

It is only at the neocortical level that we find the autonoetic emotional experiences corresponding to "our ability to travel through time and be able to look forward and backward in our minds" (Panksepp & Biven, 2012, p. 41).

These are the emotions related to reflections on us in the world, on ideals, and therefore, are more sensitive to culture and society than other knowledge.

Therefore, the *process of individuation* presents itself as a true act of creation, a continuous invention resulting from a development that, if well conducted and carried out, is capable of guaranteeing ever new and further structuring, giving rise to the realization of a part of those possibilities inherent in the coupling between the indeterminate and pre-individual plane, laden with potentials, that each person inherits from the past, even the distant past, in the form of archetypes, and the present of his specific individuality.

We can, therefore, conclude this analysis devoted to the intermediate space between inside and outside, between outside and inside, which overcomes the traditional oppositional pair in which they are considered mutually exclusive extremes, with the very significant reference to precisely this duplicity of the body, to this amphibious character of the body, which consists in its appearing as *intrinsically double* within itself, in that it is, at the same time, *subject and object*, subject springing from the object and taking on the latter as the "target" of its gaze and description. The resulting image, precisely by virtue of the placement of personal identity no longer solely and wholly on the side of one of the two components at play, in this case, the observing subject, but, as noted earlier, in the intermediate space and interface between them, does not, however, appear to be the product of a simple communication and exchange of information, or of a unidirectional process of knowledge, but rather becomes the result of a kind of κοινωνία, which is union and participation, and thus mutual involvement. This is the reason why the body cannot be reduced to a physicalistic explanation: being something that in itself translates the intrinsically conscious/intentional character of non-conceptual perceptual-motor representations, it cannot be adequately understood without taking into account the reflective dimension of which it is an expression, of its exhibiting, intrinsically, the properties of bodily consciousness, both as a manifestation of the relation between body and world, which becomes an intentional object in itself, and as a manifestation of the anomalous position that the perceptual and sense-motor body entertains with respect to itself.

The mind is also intrinsically dual; otherwise, it could not be accorded that ability to "reflect on itself", which is inherent in the moment when self-consciousness is born. To arrive at this result requires two different processes, which it is good to keep distinct:

- The ascent from a level-object to a meta-level, a second-order thought process that constitutes an appropriate, more powerful extension of the starting stage, so as to make conscious the information related to the first-order experience;
- The ability to reflect on one's own thoughts, that is, to consciously experience a thought by treating it as if it were the object of another. We are not only conscious of the stimuli of our environment, we are also conscious of ourselves, and this is the core of what Tulving, as we have seen, calls "autonoetic consciousness", a state of metacognitive awareness, a version of higher-order consciousness, specifically, a thought about oneself.

The personal identity of each individual, therefore, depends not only on what we might call "the privileged link", the one that directly feeds each particular brain, but also on the private identity of the other individuals with whom he or she interacts. Detachment from myself is fully manifested when I recognize in the other, in the interlocutor with whom I confront and dialogue, another self. Thus, this is how the gap – "being other than myself" that characterizes my way of being in the world – manifests itself. Intersubjectivity, the *between*, constitutes, once again, the real stakes: it is no coincidence that today, in the society of networks and socials, rather than collective intelligence, we tend to speak, along with Derrick De Kerckhove, of "connective intelligence" (De Kerckhove, 1998, 2001).

This type of intelligence is, according to his definition, a form of connection and collaboration between different individual and collective subjects that is the result of a sharing between them built on the basis of dialogic exchange. The distinguishing feature of this mode of thinking, which differentiates it from those that fall under "collective intelligence", is that, unlike what generally occurs in the latter, within connective intelligence, each individual or group maintains its own specific identity while within a highly articulated and extensive structure of connections. We are thus faced with a process of externalization of *intelligence*, which becomes a process supported and unveiled by the network.

Therefore, if on the basis of what has been said earlier we agree on the fundamental role of affects (which today, as we have seen, is gaining momentum in neurobiological research) – that is, their role in maintaining dynamic homeostasis – it follows that the process of individuation itself is regulated by affect and, as Carta maintains quoting Jung, by and through the experience of the *numinosum*. Affects are biologically and functionally endogenous and express the interior of the organism, not just react to external stimuli.

Let us now return, on the basis of this conclusion, to the division of consciousness into three forms, which Solms and Panksepp borrow from Tulving, and, in particular, to affective, "a-noetic" consciousness – the first evolutionary step in animal subjectivity. It has been defined as "unthinking forms of experience, which may be affectively intense without being 'known'." (Solms & Panksepp, 2012, p. 14).

This is a significant definition, which rightly presents it as the first evolutionary step of animal subjectivity, a form of non-thinking experience, which can be affectively intense without being known and which, for this very reason, raises the crucial question of the importance of the transition from the known to the understood, which is one of the still relevant aspects of Hegelian thought, of which it is one of the strong points.

According to the German philosopher, "what is *known* is not therefore already *familiar*" (Hegel, 2010, p. 11). Indeed, precisely what is known is the least known, and one must know how to see in order to know it. To know how to see, however, is to learn, and to learn, in turn, is, precisely, to detach oneself from the known and its prejudices.

The task of philosophy is to teach how to see in this way, that is, in the sense of the transition from the known to the understood, which is anything but peaceful and simple. The specific individual, in fact, quickly appropriates, "as degrees of a path already traced and paved" (Hegel, 1960, p. 22, my transl.), the work of entire generations of men because it has already been metabolized into *culture* and *language*. In this way, thinking has become for man more than a second nature – one now thinks as one digests, with the same *unconscious automatism*, with the same *instinctiveness* – so that if one wants to understand the meaning of the world and assimilate it again, one must bring to light those contents that are already unconsciously present, shed a new light on them, make them the object of reflection and understanding and reappropriate them in the form of thought that is no longer unreflective but conscious.

The same concept is expressed in an insightful form and with a series of very plastic and effective images, by the best known of the Russian formalists, Viktor Shklovsky, who, however, attributes to art, and, in particular, to literature, the task that Hegel assigned to philosophy. In his opinion, in fact:

> the writer, by interweaving, *washes the world*. The world only becomes confused and dusty. The writer, with the plot, *scrubs the mirror of consciousness*.
> (Shklovsky, 1984, p. 32)

The modalities of this operation of recovering the transparency and brilliance of reality are surely the subject of the most revolutionary text Shklovsky wrote, a landmark work of the entire *Opojaz* movement, a name referring to the *Obščestvo izučenija poetičeskogo jazyka* (Society for the Study of Poetic Language), where Russian theorists, adherents of this group, usually met. It was the article *Iskusstvo*

kak priëm (Art as a procedure), from 1917, in which the laws of prosaic language
and those of poetic language were enucleated:

> If we set out to reflect on the general laws of perception, we see that as they
> become habitual, actions become mechanical. Thus, for example, all our experi-
> ences pass into the realm of the "unconsciously automatic"; if one remembers
> the sensation he felt holding a pen for the first time or speaking for the first time
> in a foreign language, and compares this sensation with the one he feels now,
> repeating the action for the ten-thousandth time, he will agree with us. With
> the process of automation we also explain the laws of our prosaic language,
> with its unfinished sentences and half-said words. It is a process whose ideal
> expression is algebra, in which objects are replaced by symbols. In the rapidity
> of practical language, words are not uttered all the way through, and the first
> sounds of the word barely appear in consciousness. This property of thought not
> only suggested the way of algebra, but also the choice of symbols (the letters,
> specifically the initials). With this algebraic method, objects are considered in
> their number and volume, but they are not seen: we know them only by their
> first features.
>   The object passes by us as packed. We know what it is by the place it occu-
> pies, but we see only its surface. By the influence of such perception, the object
> withers away, at first only as perception, but then also in its reproduction. . . .
> And here it is that to restore the sense of life, to "feel" objects, to make stone
> out of stone, there exists what is called art. The purpose of art is to convey the
> impression of the object, as "vision" and not as "recognition": procedure of art
> is the procedure of the *estrangement* (*ostranenie*) of objects and the procedure
> of the obscure form, which increases the difficulty and duration of perception,
> since the perceptual process, in art, is an end in itself and must be prolonged;
> *art is a way of "feeling" the becoming of the object, while the "already accom-
> plished" has no importance in art.*
>
>   (Shklovsky, 1981, p. 82, my italics and transl.)

These dazzling metaphorical short-circuits of Shklovsky's help us to understand why and in what sense for Jung the libido expresses itself through an endless
process of transformations of itself and, in so doing, in the psychological realm,
proceeds from one symbol to another symbol, from one image to another image
in what seems to be an endless, or indefinite, process of self-revelation. Through
these processes of symbolization and metaphorization, the libido thus stands as
a *tertium comparationis* between different states and organizations, whose transformations are governed by what Jung called the principle of equivalence. In all
that exists, therefore, the vicissitudes of libido are virtually infinite, just as they
are in the ontological realm of psychology. Indeed, as Carta forcefully points out,
linking back to what he rightly considers one of the most effective distinguishing
features of the Jungian approach, in the course of its transmigrations, the libido is

transformed from one motivational system to another, progressing or regressing, becoming conscious or unconscious, expressing itself through one typological attitude or the other, or organizing a particular phase of the individual's life. It is, therefore, subject to continuous transformations from the known to the understood, which, when they take accomplished forms, are symbolic in character. Thus, the energetic value expressed by a given motivation can be transformed into a *different but equivalent* motivation. This process is made possible by what Jung calls the *transcendent function*, to which, for this very reason, the author devotes special attention.

The general framework that is thus proposed is the key to deepening and adequately understanding the concept of co-evolution, based on a process, that of psychization, which, for Jung, involves the assimilation of the biological "instinct" (rooted in the structure of the body and autonomic, peripheral and central nervous systems) to the individual psychic environment. The immediate determinant is, therefore, not the ectopsychic instinct but the structure resulting from the interaction between the instinct and the psychic situation of the moment, that is, a modified instinct. This is an important clarification, as it allows for a significant dislocation of the archetypes, making it something that is located not already in the mind of the organism, or in the body-mind, but in the interface between the latter and its double, that is, the environment at each of the levels of articulation and complexity discussed earlier. The general framework of analytical psychology thus connects in a way that is anything but forced with current developments in the model of the brain and its relationship to "its" environment on the basis of reference to quantum field theory, in that archetypes can be presented not only as a crucial source of symbolic images but also as emergent structures resulting from an evolutionary interaction between genes and environment that is unique to each person.

A final point worth emphasizing about the relationship between the knowing subject and external reality is that the work of observation and exploration that is carried out on the latter in order to "get a grip" on external reality requires a strategy of looking, new eyes, as is increasingly emphasized not only by research in the field of neuroscience but also by physicists.

Carlo Rovelli, for example, points out that our brain:

> processes an image of what it *predicts* the eyes should see. [. . .] This information is sent from the brain toward the eyes through intermediate states. If a discrepancy is detected between what the brain expects and the light that reaches the eyes, *only* then do the neural circuits send signals toward the brain.
>
> (Rovelli, 2020, p. 190, my transl.)

It is thus reaffirmed that it is not the image of the observed environment that travels from the eyes to the brain but only the information relating to any discrepancies, to deviations, from what the brain expects. What is relevant, therefore, for the ability to see, is precisely the gap, a tool, at the same time, of *exploration* and *control*, of the connection between the sense of possibility and the sense of reality, between what is expected and predicted and what actually occurs, a gap that eventually brings out a possible other, operating, in continuous tension with past experience and lived experience, and that marks a distance by virtue of which one always remains open to the other and the elsewhere.

The gaze that discovers, the gaze that cares, is not the direct gaze, which claims to go straight to things, but the "gaze through", which is characterized by that "*dia*", which, in Greek, expresses both the gap and the crossing.

The reason why is explained by the philosopher, mathematician and theologian Pavel Florensky in his reflections on how he believes Plato's allegory of the cave should be interpreted. Florensky disagrees with the usual meaning attributed to it, a metaphor that refers to the prisoner's effort to emerge from the place of self-enclosed darkness in which things lose their contours into the clear light of the sun and transcendent Truth, in accordance with a vision whereby the violent ascent towards the light is countered by the risk of perceiving the abyss of the unknown. He proposes an alternative reading, based on the idea that the invisible and salvation can only be accessed by placing oneself in an *intermediate space* between the darkness and opacity of the cave and the full light that blinds, a space in which darkness and light converge, generating that primordial penumbra in which truth is revealed to an extent that corresponds to the human capacities of the moment. If one is properly initiated and equipped, the cavern, thus understood, is first and foremost the place of passage from *outside* to *inside*, from external reality to the inner universe, the space that represents the reality of symbol and human inhabiting and knowing, the threshold that encompasses, connects and unites the two worlds in which our lives unfold, that of the visible and solid anchorage to the earth and that of the invisible and the gaze turned towards heaven.

The allegory of the cave, in his view, thus constitutes the account of the process by which man attempts to connect these two worlds through a transitive capacity that takes place in the boundary space between them, which, in order to be adequately perceived, requires an articulation between light and shadow, between the visible and the invisible that Florensky expresses with the term *skvoznoj*, a concept of inner luminosity that F. Malcovati (1983) correctly renders with "translucency".

Translucency, or that degree of transparency of a body that allows one to distinguish approximately the shape, but not the contours, of an object placed behind it, is the typical condition of boundary realities, i.e., of everything that, while foreign to consciousness, is nonetheless capable of entering into some kind of relationship with it, demonstrated by the fact that it is nonetheless capable of resonating and producing meanings within it, although, of course, not in an immediate way, by virtue of an always available transparency, but through prolonged work of excavation and deepening. In order to access the invisible, one must rely on the symbol and its residue of irreducible opacity and not think of relying on the transparency of the sign: that is why translucency implies a "seeing through" a medium and not in a direct way free of barriers and waste.

Moving into the intermediate space, one can take the *limes*, the way, the road, the path, each of which always has an end point and directs the view towards the conclusion of each individual stage of the journey, which, however, simultaneously also represents a *limen*, a threshold, an entrance, the beginning of a new phase, as is evident from the dual meaning of the boundary to which, not surprisingly, attention has already been drawn.

*Silvano Tagliagambe is Professor Emeritus of Philosophy of Science at the University of Sassari, Italy. A physicist and a philosopher, he previously taught at the universities of Pisa, Cagliari, "Sapienza" University of Rome and Sassari, Italy.

Notes

1　Pauli, W. (1948/2006). *Hintergrundsphysik* (trans *Psiche e natura*). Milano: Adelphi.
2　Jung (1952), but on the topic, see, in particular, the research of Tagliagambe & Malinconico, 2018.
3　The book by M.R. Bennett e P.M.S. Hacker del 2003 to which the authors refer: *Philosophical Foundations of Neuroscie*nce. Malden, MA: Blackwell.

References

Alfinito, E., Vitiello, G. (2000). Formation and lifetime of memory domains in the dissipative quantum model of brain. *International Journal of Modern Physics*, B14, 853–868; Erratum-Ibid. B14, p. 1613.
Anderson, P.W. (1984). *Basic Notions of Condensed Matter Physics.* Menlo Park: Benjamin.
Atmanspacher, H. (2018). Walter Freeman – I did it my way. *Journal of Consciousness Studies*, 25, 39–44.
Atmanspacher, H., Scheingraber, H. (1990). Pragmatic information and dynamical instabilities in multi-mode continuous-wave laser systems. *Canadian Journal of Physics*, 68, 728–737.
Barkow, J., Cosmides, L., Tooby, J. (eds) (1992). *The Adapted Mind: Evolutionary Psychology and the Generation of Culture.* Oxford, New York, Toronto: Oxford University Press.
Cacciari, M. (2023). *Metafisica Concreta.* Milano: Adelphi.
Cannon, W.B. (1929/1932). Organization for physiological homeostasis. *Physiological Reviews*, 9, 399–427. ID. *The Wisdom of the Body.* New York: W.W. Norton & CO.
Ceruti, M. (2018). *Il Tempo della Complessita.* Milano: Raffaello Cortina.
De Kerckhove, D. (1998). *Connected Intelligence: The Arrival of the Web Society* (ed Wade Rowland). London: Kogan Page.
De Kerckhove, D. (2001). *The Architecture of Intelligence.* Basel-Boston: Birkhäuser.
Freeman, W.J. (2004a). Origin, structure, and role of background EEG activity, Part 1, Phase. *Clinical Neurophysiology*, 115, 2077–2088.
Freeman, W.J. (2004b). Origin, structure, and role of background EEG activity, Part 2, Amplitude. *Clinical Neurophysiology*, 115, 2089–2107.
Freeman, W.J. (2005a). Origin, structure, and role of background EEG activity, Part 3, Neural frame classification. *Clinical Neurophysiology*, 116, 1117–1129.
Freeman, W.J. (2005b). Volume transmission, and self-organization in brain dynamics. *Journal of Integrative Neuroscience*, 4(4), 407–421.
Freeman, W.J. (2006). Origin, structure, and role of background EEG activity, Part 4, Neural frame simulation. *Clinical Neurophysiology*, 117, 572–589.
Freeman, W.J., Vitiello, G. (2005). Nonlinear brain dynamics and many-body field dynamics. *Electromagnetic Biology and Medicine*, 24, 1–9.
Freeman, W.J., Vitiello, G. (2006). Nonlinear brain dynamics as macroscopic manifestation of underlying many-body field dynamics. *Physics of Life Review*, 3, 93–118.

Freeman, W.J., Vitiello, G. (2008). Dissipation and spontaneous symmetry breaking in brain dynamics. *Journal of Physics A: Mathematical and Theoretical*, 41, 1–17.

Freeman, W.J., Vitiello, G. (2016). Matter and mind are entangled in two streams of images that guide behavior and inform the subject through awareness. *Mind and Matter*, 14(1).

Freud, S. (1915/1957). Triebe Und Triebschicksale (Pulsioni e Loro Destini). Instincts and Their Vicissitudes. In: *The Complete Works of Sigmund Freud*. London: Hogart Press.

Hegel, G.W.F. (1960). *Fenomenologia Dello Spirito*, vol. I. Firenze: la Nuova Italia.

Hegel, G.W.F. (2010). *The Science of Logic* (trans & ed George Di Giovanni). Cambridge: Cambridge University Press, p. 11.

Humphrey, N. (2006). *Seeing Red: A Study in Consciousness (Mind/Brain/Behavior Initiative)*. Cambridge, MA: Belknap Press of Harvard University Press.

Jung, C.G. (1952). Synchronicity: An Acausal Connecting Principle. In: *The Collected Works of C.G. Jung*, vol. 8. London, New York, NY: Routledge.

Lacan, J. (1974). *Scritti*, vol. 2. Torino: Einaudi, p. 512.

Lacan, J. (2007). *Il Seminario. Libro X. L'angoscia*. Torino: Einaudi.

Lacan, J. (2008). *Il Seminario. Libro VII. L'etica della Psicoanalisi* (2a ed.). Torino: Einaudi, p. 165.

Laland, K.N., Odling-Smee, F.J., Feldman, M.W. (2000). Niche construction, biological evolution, and cultural change. *Behavioral and Brain Sciences*, 23(1), 131–175.

Lewontin, R. (2022). *The Triple Helix. Gene, Organism and Environment*. Cambridge, London: Harvard University Press.

Malcovati, F. (1983). *Vjačeslav Ivanov: Estetica e Filosofia*. Firenze: la Nuova Italia.

Merlini, F. (2022). *Ritornare in Sé. L'interiorità Smarrita e L'infinita Distrazione*. Torino: Aragn.

Panksepp, J., Biven, L. (2012). *The Archeology of Mind. Neuroevolutionary Origins of Human Emotions*. New York: W.W. Norton & Company.

Pessa, E., Vitiello, G. (1999). Quantum dissipation and neural net dynamics. *Bioelectrochemistry and Bioenergetics*, 48, 339.

Pessa, E., Vitiello, G. (2004). Quantum noise induced entanglement and chaos in the dissipative quantum model of brain. *International Journal of Modern Physics*, B18, 841–858.

Reid, T. (1785/1975). *Essays on the Intellectual Powers of Man*. Printed for John Bell and D.G.G.J. & J. Robinson, Edinburgh (trans Antonio Santucci, *Ricerca Sulla Mente Umana e Altri Scritti*). Torino: UTET.

Rovelli, C. (2020). *Helgoland*. Adelphi: Milano.

Simondon, G. (2020). *Individuation in Light of Notions of Form and Information*. Minneapolis, London: The University of Minnesota Press.

Shklovsky, V. (1981). Iskusstvo Kak Priĕm (L'arte Come Procedimento). In: De Michelis, Di C.G., Oliva, R. (Trad) *O Teorii Prozy (Teoria della Prosa)*. Milano: Einaudi.

Shklovsky, V. (1984). *Energija Zabluzdenija (L'energia Dell'errore)* (trans M. Di Salvo). Roma: Editori Riuniti.

Solms, M., Panksepp, J. (2012). The "Id" knows more than the "ego" admits: Neuropsychoanalytic and primal consciousness perspectives on the interface between affective and cognitive neuroscience. *Brain Sciences*, 2, 147–175.

Tagliagambe, S. (1997). *Epistemologia Del Confine*. Milano: Il Saggiatore.

Tagliagambe, S., Malinconico, A. (2018). *Tempo e Sincronicità. Tessere Il Tempo*. Milano-Udine: Mimesis.

Tulving, E. (2002). Episodic memory: From mind yo brain. *Annual Review of Psychology*, 53, 1–25.

Umezawa, H. (1993). *Advanced Field Theory: Micro, Macro and Thermal Concepts*. New York: American Institute of Physics.

Vallortigara, G. (2023). *Il Pulcino Di Kant*. Milano: Adelphi.

Vallortigara, G. (2021). *Pensieri della Mosca con la Testa Storta*. Milano: Adelphi.

Vitiello, G. (1995). Dissipation and memory capacity in the quantum brain model. *International Journal of Modern Physics*, B9, 973.

Vitiello, G. (1997). Dissipazione e Coscienza. *Atque*, 6, 171–198.

Vitiello, G. (2001). *My Double Unveiled*. Amsterdam: John Nenjamins.

Von Uexküll, J.J. (1962). *Streifzüge Durch Die Umwelten Von Tieren Und Menschen. Eine Bedeutungslehre* (Mit G. Kriszat). Hamburg: Rowohlt (English trans (2010). *A Foray into the Worlds of Animals and Humans: With a Theory of Meaning*, trans Joseph D. O'Neil). Minneapolis/London: University of Minnesota Press.

Yong, E. (2022). *An Immense World: How Animal Senses Reveal the Hidden Realms Around us*. Dublin: Penguin Random House.

Index

abductive: cognition 56–57, 74n3; reasoning 10n1, 71
Abelson, Robert 80
ability: domain-specific 55, 69–70; of self-reflection 191
action system 24–25
actor 80
Adler, Alfred 154
affect(s): a-noetic 25, 30, 32–33, 65; disposition 1, 11–12, 19, 25, 63, 74n4; emotional 23; innate 2; intentions-in-action 23, 25; motion and 24; primacy 11, 93, 141, 169; primary 9, 22, 30, 33, 65, 90, 95, 115, 117, 121, 124, 125, 187; proper 26; role of 13, 23, 25, 61, 99n4, 116, 140–141, 183, 191
affectivity 7, 14, 25, 72, 75n6, 106, 183, 185, 188
agency 72, 160
agent 39, 48, 68
agriculture 9
Aion (deity) 155
Alcaro, Antonio 16, 22, 30, 32
analogy 70, 102–103, 110, 118
analysand (person who is undergoing psychoanalysis) 56–57
analysis: historical 3; levels of 12, 39, 91, 156, 170; neurological 22; perceptual 23, 33, 47, 109, 116, 133
animal: behavior 24–25, 29, 54, 134, 189; endothermic 29, 32, 111n2; homeotherm 17; human 85, 149, 151, 160; ritual slaughter 79
anthropology 2, 4, 39; cognitive 13–14, 40–41, 43, 48–49, 138, 141; disciplines of 42, 48
antiquity 45

anxiety 8, 83–84, 88, 91, 95, 108, 188
apparatus: mental 188; perceptive 19, 34n3, 44; sensory/sensory-motor 1, 19, 63, 69, 98, 112–115, 117, 135, 142n1
apprehension, modes of 1, 13, 34n3, 61, 65, 181
archaic: structures 15–16; unconsciousness 19, 65
archetypal: constrained emotional apprehension 65; evolutionary history 25; hypothesis 11–13, 124; nature 43, 139; structure 77, 82, 91
archetypal image: complex 31, 47, 66–67, 117; managing 147–148; universality 102, 104, 106, 124
archetypes: in-between 12, 59, 65, 106, 114, 176; nature of 11, 13, 57, 65, 92
art 45–46, 69, 129, 192–193
artifact: character of 9, 41; cultural 41, 56–57, 70–71, 120, 127
Ashanti (ethnic peoples) 94
assumptions 65–66, 103, 170
Atran, Scott 47, 58, 68
attachment 32, 115, 162n6
attractors: bottom-up/top-down process 152–153; developmental 40, 61, 63–64, 68–69; evolution 38, 40, 179; of human cognition 48, 53; neurobiological 22; teleological 113–114, 117
Austin, John L. 92
autism 50, 85, 115

Barkow, Jerome H. 113, 179
behavior: animal 25, 54, 134, 189; consequences of 57–58; de-humanizing 65; human 38, 66, 97, 104; pattern of 3, 38, 71, 78, 81, 87, 91, 96–98; social 21, 72; universal 77–78

For Product Safety Concerns and Information please contact our EU
representative GPSR@taylorandfrancis.com
Taylor & Francis Verlag GmbH, Kaufingerstraße 24, 80331 München, Germany

www.ingramcontent.com/pod-product-compliance
Lightning Source LLC
Chambersburg PA
CBHW070327270326
41926CB00017B/3800

* 9 7 8 1 0 3 2 9 5 7 6 7 8 *